RURAL RIDES

an abridgement

William Cobbett

RURAL RIDES

An abridgement with
biographical Introduction by
E. R. CHAMBERLIN

Constable · London

First published in Great Britain 1982
by Constable and Company Ltd
10 Orange Street London WC2H 7EG
Introduction copyright © 1982 by E. R. Chamberlin
All rights reserved
ISBN 0 09 464060 2
Set in Monophoto Baskerville 11pt by
Servis Filmsetting Ltd Manchester
Printed in Great Britain by
St Edmundsbury Press
Bury St Edmunds
Suffolk

The illustrations on pages 40, 52, 73, 77 and 79
are reproduced from woodcuts by John Nash.
The remaining illustrations are from woodcuts
by Thomas Bewick.

Introduction

On a June morning in the year 1777 a fourteen-year-old boy set out to walk the eighteen-odd miles from his home in Farnham, Surrey to Kew. A countryman's son, he had heard tales of the fabulous new gardens established at Kew and determined to find work there. He was a solid lad, high-coloured, fair-haired with small, grey, twinkling eyes. He was wearing a blue linen smock and cross garters of scarlet. He had sixpence halfpenny upon him, of which he spent threepence for his mid-day meal of bread, cheese and beer, and then lost the odd halfpenny. The remaining threepence, intended for his evening meal, was spent on impulse on a copy of Swift's *Tale of a Tub* which he found in a bookshop in Richmond. He went supperless but cheerful to bed in a haystack and, on the following morning, walked to Kew. There, the Scots gardener gave him a job and he worked contentedly and efficiently in the Gardens until his father came to take him home.

The boy was, of course, William Cobbett and it is possible to give such a remarkably detailed account of one day in his life because he was one of the most prolific self-revelators who ever put pen to paper. He published his first identifiable work in 1792: he died in 1835 and he scarcely ever ceased writing during those forty-three years. Technically, what he produced was journalism for it was all written at high speed, published in mostly ephemeral media and was intended for immediate effect. He was totally blind to much of what passes for culture: he rarely mentions painting; music was for him songs in an alehouse or a fiddler on the green; he was contemptuous alike of William Shakespeare and Samuel Johnson. But by virtue of an eye for living detail and a plain but polished and vigorous prose he was to join their company as one of the grand masters of English literature – a fact which would have amused him enormously.

Cobbett was born in Farnham in 1762. The little town has changed less than most. The hops that were its main industry have ceased, but only a few years ago. The inn where Cobbett was born has changed its name in his honour from *The Jolly Farmer* to the *William Cobbett* but it still follows its ancient trade. His father was a small farmer, eking out his income with that derived from the inn. The family lived in decent, if modest circumstances: all his life, indeed, Cobbett was to have the inestimable benefit of a happy family life, first as child, then as husband and father.

As a boy and as a man, he was a creature of impulses. After his father brought him back from Kew, he went off again to Portsmouth to try and go to sea. Failing, in 1783 – again on impulse – he went to London and spent nine mortifying months in an attorney's office from which he rescued himself by taking the King's Shilling. In 1784, at the age of twenty-one, he was sent to join his regiment – the Fifty-Fourth Foot, in Nova Scotia. A year later, he was RSM and virtually running the regiment in place of the arrogant, virtually illiterate and incompetent adjutant.

Cobbett taught himself to read and write. 'I learned grammar when I was a private soldier on the pay of sixpence a day. The edge of my berth, or that of my guard-bed, was my seat to study in; my knapsack was my bookcase, a bit of board lying on my bed was my writing table. I had no money to purchase candle or oil; in winter time it was rarely that I could get any evening light but the fire. To buy pen or a sheet of paper I was compelled to forego some portion of my food, though in a state of semi-starvation'.

His account of his eight years soldiering is scattered through his voluminous works and it is possible to build up a lively picture of the ordinary life of an ordinary soldier in an undistinguished regiment. From the beginning he had the ability to sketch life-like little vignettes. His courtship of his future wife is delightful, a mixture of romance and hard-headed practicality. They first met when she was thirteen, and he twenty-one. He and a companion were out riding shortly after daybreak on a winter's morning when they saw the girl. 'It was hardly light, but she was out in the snow scrubbing out a washing tub. "That's the girl for me," I said.'

And so she was. Later she returned to England, ahead of Cobbett, with her father's regiment. Her lover gave her the hundred and fifty guineas he had painstakingly amassed so that she could 'buy herself good clothes and live without hard work' until he himself returned to England. He returned with his regiment in 1791 and immediately went in search of her. 'I found my little girl *a servant of all work* (and hard work it was) at *five pounds a year* and, without saying hardly a word about the matter she put into my hands *the whole of my hundred and fifty guineas unbroken!*' They were married shortly afterwards.

Immediately on his return to England Cobbett, with his usual impulsiveness, embarked upon a project which, while it marked his debut in polemics, also left something of a slur upon his name. Throughout his time in the army this highly intelligent, efficient, truculent man had developed a thoroughgoing contempt for his officers, later castigating their ignorance, their arrogance and their indolence. But above all it was their corruption that enraged him: he calculated that the QM was holding back illegally at least a quarter of the men's scanty rations. As soon as he was discharged from the Army, he formally accused certain officers of peculation, providing impressive documentary material to back up his charges. Reluctantly, the War Office arranged a court martial – but Cobbett failed to put in an appearance and the undoubtedly guilty men were discharged.

Both during his lifetime and afterwards Cobbett was condemned for what seems an act of cowardice. More likely, however, it was a failure of confidence rather than courage. He was in the position of a man who, seeking to remove what appears to be a moderate-sized boulder discovers that it is, in fact, the visible tip of a vast buried rock. Corruption was virtually an intrinsic, inalienable part of the army system. It was not simply a case of an ex-sergeant major impugning three corrupt officers but of an unknown ex-countryman taking on a system created by, and for, a powerful aristocracy. He was to spend the rest of his life fighting that THING, as he was to call it, but now was not the time.

In October 1792 Cobbett and his young wife were back in America. He had spent a few months in France learning French and now, in Philadelphia, he set himself up as a teacher of English to French immigrants. Chance and skill had given him the ideal opportunity to hone the weapon which he was to use with ever-increasing skill throughout his life, for there is nothing quite like teaching one's language to a foreigner to gain an intimate knowledge of it. At the same time, he threw himself into the propaganda war raging in the infant republic. In 1794, Joseph Priestley had arrived in America as a species of refugee from England, and continued his attacks on the Pitt government condemning the war against revolutionary France. Cobbett was incensed at what he deemed to be treachery and attacked Priestley in his first, identifiable political pamphlet *Observations on the Emigration of Joseph Priestley*. The pamphlet attracted the gratified attention of the British government and the enraged attention of the American republicans and, in responding to them, Cobbett finally launched himself on his career as political journalist.

Cobbett's seven years in America were active, fruitful and, on the whole, happy; certainly he was to return to them in memory again and again with affection. He earned his living partly as publisher, partly as bookseller, partly as pamphleteer and by the time he returned to England with his growing family he had served his apprenticeship in the craft which was to bring him a modest fortune and undying fame. He found England passing through a crucial period. Napoleon had just become First Consul, the Revolutionary War with France transforming itself into what history would come to know as the Napoleonic Wars. Pitt's coalition was collapsing and his supporters – William Windham in particular – were seeking any means to prop it up. The arrival of the rising young journalist from America was most opportune: he was promptly invited to dine with leading members of the Government to discuss how his pen could best be employed.

It was a signal honour, and Cobbett basked in it. A few days later, riding back to his old home in Farnham, he mused on all that had happened since he left over 17 years before. 'What scenes I had gone through. How altered my state. I had dined the day before at the Secretary of State's (William Windham) in company with Mr Pitt, and had been waited on by men in gaudy livery. I had had no one to assist me in the world. No teachers of any sort. I felt proud. The distinction of birth and rank and wealth became nothing in my eyes. And from that moment, less than a month after my arrival in England, I resolved never to bend before them.'

It was a resolve which he kept. During the negotiations over that, and subsequent dinner tables, he was offered control of one of the Government's two daily papers. He refused, citing the fable of the hungry, but free wolf and the well-fed, but chained, household dog. The first publication which he launched – the *Porcupine* – failed but its successor, the *Political Register* ran from its first publication in 1802, even surviving his death in 1835. Much of it he wrote himself. It was a runaway success: in its later period, when he reduced its price to twopence it became in effect the eyes, ears and, above all, the voice of the working class. It sold some sixty thousand copies and assuming that at the very least there would have been four or five readers for every copy, its impact would have reached virtually every literate working class household in the country, quite apart from the circles of the literate élite. And it was in the *Political Register* that the spontaneously written notes known as *Rural Rides* were first published.

Cobbett's objective in setting forth on his Rides was limited and pragmatic: he wanted to have first-hand experience of the rural conditions of England in order to refute a government which, he was convinced, was dedicated to the ruin of the country. Fortunately for posterity, the writer and the observer in him triumphed over the statistician and the propagandist, *Rural Rides* becoming, despite their author, a work of literature.

William Cobbett's honeymoon with the Establishment did not last long. In due course those friends and supporters of Pitt who had tried to enlist this radical in their ranks in their turn became the government – the so-called Ministry of all the Talents – and Cobbett discovered what many a voter has sadly discovered since: a party in opposition tends to change its colours when it, at last, lays its hands on the helm of state. In vain, Cobbett waited for the attack on corruption, on the complex, tottering, self-supporting system of placemen and sinecures and pensioners – above all, on the paper currency which was inflating prices grievously to the harm of the ordinary man – all of which had been developed under pressure of war. In

1815, that long drawn-out war came to an end – and the lot of the common man was worsened by far. The pensioners and placemen and sinecurists still flourished but war production came to an end, discharged soldiers flooded the labour market, farm prices – Cobbett's particular interest – tumbled. In a well-meaning attempt to alleviate distress the magistrates of Speenhamland introduced a system that was to become a byword and particularly attracted Cobbett's rage: the level of relief was pegged to the price of the gallon loaf. In effect, the poorlaws subsidised the farmer: he could reduce wages, confident that the parish would make them up. But Cobbett put his finger on the glaringly obvious weakness of the system: again and again he describes situations where able-bodied men were improving roads in order to allow the hated 'jews and jobbers' to travel comfortably in their carriages while the fields lie untilled. Throughout this period, too, is the growing movement of violence now known as the Luddite movement and the corresponding rural unrest led by the mythical 'Captain Swing' with its accompaniment of rick-burning and threats of violence to landowners who were turning over to the use of threshing machines – threats which remained only threats.

So, on a foggy October morning in 1821, William Cobbett, a hale and hearty yeoman farmer not quite sixty years old, set out from his seed farm in Kensington to see for himself how the countryman fared. Sometimes he would be accompanied by a friend, or a servant, or his little son Richard, whose brother James would, in due course, edit the *Rides* and give them to a larger public even than those who subscribed to the weekly *Register*. One can only marvel at the man's sure powers of endurance. After a ride of perhaps thirty or forty miles, sustained by nothing more than a hunk of bread and cheese bought from a cottager, as often as not soaking wet from rain and mist, he will pick up pen and paper and dash off several hundred words of invective or observation or reminiscence while waiting for his mutton chop. He is a violent, intemperate writer. 'People have about Cobbett as substantial an idea as they have of Cribb,' William Hazlitt noted. 'His blows are as hard, and he himself is as impenetrable. One has no notion of him making use of a fine pen, but a great mutton fist. His style stuns his readers.' Certain key words and

phrases appear again and again almost as leitmotifs. Predomin-
ant is THE THING. His hatred of the Pitt system of government with its swarm of pensioned hangers-on is so great as to
give it almost visual form – something that Doré or Fuseli might
illustrate, a vile, shapeless, oozing, tenacious ubiquitous monster
against whom he must fight. Repeated as counterpoint to this
motif are the endless litanies of hatred directed against, Jews,
loan-jobbers, stock-jobbers – all those who derived a living other
than from the land or manufacture. He is anti-semite as a matter
of course, using the word 'jew' in lower case quite casually as a
definition of a sly rogue. In his political infighting justice or
mercy or common fairness means absolutely nothing to him:
there can be few more unpleasant pictures of political hatred
than the manner in which he dances on the corpse of Castlereagh (page 90). He might fairly be called a professional
John Bull, as with his description of the market place in Norwich
where he compares the trim, neat Norfolk women and their
wholesome produce with the French whose 'meat is lean and
bloody and nasty and the people snuffy and grimy in hands and
face' (page 21).

But there was another side to the man, a side which he turned
towards those he loved, or who depended on him, and which can
only be called lovable. Miss Mitford, the author of *Our Village*,
visited him at his farm in Botley and left a delightful portrait of a
happy household. 'There was not the slightest attempt at finery
or display. They called it a farmhouse. Everything was excellent, everything abundant – all served with the greatest nicety
by trim waiting damsels. I need not say a word more in praise of
the good wife to whom this admirable order was mainly due. She
was a sweet, motherly woman.' He was an excellent master. He
boasted that, although he employed only by the week, his men
stayed with him for years. His biographer, Edward Smith,
provides a delightful vignette of him and his men one Sunday:
he had arranged with them to work for double pay on that day
and gave them a good dinner at the end of the day, putting each
man's pay before him. 'Now, if you go to hell for working on
Sunday, don't you go and say you b'ent been paid!'

But it was the land he loved. He 'reads' it, as a geologist reads
strata or an archaeologist reads deposits. He is aware, and makes

the reader aware, of the bones and structure underfoot; that the soil, being like this, will produce such-and-such a crop and will look in this or that manner after winter's rains, after summer's drought. He describes trees not in the vague way of the urban nature lover, nor the precise manner of the botanist but in terms of the working farmer – this kind of tree, planted in that kind of place will yield so much timber suitable for such and such a purpose in a particular time. But he is aware, too, of their beauty. His love of nature can inspire him, as in the entry (page 26) where he graduates from a consideration of woodland technique to a passage of considerable poetic power. He appraises a town as he would a good dinner – 'solid, substantial, clean, neat' these are his words of praise. He has an eye always for pretty young women, seeming to regard them as though they were a particularly attractive and valuable crop. History is for him a real and living, though thoroughly garbled presence. Passing Blickling Hall in Norfolk he is moved to speculate on Anne Boleyn, then by natural association to Catherine of Aragon, thence to Cranmer and Foxe's *Book of Martyrs*, commiserating with the one and trouncing the other with gusto. England before the Reformation is, for him, the Golden Age and he is again and again comparing the kindly monks and friars of that mythical age of piety with the greedy, lazy degenerate parsons of his own time. He has a fixed idea that the population of England had declined disastrously since the Middle Ages, again and again and again citing the vast size of churches in tiny villages as evidence.

A page of Cobbett's text presents a somewhat spiky, rather daunting appearance with its liberal sprinkling of italics and capital letters. These typographical devices are not, by any means, randomly scattered. What he is attempting to do is to transcribe his actual pattern of speech and succeeds very well in this. The reader is left with the unforgettable impression of the vigorous, impulsive man riding on horseback beside him, pointing out this or that scene of interest, reminiscing, as often as not at the top of his voice, frequently infuriating, often wrong-headed, but never boring.

The total text of the *Rural Rides* runs into some hundreds of thousands of words: the present edition runs to some eighty thousand words. The labour of reducing this vast mass of words has been considerably lightened by the fact that Cobbett may fairly be described as the master of the non sequitor. Thus, after a sweeping, venomous attack on 'jews and jobbers' ending with the bloodthirsty statement, 'It is time that these degenerate dogs were swept away', in the very next sentence he goes on 'The blackthorns are full in flower and make a grand show'. The present editor has taken full advantage of this amiable indifference to sequence. The text, however, is not a selection but an abridgement, Cobbett's own words being used to link the sections. Again, his habit of precisely dating and identifying the locality and the time at which he is writing, and the route he has just taken, helps to establish a natural flow. Sometimes these itineraries are frankly tedious, consisting simply of a list of place names, but by judicious selection of these names it is possible to plot the author's path across the country, and so create the impression of continuity.

Nothing whatsoever has been added to the text, the only editing being that of elimination. The student of late eighteenth- and early nineteenth-century political history would be reluctant to lose a single word of Cobbett's. But very much of what he wrote was intended as current political propaganda and it is this material, strictly irrelevant to 'rural rides', that has been eliminated. In addition, Cobbett repeats himself time and again – as with his insistence that each large, empty country church is an indication of a dwindling population, and after the first two or three such entries, further references to the subject can be removed without much loss. The principle of inclusion, of choosing what to preserve among a mass of delectable choices is obviously more difficult. In general, wherever Cobbett describes something that has disappeared completely – for example, the gunpowder mills at Chilworth or, by contrast, where he describes the origins of a process, such as the beginning of London to Brighton commuting (which predictably attracts his spitting rage), these entries have been preserved.

Bibliographical note

The printing of *Rural Rides* has had a curious history. In 1853, eighteen years after Cobbett's death, his son James assembled an edition in book form. This is the edition usually cited as the *Rural Rides* but, far from being complete, large sections have been omitted without any discernible reason. These include the entire Irish Tour of 1834 – giving an horrific picture of Irish poverty and written in the form of letters to Cobbett's employee, Charles Marshall – and most of the northern and Scottish tours of 1832. The Scottish section does not, admittedly, show Cobbett at his best. There is evidence that he was working under considerable pressure. For example, instead of following his usual habit, and writing up his impressions within a few hours of their occurring – or even while they were occurring – he will put the task off for days together before embarking on a marathon stint, with some loss of spontaneity. The quality of the grammar, too, falls short of his usual meticulous care. And one gets the impression at times that he is whistling in the dark, as evidenced by the endless, tedious Addresses of Welcome which he reproduces verbatim despite their length and, not satisfied with that, tacks on endless lists of signatures to the addresses. And his constant diatribes against Scotch 'fellosofers', though spiced with invective eventually begin to pall.

But there is also much excellent material here: his witty, if predictably ungenerous description of Robert Owen's experiment at New Lanark: the appalling picture of the condition of Scottish agricultural labourers which he paints in his Address to the Chopsticks of the South – above all, the lively, penetrating but on the whole sympathetic description he gives of Scotland as being virtually a foreign country emphasises the difference between the two races and certainly deserves to be included in any edition of the *Rides*.

Whatever the cause for these omissions, modern readers without access to the volumes of *Cobbett's Weekly Register* would have been unaware of missing many of the *Rides* even in England, including that containing the splendid if thoroughly reprehensible description of the author's gloating over Castlereagh's death (page 90). In 1930, G.D.H. and Margaret Cole produced their beautiful but, alas, short-lived three volume edition of the *Rides* in which they brought together, at last, the whole collection, augmenting it with an exhaustive index of all major characters to whom Cobbett makes reference.

The present edition has been edited from the original *Registers*, grateful use being made of the Coles' edition to clear up uncertain issues.

Chronology

1762 Born at Farnham

1777 Walks to Kew Gardens and takes service there

1783 Works in London as lawyer's clerk

1784 Enlists in 54th Foot at Chatham barracks

1785 Joins regiment in Nova Scotia

1791 Returns to England: is discharged

1792 Marries. Begins action accusing his officers of corruption. Goes to France

1792 (October) Takes up residence in America. Publishes, *inter alia* Porcupine's Gazette and Daily Advertiser advocating English Alliance

1800 Returns to England: offered and refuses editorship of government newspaper

1802 Launches weekly *Political Register*. Begins *Cobbett's Parliamentary Debates* which in due course is taken over by Luke Hansard

1805 Buys farm in Botley, Hampshire

1806 Death of Pitt. Ministry of all the Talents

1809 Publishes article in *Register* condemning flogging of soldiers by Hanoverian guard

1810 Convicted of seditious libel: fined £1,000 and sentenced to two years imprisonment during which he continues *Register*

1812 Released

1816 Publishes *Letter to the Luddites* condemning violence

1817 Habeas corpus Act suspended. Cobbett escapes to America

1819 Returns to England, bringing bones of Tom Paine

1820 Becomes bankrupt, partly as result of stamp duty imposed on periodicals

1821 October. First Rural Ride. The Rides continue intermittently until 1832, accounts being published in the *Register*. Other publications include *Cottage Economy* and *Advice to Young Men*

[October 30, 1821, Tuesday (Evening)]
Fog that you might cut with a knife all the way from London to
Newbury. The fog prevented me from seeing much of the fields
as I came along yesterday: but the fields of Swedish turnips were
good; pretty good: though not clean and neat like those in
Norfolk. The farmers here, as everywhere else, complain most
bitterly: but they hang on like sailors to the mast or hull of a
wreck.

Came through a place called 'a park' belonging to a Mr
Montague, who is now *abroad*. Of all the ridiculous things I ever
saw in my life, this place is the most ridiculous. The house looks
like a sort of church, in somewhat of a gothic style of building,
with *crosses* on the tops of different parts of the pile. There is a sort
of swamp, at the foot of a wood, at no great distance from the
front of the house. This swamp has been dug out in the middle to
show the water to the eye: so that there is a sort of river or chain
of diminutive lakes, going down a little valley about 500 yards
long. By the sides of these lakes there are little flower gardens
laid out in the Dutch manner: that is to say, cut out into all
manner of superficial geometric figures.

Here is the *grand en petit*, or mock magnificence more complete
than I ever beheld it before. Here is a *fountain*, the basin of which
is not four feet over, and the water spout not exceeding the pour
from a teapot. Here is a *bridge* over a *river* of which a child four
years old would clear the banks at a jump. In another part there
was a *lion's mouth* spouting out water into the lake, which was so
much like the vomiting of a dog, that I could almost have pitied
the poor Lion. In short, such fooleries I never before beheld. But
what I disliked most was the apparent impiety of a part of these
works of refined taste. I did not like the crosses on the dwelling
house; but, in one of the gravel walks, we had to pass under a
gothic arch, with a cross on the top of it, and in the point of the
arch a niche for a saint or a virgin, the figure being gone through
the lapse of centuries, and the pedestal only remaining. But the
good of it was, this gothic arch, disfigured by the hand of old
Father Time, was composed of Scotch fir wood, as rotten as a
pear, nailed together in such a way as to make the thing appear,
from a distance, like the remnant of a ruin! I wonder how long

this sickly, this childish taste is to remain? I do not know who this gentleman is. I suppose he is some honest person from 'Change or its neighbourhood: and that these *gothic arches* are to denote the *antiquity of his origin!*

At the end of this scene of mock grandeur and mock antiquity, I found something more rational: namely some hare-hounds, and, in half an hour after, we found, and I had the first hare hunt that I had had since I wore a smock-frock! We killed our hare after good sport, and got to Burghclere in the evening to a nice farm-house in a dell, sheltered from every wind, and with plenty of good living; though with no gothic arches made of Scotch-fir!

[October 31, Wednesday]

A fine day. Too many hares here, but our hunting was not bad: or, at least, it was a great treat to me who used, when a boy, to have my legs and thighs so often filled with thorns when running after the hounds, anticipating with pretty great certainty, a '*waling*' of the back at night. We had grey-hounds a part of the day: but the ground on the hills is so flinty, that I do not like the country for coursing. The dogs' legs are presently cut to pieces.

HURSTBOURN TARRANT, HANTS
[Nov. 2, Friday]

This place is commonly called *Uphusband*, which is, I think, as decent a corruption of names as one would wish to meet with. However, Uphusband the people will have it, and Uphusband it shall be for me.

I came from Burghclere this morning, and through the park of Lord Caernarvon, at Highclere. It is a fine season to look at woods. The oaks are still covered, the beeches in their best dress, the elms yet pretty green, and the beautiful ashes only beginning to turn off. This is, according to my fancy, the prettiest park that I have ever seen. A great variety of hill and dell. I like this place better than *Fonthill, Blenheim, Stowe*, or any other gentleman's grounds that I have seen. The *house* I did not care about, though it appears to be large enough to hold half a village. The great beauty of the place is the *lofty downs*, as steep, in some places, as the roof of a house, which form a sort of boundary, in the form of a part of a crescent, to about a third part of the park, and then slope off and get more distant, for about half another third part.

[Nov. 5, Monday]
A *white frost* this morning. The hills round about beautiful at sunrise, the rooks making that noise which they always make in winter mornings. The starlings are come in large flocks; and, which is deemed a sign of a hard winter, the fieldfares are come at an early season. The haws are very abundant; which, they say, is another sign of a hard winter. The wheat is high enough here, in some fields, 'to hide a hare', which is, indeed, not saying much for it, as a hare knows how to hide herself upon the bare ground. The fuel here is wood. Little coal is brought from Andover. A load of faggots does not cost above 10s. So that, in this respect, the labourers are pretty well off. The wages here, and in Berkshire, about 8s a week; but the farmers talk of lowering them.

MARLBOROUGH
[Tuesday noon, Nov. 6]
I left Uphusband this morning at 9, and came across to this place (20 miles) in a post chaise. Came up the valley of Uphusband, which ends at about 6 miles from the village, and puts one out upon the Wiltshire downs.

After about half a mile of down we came down into a level country. The labourers along here seem very poor indeed. A group of women labourers, who were attending the measurers to measure their reaping work, presented such an assemblage of rags as I never before saw even amongst the hoppers at Farnham, many of whom are country beggars. There were some very pretty girls, but ragged as colts and as pale as ashes. The day was cold, too, and frost hardly off the ground: and their blue arms and lips would have made any heart ache but that of a seat seller or loan-jobber.

A little after passing by these poor things, whom I left, cursing, as I went, those who had brought them to this state, I came to a group of shabby houses on a hill. The whole of the houses are not intrinsically worth a thousand pounds. There stood a thing out in the middle of the place, about 25 feet long and 15 wide, being a room stuck up on unhewed stone pillars about 10 feet high. It was the Town Hall where the ceremony of choosing *two members* is performed. 'This place sends members to parliament, don't it?' said I to the ostler. 'Yes, sir.' 'Who are members *now*?' 'I don't know, indeed, sir.'

In quitting this villainous place we see the extensive and uncommonly ugly park and domain of Lord Aylesbury, who seems to have tacked park on to park, like so many outworks of a fortified city. I suppose here are 50 or 100 farms of former days swallowed up. They have been bought, I dare say, from time to time; and it would be a labour very well worthy of reward by the public, to trace to its source the money by which these immense domains, in different parts of the country, have been formed!

Marlborough, which is an ill-looking place enough, is succeeded on my road to Swindon by an extensive and very beautiful down about 4 miles over. The fine short grass has about 9 inches of mould under it, and then comes the chalk. The water that runs down the narrow hill-side valleys is caught, in different parts of the down, in basins made on purpose and lined with clay, apparently. This is for watering the sheep in summer; sure signs of a really dry soil, and yet the grasses never *parch* on these downs. The chalk holds the moisture, and the grass is fed by the dews in hot and dry weather.

At the end of this down the high-country ends. The hill is high and steep; and from it you look immediately down into a level farming country; a little further on, into the dairy-country, whence the North-Wilts cheese comes; and, beyond that, into the vale of Berkshire, and even to Oxford, which lies away to the north-east from this hill.

The land continues good, flat and rather wet to Swindon, which is a plain country town, built of the stone which is found at about 6 feet under ground about here. I come on now towards Cirencester, through the dairy country of North Wilts.

CIRENCESTER
[Wednesday (Noon), 7 Nov.]
I slept at a dairy-farm house at Hannington, about eight miles from Swindon. I passed through that villainous hole Cricklade, about two hours ago; and certainly a more rascally looking place I never set my eyes on. I wished to avoid it, but could get along no other way.

All along here the land is a whitish stiff loam upon a bed of soft stone which is found at various distances from the surface, sometimes two feet and sometimes ten. Here and there a field is fenced with this stone, laid together in walls without mortar or earth. All the houses and outhouses are made of it, and even covered with the thinnest of it formed into tiles. The stiles in the fields are made of large flags of this stone, and the gaps in the hedges are stopped with them.

There is very little wood all along here. The labourers seem miserably poor. Their dwellings are little better than pig-beds, and their looks indicate that their food is not nearly equal to that of a pig. Their wretched hovels are stuck upon little bits of

ground *on the road side* where the space has been wider than the road demanded. Yesterday morning was a sharp frost; and this had set the poor creatures to digging up their little plats of potatoes. In my whole life I never saw such wretchedness equal to this; no, not even amongst the free negroes of America who, on an average, do not work one day out of four. The land all along here is good. Fine fields and pastures all around; and yet the cultivators of those fields so miserable!

GLOUCESTER
[Thursday (morning) Nov. 8]
In leaving Cirencester, which is a pretty large town, a pretty nice town, and which the people call *Cititer*, I came up hill into a country, apparently formerly a down or common, but now divided into large fields by stone walls. Anything so ugly I have never seen before. The stone, which on the other side of Cirencester, lay a good way underground, here lies very near to the surface. The plough is continually bringing it up, and thus, in general, come the means of making the walls that serve as fences.

With the exception of a little dell about eight miles from Cititer, this miserable country continued to the distance of ten miles when, all of a sudden, I looked down from the top of a high hill into the *vale of Gloucester*. Never, surely, was there such a contrast in this world. This hill is called Burlip Hill; it is much about a mile down it, and the descent so steep as to require the wheel of the chaise to be locked; and even with that precaution I did not think it over and above safe to sit in the chaise.

From this hill you see the Morvan Hills in Wales. You look down into a sort of *dish* with a flat bottom, the Hills are the sides of the dish, and the City of Gloucester, which you plainly see, at seven miles distance from Burlip Hill, appears to be not far from the centre of the dish. All here is fine; fine farms; fine pastures; all inclosed fields; all divided by hedges; orchards a plenty. Gloucester is a fine, clean, beautiful place; and, which is of a vast deal more importance, the labourers' dwellings, as I came along, looked good, and the labourers themselves pretty well as to dress and healthiness. The girls at work in the fields (always my standard) are not in rags, with bits of shoes tied on their feet and rags tied round their ankles, as they had in Wiltshire.

BOLLITREE CASTLE, HEREFORDSHIRE
[Friday, 9 Nov., 1821]
I got to this beautiful place (Mr William Palmer's) yesterday from Gloucester. This is in the parish of *Weston*, two miles on the Gloucester side of Ross.

On quitting Gloucester I crossed the Severne, which had overflowed its banks and covered the meadows with water. At about seven miles from Gloucester I came to hills, and the land changed from whitish soil to a red brown, with layers of flat stone of a reddish cast under it.

The spot where I now am is peculiarly well suited in all respects. The land very rich, the pastures the finest I ever saw, the trees of all kinds surpassing upon an average any that I have before seen in England. From the house you see, in front and winding round to the left, a lofty hill called *Penyard Hill*, at about a mile and a half distance, covered with oaks of the finest growth. Along at the foot of this wood are fields and orchards continuing the slope of the hill down for a considerably distance, and as the ground lies in a sort of *ridges* from the wood to the foot of the slope, the hill and dell is very beautiful. One of these dells with the two adjoining sides of hills is an orchard belonging to Mr Palmer. Sheltered by a lofty wood; the grass fine beneath the fruit trees; the soil dry under foot though the rain has scarcely ceased to fall; no moss on the trees; the leaves of many of them yet green. No wonder that this is a country of *cider* and *perry*. But what a shame it is that here, at any rate, the owners and cultivators of the soil, not content with these, should for mere fashion's sake, waste their substance on *wines* and *spirits*. They really deserve the contempt of mankind and the curses of their children.

I was much amused for an hour after daylight this morning in looking at the *clouds*, rising, at intervals, from the dells on the side of Penyard Hill, and flying to the top and then over the Hill. Some of the clouds went up in a roundish and compact form. Others rose in a sort of string or stream, the tops of them going

over the hill before the bottoms were clear of the place whence
they had arisen. Sometimes the clouds gathered themselves
together along the top of the hill, and seemed to connect the
topmost trees with the sky.

OLD HALL
[Saturday night, Nov. 10]
Went to Hereford this morning. It was market day. My arrival
became known, and, I am sure, I cannot tell how. A sort of *buz*
got about. I could perceive here, as I always have elsewhere,
very ardent friends and very bitter enemies; but all full of
curiosity. One thing could not fail to please me exceedingly: my
friends were *gay* and my enemies *gloomy*. The former smiled, and
the latter, in endeavouring to screw their features into a sneer,
could get them no further than the half sour and the half sad: the
former seemed, in their looks, to say 'Here he is', and the latter to
respond 'Yes, g-d d- him!' I went into the market place, amongst
the farmers with whom, in general, I was very much pleased. If I
were to live in the country two months, I should become
acquainted with every man of them.

   In coming to this place, which lies about two miles distant
from the great road, and at about equal distance from Hereford
and from Ross, we met with something, the sight of which
pleased me exceedingly: it was that of a very pretty pleasant-
looking lady (and *young* too) with two beautiful children, riding
in a little sort of chaise cart, drawn by an *ass* which she was
driving in reins. She appeared to be well known to my friends who
drew up and spoke to her, calling her Mrs *Lock* or *Locky* or some
such name. Her husband who is, I suppose some young farmer of
the neighbourhood, may well call himself Mr *Lucky*; for to have
such a wife to have the good sense to avoid, as much as possible,
feeding those cormorants who gorge on the taxes, is a blessing
that falls, I am afraid, to the lot of very few rich farmers. Let me
hope that Mr *Lock* does not indulge in the use of wine and spirits,
while Mrs Lock and her children ride in a jack-ass gig; for, if he
do, he wastes in this way the means of keeping her a chariot and
pair. For the husband to indulge in the guzzling of expensive,
unnecessary and really injurious drink to the tune, perhaps, of

50 or 100 pounds a year, while he preaches economy to his wife, is not only unjust but *unmanly*.

BOLLITREE
[Monday, 12 Nov.]
Returned this morning and rode about the farm, and also that of Mr Winnal, where I saw, for the first time, a plough going *without being held*. The man drove the three horses that drew the plough, and carried the plough round at the ends; but left it to itself the rest of the time. There was a skim coulter that turned the sward in under the furrow; and the work was done very neatly.

BOLLITREE
[Wednesday, 14 Nov.]
Rode to the Forest of Dean, up a very steep hill. The lanes here are between high banks, and, on the sides of the hills, the road is a rock, the water having long ago washed all the earth away.

The only good purpose that these forests answer is that of furnishing a place of being to labourers' families on their skirts. And here their cottages are very neat, and the people look hearty and well, just as they do round the forests in Hampshire. Every cottage has a pig, or two. These graze in the forest, and, in the fall, eat acorns and beech-nuts and the seed of the ash; for these last, as well as the others, are very full of oil, and a pig that is put to his shifts will pick the seed very nicely out from the husks. Some of these foresters keep cows, and all of them have bits of ground cribbed, of course, at different times from the forest. The dead limbs and old roots of the forest give *fuel*. And how happy are these people, compared with the poor creatures about Great Bedwin and Cricklade, where they have neither land nor shelter, and where I saw the girls carrying home bean and wheat stubble for fuel!

In returning from the forest we were overtaken by my son, whom I had begged to come from London to see this beautiful country. On the road-side we saw two lazy-looking fellows, in long coats and bundles in their hands, going into a cottage.

'What do you deal in?' said I to one of them, who had not yet entered the house. 'In the *medical way*,' said he. And I find that vagabonds of this description are seen all over the country with tea-licenses in their pockets. They vend *tea*, *drugs* and *religious tracts*. The first to bring the body into a debilitated state; the second to finish the corporeal part of the business; and the third to prepare the spirit for its separation from the clay!

OLD HALL
[Thursday, 15 Nov.]
We came this morning from Bollitree to Ross-Market, and thence to this place. Ross is an old-fashioned town, but it is very beautifully situated and if there is little of *finery* in the appearance of the inhabitants, there is also little of *misery*. It is a good, plain, country town or settlement of tradesmen, whose business is that of supplying the wants of the cultivators of the soil. It presents to us nothing of rascality and roguishness of look, which you see on almost every visage in the *borough-towns*, not excepting the visages of the women. I can tell a borough-town from another upon my entrance into it by the nasty, leering, cunning, designing look of the people, a look between that of a bad (for *some* are good) Methodist parson and that of a pickpocket. Some people say 'O, poor fellows! It is not *their* fault.' No? Whose fault is it, then? The miscreants who bribe them? True that these deserve the halter (and some of them may have it yet). But are not the takers of the bribes *equally* guilty?

This is the town to which Pope has given an interest in our minds by his eulogium on '*The Man of Ross*', a portrait of whom is hanging up in the house in which I am now.

[Friday, 16 Nov.]
A whole day most delightfully passed a hare-hunting, with a pretty pack of hounds kept here by Messrs. Palmer. They put me upon a horse that seemed to have been made on purpose for me, strong, tall, gentle and bold, and that carried me either over or through everything. I, who am just the weight of a four-bushel sack of good wheat, actually sat on his back from daylight in the morning to dusk (about nine hours) without once setting my foot on the ground.

Our ground was at Orcop, a place about four miles distant from this place. We found a hare in a few minutes after throwing off, and in the course of the day we had to find four and were never more than ten minutes in finding. A steep and naked ridge, lying between two flat valleys, having a mixture of pretty large fields and small woods, formed our ground. The hares crossed the ridge forward and backward, and gave us numerous views and very fine sport. I never rode on such steep ground before and, really, in going up and down some of the craggy places, where the rains had washed the earth from some of the rocks, I did think, once or twice, of my neck, and how Sidmouth would like to see me.

OXFORD
[Saturday, 17 Nov.]
We left Old Hall (where we always breakfasted by candlelight) this morning after breakfast; returned to Bollitree; took the Hereford coach as it passed about noon and came in it through Gloucester, Cheltenham, Northleach, Burford, Whitney and on to this city, where we arrived about ten o'clock. I could not leave Herefordshire without bringing with me the most pleasing impressions. It is not for one to descend to particulars in characterising one's personal friends, and therefore I will

content myself with saying that the treatment I met with in this beautiful county, where I saw not one single face that I had, to my knowledge, ever seen before, was much more than sufficient to compensate to me, personally, for all the atrocious calumnies which, for twenty years, I have had to endure.

At *Gloucester*, (as there were no meals on the road) we furnished ourselves with nuts and apples. They say that nuts of all sorts are unwholesome. If they had been, I should never have written Registers, and, if they were now, I should have ceased to write ere this, for upon an average, I have eated a pint a day since I left home. In short, I could be well content to live on nuts, milk and home-made bread.

Cheltenham is a nasty, ill-looking place, half clown and half cockney. The town is one street about a mile long. But then at some distance from this street there are rows of white tenements, with green balconies, like those inhabited by the tax-eaters around London. Indeed, this place appears to be the residence of an assemblage of tax-eaters. These vermin shift about between London, Cheltenham, Bath, Bognor, Brighton, Tunbridge, Ramsgate, Margate, Worthing and other spots in England, while some of them get over to France and Italy.

BURGHOLERE (Hants)
[Sunday, 18 Nov.]
We left Oxford early, and went on through Abingdon (Berks) to Market Ilsey. We pushed on through Ilsey towards Newbury, breakfasting upon the residue of the nuts, aided by a new supply of apples bought from a poor man, who exhibited them in his window. Inspired, like Don Quixote, by the *sight of the nuts*, and recollecting last night's bill, I exclaimed 'Happy! thrice happy and blessed that golden age when men lived on the simple fruits of the earth. Happy age, when no Oxford landlord charged two men, who had dropped into a common coach-passenger room and who had swallowed three pennyworths of food, 'four shillings for *teas*' and 'eighteen pence for *cold meat*', 'two shillings for *moulds and fire*' in this common coach room and 'five shillings for *beds*'.

Upon beholding the masses of buildings at Oxford, devoted to what they call *learning*, I could not help reflecting on the drones that they contain and the wasps they send forth. One half of the fellows who are what they call *educated* here are unfit to be clerks in a grocer's or mercer's shop. As I looked up at what they call *University Hall*, I could not help reflecting that what I had written, even since I had left Kensington on the 29th October, would produce more effect, and do more good in the world, than all that had for a hundred years been written by all the members of this University.

Between Ilsey and Newbury the land is enclosed. In going along we saw a piece of wheat with cabbage leaves laid all over at the distance, perhaps, of eight or ten feet from each other. It was to catch *slugs*. The slugs, which commit their depredation in the *night*, creep under the leaves in the morning and by turning up the leaves you come at the slugs, and crush them or carry them away. But besides the immense daily labour attending this, the slug, in a field sowed with wheat, has a *clod* to creep under at every root, and will not go five feet to get under a cabbage leaf. Then, if the day be *wet*, the slug works by day, as well as night. It is the sun and drought that he shuns, not the light. Therefore the only effectual way to destroy slugs is to sow lime, in dust, and *not slaked*. The slug is wet, he has hardly any skin, his slime is his covering; the smallest dust of hot lime kills him, and few bushel to the acre are sufficient. We got about three o'clock to this nice, snug little farm-house and found our host, Mr Budd, at home.

BURGHCLERE
[Monday, 19 Nov.]
A thorough wet day, the only day the greater part of which I have not spent out of doors, since I left home.

BURGHCLERE
[Tuesday, 20 Nov.]
With Mr Budd we rode today to see the *Farm* of Tull at Shalborne, in Berkshire. Mr Budd did the same thing with Arthur Young twenty-seven years ago. It was a sort of *pilgrimage*,

but as the distance was ten miles we thought it best to perform it on horseback. At about two miles from Inkpen we came to the end of our pilgrimage: the farm, which was Mr Tull's, where he used the first drill that ever was used, where he practised his husbandry, where he wrote that book which does so much honour to his memory and to which the cultivators of England owe so much. This farm is on an open and somewhat bleak spot in Berkshire, on the borders of Wiltshire and within a very short distance of Hampshire. The house, which has been improved, is still but a plain farm-house. We returned, not along the low land but along the top of the downs, and through Lord Caernarvon's park, and got home after a very pleasant day.

BURGHCLERE
[Wednesday, 21 Nov.]
We intended to have a hunt; but the fox-hounds came across and rendered it impracticable. As an instance of the change which rural customs have undergone since the hellish paper system has been so furiously at work, I need only mention the fact that, forty years ago, there were *five* packs of *fox-hounds* and *ten* packs of harriers kept within *ten miles* of Newbury and that there is now *one* of the former (kept, too, by *subscription*) and *none* of the latter, except the few couples of dogs kept by Mr Budd. 'So much the better,' says the shallow fool who cannot duly estimate the difference between a *native* gentry, attached to the soil, and a gentry only now and then residing at all, having no relish for country-delights, foreign in their manners, distant and haughty in their behaviour, looking to the soil only for its rents, viewing it as a mere object of speculation, unacquainted with its cultivators, despising them and their pursuits and relying for influence, not upon the good will of the vicinage, but upon the dread of their power.

The war and paper system has brought in nabobs, negro-drivers, generals, admirals, governors, commissaries, contractors, pensioners, sinecurists, commissioners, loan-jobbers, lottery dealers, bankers, stock-jobbers. You can see but a few good houses not in possession of one or other of these. These, with the parsons, are now the magistrates.

KENSINGTON
[Friday, 23 Nov.]
Got home by the coach. I see that they are planting oaks on the
'*wastes*', as the *Agriculturasses* call them, about Hartley Row. The
planter here is Lady Mildmay, who is, it seems, Lady of the
Manors about here. It is impossible to praise this act of hers too
much, especially when one considers her *age*: I beg a thousand
pardons! I do not mean to say that her ladyship is *old*, but she has
long had grand-children. If her ladyship had been a reader of
old dread-death and dread-devil Johnson, that teacher of
moping and melancholy, she never would have planted an oak
tree. If the writings of this time-serving, mean, dastardly old
pensioner had got a firm hold of the minds of people at large,
these people would have been bereft of their very souls. These
writings, aided by the charm of pompous sound, were fast
making their way, till light, reason and the French revolution
came to drive them into oblivion.

KENTISH JOURNAL
[Tuesday, 4 December, 1821]
Elverton Farm, near Faversham, Kent.
This is the first time since I went to France in 1792 that I have
been on this side of *Shooter's Hill*. The land, generally speaking,
from Deptford to Dartford is poor and the surface ugly by
nature, to which ugliness there has been made, just before we
came to the latter place, a considerable addition by the inclosure
of a common, and by the sticking up of some shabby-genteel
houses, surrounded with dead fences and things called gardens,
in all manner of ridiculous forms.

After you leave Dartford, the land becomes excellent. Along
through Gravesend towards Rochester, the country presents a
sort of gardening scene. Rochester is a small but crowded place,
lying on the south bank of the beautiful Medway, with a rising
ground on the other side of the city. *Stroud*, which you pass
through before you come to the bridge over which you go to
enter Rochester, *Rochester* itself, and *Chatham* form, in fact, one
main street of about two miles and a half in length. Here I was
got into the scenes of my cap-and-feather days! Here, at between

sixteen and seventeen, I enlisted for a soldier. Upon looking up towards the fortifications and the barracks, how many recollections crowded into my mind. The girls in these towns do not seem to be *so pretty* as they were thirty-eight years ago, or am I not so quick in discovering beauties as I was then? Have thirty-eight years corrected my taste, or made me a hypercritic in these matters?

This Chatham has had some monstrous *wens* stuck on to it by the lavish expenditure of the war. These will moulder away. It is curious enough that I should meet with a gentleman in an inn at Chatham to give me a picture of the house-distress in that enormous wen which, during the war, was stuck on to Portsmouth. Not less than fifty thousand people had been drawn there! These are now dispersing. The coagulated blood is diluting and flowing back through the veins. Whole streets are deserted, and the eyes of the houses knocked out by the boys that remain. We shall see the whole of these wens abandoned by the inhabitants and, at last, the cannon on the fortifications may be of some use in battering down the buildings. But what is to be the fate of the greatest wen of all? The monster, called by the silly coxcombs of the press 'the metropolis of the empire'? What is to become of the multitude of towns stuck up around it? The village of Kingston was smothered in the town of Portsea. And why? Because taxes, drained from other parts of the kingdom, were brought thither. The dispersion of the wen is the only real difficulty that I see in settling the affairs of the kingdom, and restoring it to a happy state. But dispersed it *must* be.

[Wednesday, 5 December]
Mr William Waller, at whose house I am, has grown this year mangel-wurzel the roots of which weigh, I think, on an average twelve pound. In short, as far as *soil* goes it is impossible to see a finer country than this. You frequently see a field of fifty acres, level as a die, clean as a garden and as rich. This is a country of hop-gardens, cherry, apple, pear and filbert orchards, and quickset hedges. But alas! what, in point of beauty, is a country without woods and lofty trees? Rich fields, pastures and orchards lie all round me and yet, I declare, that I a million times to one prefer, as a spot to *live on*, the heaths, the miry

coppices, the wild woods and the forests of Sussex and Hampshire.

[Saturday, 8 Dec.]

Came home very pleased with my visit to Mr Walker [sic] in whose house I saw no drinking of wine, spirits or even beer, where all, even the little children, were up by candlelight in the morning, and where the most perfect sobriety was accompanied by constant cheerfulness. *Kent* is in a deplorable way. The farmers are skilful and intelligent, generally speaking. But there is infinite *corruption* in Kent, owing to the swarms of West Indians, nabobs, commissioners and others of nearly the same description that have selected it for the place of their residence, but owning still more to the immense sums of public money that have, during the last thirty years, been expended in it. This country, so blessed by providence, has been cursed by the system in a peculiar degree. It has been the *receiver* of immense sums, raised on the other counties. This has puffed its *rents* to an unnatural height, and now that the drain of other counties is stopped, it feels like a pampered pony, turned out in winter to live upon a common.

NORFOLK AND SUFFOLK JOURNAL
Bergh Apton, near Norwich
[Monday, 10 Dec, 1821]

From the *Wen* to Norwich, from which I am now distant seven miles, there is nothing in Essex, Suffolk or this county that can be called a *hill*. Essex, when you get beyond the immediate influence of the gorgings and disgorgings of the Wen, that is to say, beyond the demand for crude vegetables and repayment in manure, is by no means a fertile county. There appears generally to be a bottom of *clay*, not *soft chalk* which they persist in calling clay in Norfolk. I wish I had one of these Norfolk men in a coppice in Hampshire or Sussex, and I would show him what *clay* is. Clay is what pots and pans and tiles are made of, and not soft, whitish stuff that crumbles to pieces in the sun instead of baking as hard as a stone and which, in dry weather, is to be broken to pieces by nothing short of a sledge-hammer.

Bury, formerly the seat of an abbot, the last of whom was, I think, hanged or somehow put to death by that matchless tyrant Henry VIII, is a very pretty place; extremely clean and neat, no ragged or dirty people to be seen and women (*young* ones I mean) very pretty and very neatly dressed. The farming all along to Norwich is very good. The land clean, and everything done in a masterly manner.

GROVE, NEAR HOLT
[Thursday, 13 Dec.]
Came to the Grove (Mr Wither's), near Holt. Through *Norwich* to *Aylsham* and then to *Holt*. On our road we passed the house of the late *Lord Suffield*. This house, which is a very ancient one, was, they say, the birth place of Ann de Boleyne, the mother of Queen Elizabeth. Not much matter, for she married the king while his real wife was alive. I could have excused her, if there had been no marrying in the case, but hypocrisy, always bad, becomes detestable when it resorts to religious ceremony as a mask. She, no more than Cranmer, seems to have remembered her sins against her lawful queen. Foxe's *Book of Martyrs*, that ought to be called the *Book of Liars*, says that Cranmer, the recanter and re-recanter, held out his offending hand in the flames and cried out 'that hand, that hand!' If he had cried out '*Catherine! Catherine!*' I should have thought better of him, but it is clear that the whole story is a lie, invented by the protestants and particularly by the sectarians, to whitewash the character of this perfidious hypocrite and double apostate who, if bigotry had something to do with bringing him to the stake, certainly deserved his fate if any offences committed by man can deserve so horrible a punishment.

The present Lord Suffield is that Mr Edward Harbord whose father-in-law left him £500 to buy a seat in parliament and who refused to carry an address to the late beloved and lamented queen, because Mr Cartwright and myself were chosen to accompany him! Never mind, my lord, you will grow less fastidious! They say, however, that he is really good to his tenants and has told them he will take anything that they can give.

There are some oak woods here, but very poor. All this eastern coast seems very unpropitious to trees of all sorts. Holt is a little, old-fashioned, substantially-built market town. The land just about it, or at least towards the east, is poor and has been lately enclosed.

[Friday, 14 Dec.]
Went to see the estate of Mr Hardy at Leveringsett, a hamlet about two miles from Holt. This is the first time I have seen a *valley* in this part of England. From Holt you look, to the distance of seven or eight miles, over a very fine valley having a great deal of inferior hill and dell within its boundaries. At the bottom of this general valley, Mr Hardy has a very beautiful estate of about four hundred acres. His house is at one end of it near the high road, where he has a malt-house and brewery, the neat and ingenious method of managing which I would detail if my total unacquaintance with machinery did not disqualify me for the task. His estate forms a valley of itself, somewhat longer than broad. The tops and the sides of the hills round it, and also several little hillocks in the valley itself, are judiciously planted with trees of various sorts, leaving good wide roads so that it is easy to ride round them in a carriage.

[Saturday, 15 Dec.]
Spent the evening amongst the farmers, at their market room at Holt, and very pleased at them I was. We talked over *the cause of the low prices* and, as I have done everywhere, endeavoured to convince them that prices must fall a great deal lower yet. They heard me patiently and, I believe, were well convinced of the truth of what I said.

Here, as everywhere else, I hear every creature speak loudly of Mr Coke. It is well known to my readers that I think nothing of him as a *public* man, that I think even his good qualities an injury to his country because they serve the knaves he is duped by, to dupe the people more effectually. But it would be base of me not to say, that I hear, from men of all parties and sensible men too, expressions made use of towards him that affectionate children use towards their parents. I have not met with a single exception.

BERGH APTON
[Sunday, 16 Dec.]

Came from Holt through Saxthorpe and Cawston. At the former village were on one end of a decent white house these words 'Queen Caroline; for her Britons mourn', and a crown over all in black. I need not have looked to see. I might have been sure that the owner of the house was a shoe-maker, a trade which numbers more men of sense and of public spirit than any other in the kingdom.

At Cawston, we stopped at a public house, the keeper of which had taken and read the Register for years. I shall not attempt to describe the pleasure I felt at the hearty welcome given us by Mr Pern and his wife, and by a young miller of the village who, having learned at Holt that we were to return that way, had come to meet us.

GREAT YARMOUTH
[Friday (morning), 21 Dec.]

The day before yesterday, I set out for Bergh Apton with Mr Clarke, to come hither by way of Beccles in Suffolk. This Beccles is a very pretty place, has watered meadows near it and is situated among fine lands. We slept at the house of a friend of Mr Clarke on our way, and got to this very fine town of Great Yarmouth yesterday about noon. A party of friends met us and conducted us about the town, which is a very beautiful one indeed. What I liked best, however, was the hearty welcome I met with, because it showed that the reign of calumny and

delusion was passed. A company of gentlemen gave me a dinner in the evening, and in all my life I never saw a set of men more worthy of my respect and gratitude. I leave Great Yarmouth with sentiments of the sincerest regard for all those whom I saw there and conversed with; nay, even the *parsons* not excepted, for, if they did not come to welcome me, they collected in a group to *see* me and that was one step towards doing justice to him whom their order have so much, so foully and, if they knew their own interest, so foolishly slandered.

BERGH APTON
[21 Dec. (night)]
After returning from Yarmouth yesterday, went to dine at Stoke-Holy-Cross, about six miles off; got home at midnight, and came to Norwich this morning, this being market-day, and also the day fixed on for a Radical Reform Dinner at the Swan Inn, to which I was invited. Norwich is a very fine city, and the castle, which stands in the middle of it on a hill, is truly majestic. The meat and poultry and vegetable market is beautiful. It is kept in a large open square in the middle, or nearly so, of the city. The ground is a pretty sharp slope. It resembles one of the French markets, only *there* the vendors are all standing and gabbling like parrots, and the meat is lean and bloody and nasty, and the people snuffy and grimy in hands and face, the contrary, precisely the contrary, of all which is the case in this beautiful market at Norwich, where the women have a sort of uniform brown great coats, with white aprons and *bibs* (I think they call them) going from the apron up to the bosom. They equal in neatness (for nothing can surpass) the market women in Philadelphia.

The cattle market is held on the hill by the castle, and many *fairs* are smaller in bulk of stock. The corn market is held in a very magnificent place, called St Andrews' Hall, which will contain two or three thousand persons.

KENSINGTON
[Monday, 24 Dec.]
Went from Bergh Apton to Norwich in the morning, and from

Norwich to London during the day, carrying with me great
admiration of and respect for this county of *excellent farmers*, and
hearty, open and spirited men. The Norfolk people are quick
and smart in their motions and in their speaking. Very neat and
trim in all their farming concerns, and very skilful. Their land is
good, their roads are level and at the bottom their soil is dry, to
be sure. And these are great advantages, but they are diligent
and make the most of everything. Their management of all sorts
of stock is most judicious; they are careful about manure, their
teams move quickly and, in short, it is a county of most excellent
cultivators.

The churches in Norfolk are generally large and the towers
lofty. They have all been well built at first. Many of them are of
the Saxon architecture. They are almost all (I do not remember
an exception) placed on the *highest* spots to be found near where
they stand. And it is curious enough that the contrary practice
should have prevailed in *hilly* countries, where they are
generally found in valleys and in low, sheltered dells even in
those valleys. These churches prove that the people of Norfolk
and Suffolk were always a superior people in point of wealth,
while the size of them proves that the country parts were, at one
time, a great deal more populous than they are now. The great
drawbacks on the beauty of these counties are their flatness and
their want of fine woods. But to those who can dispense with
these, Norfolk, under a wise and just government, can have
nothing to ask more than Providence and the industry of man
have given.

SUSSEX JOURNAL
Battle
[Wednesday, 2 Jan., 1822]
Came here today from Kensington, in order to see what goes on
at the meeting to be held here tomorrow of the 'gentry, clergy,
freeholders and occupiers in the Rape of Hastings, to take into
consideration the distressed state of the agricultural interest'. I
shall, of course, give an account of this meeting after it has
taken place.

You come through part of *Kent* to get to *Battle* from the great

Wen on the Surrey side of the Thames. The first town is Bromley, the next Seven-Oaks, the next Tunbridge and between Tun-bridge and this place you cross the boundaries of the two counties. From the Surrey Wen to Bromley the land is generally a deep loam on gravel, and you see few trees except elm. A very ugly country. On quitting Bromley, the land gets poorer. There is a frost this morning, some ice and the women look rosy-cheeked.

Here (before you come to Seven-Oaks) is a most beautiful and rich valley, extending from east to west, with rich cornfields and fine trees. Then comes sandstone again, and the hop-gardens near Seven-Oaks, which is a pretty little town with beautiful environs, part of which consists of the park of *Knowle*, the seat of the Duchess of Dorset. It is a very fine place. And there is another park, on the other side of the town. So that this is a delightful place, and the land appears to be very good. The gardens and houses all look neat and nice.

Tunbridge is a small but very nice town, and has some fine meadows and a navigable river. The rest of the way to Battle presents, alternately, clay and sandstone. Of course, the cop-pices and oak woods are very frequent. There is now and then a hop-garden spot, but these are poor indeed compared with what you see about Canterbury and Maidstone.

As 'God has made the back to the burthen' so the clay and coppice people make the dress to the stubs and bushes. Under the sole of the shoe is *iron*; from the sole six inches upwards is a high-low; then comes a leather bam to the knee; then comes a pair of leather breeches, then comes a stout doublet; over this comes a smock frock, and the wearer sets brush and stubs and thorns and mire at defiance. I have always observed that woodland and forest labourers are best off in the main. The coppices give them pleasant and profitable work in winter. If they have not so great a corn harvest they have a three weeks harvest in April or May, that is to say, in the season of barking, which in Hampshire is called *stripping*, and in Sussex *flaying*, which employs women and children as well as men. And then in the great article of *fuel*! They *buy* none. It is miserable work where this is to be bought and where, as at Salisbury, the poor take by turns the making of fires at their houses to boil four or five kettles. What a winter-life must those lead, whose turn it is not to make the fire! At Launceston in Cornwall, a tradesman, too, told me that the people in general could not afford to have fire in ordinary, and that he himself paid 3*d*. for boiling a leg of mutton at another man's fire!

BATTLE
[Thursday (night), 3 Jan., 1822]
Today there has been a *meeting* here of the landlords and farmers in this part of Sussex, which is called the Rape of Hastings. The object was to agree on a petition to parliament praying for *relief*! Good God! Where is this to *end*? We now see the effect of those *rags* which I have been railing against for the last twenty years. Here were collected together not less than 300 persons, principally landlords and farmers, brought from their homes by their distresses and by their alarms for the future. Never were such things heard in any country before, and it is useless to hope, for terrific must be the consequences if an effectual remedy is not speedily applied. The town, which is small, was in a great bustle before noon and the meeting (in a large room in the principal inn) took place about one o'clock.

After the business of the day was ended, there was a dinner in the inn where the meeting had been held. I was at this dinner. And Mr Britton having proposed my health and Mr Curteis, who was in the chair, having given it, I thought it would have looked like mock modesty, which is in fact only another name for hypocrisy, to refrain from expressing my opinions upon a point or two connected with the business of the day. I shall now insert a substantially correct sketch of what the company was indulgent enough to hear from me at the dinner.*

KENSINGTON
[Friday, 4 Jan., 1822]
Got home from *Battle*. I had no time to see the town, having

---

* Here Cobbett inserts a lengthy report, taken from the *Morning Chronicle*, whose general theme is 'A Corn Bill of no description can do either landlord or tenant any good'.

entered the inn on Wednesday in the dusk of the evening, and having come out of it only to get into the coach this morning. I had no time to see *Battle Abbey*, the seat of the Webster family, now occupied by a man of the name of *Alexander*! Thus they *replace them*! It will take a much shorter time than most people imagine to put out all the ancient families. The greatness of the estate is no protection for the owner for, great or little, it will soon yield him no rents. Mr Curteis said that the *land* was *immovable*. Yes; but the *rents are not*.

I cannot quit Battle without observing that the country is very pretty all about it. All hill or valley. A great deal of woodland, in which the underwood is generally very fine, though the oaks are not very fine and a good deal covered with *moss*. This shows that the clay ends before the *tap*-root of the oak gets as deep as it would go, for when the clay goes the full depth, the oaks always are fine. The woods are too large and too near each other for hare coursing. But it is a fine country for shooting and for harbouring game of all sorts.

It was rainy as I came home but the woodmen were at work. A great many hop-poles are cut here, which makes the coppices more valuable than in many other parts. The women work in the coppices, shaving the bark of the hop-poles and, indeed, at various other parts of the business. These poles are shaved to prevent *maggots* breeding in the bark and accelerating the destruction of the poles. It is curious that the bark of trees should generate maggots but it has, as well as the wood, a *sugary* matter in it. The hickory wood in America sends out from the ends of the logs when these are burning, great quantities of the finest syrup that can be imagined. Accordingly, that wood breeds maggots, or worms as they are usually called. Surprisingly, our *ash* breeds worms very much.

Little boys and girls shave hop-poles and assist in other work very nicely. And it is pleasant work when the weather is dry overhead. The woods, bedded with leaves as they are, are clean and dry underfoot. They are warm, too, even in the coldest weather. When the ground is frozen several inches deep in the open fields, it is scarcely frozen at all in a coppice where the underwood is a good plant, and where it is nearly high enough to cut. So that the woodman's is really a pleasant life. We are apt to think that the birds have a hard time of it in winter. But we forget the warmth of the woods, which far exceeds anything to be found in farmyards.

Woodland countries are interesting on many accounts. Not so much on account of their masses of green leaves, as on account of the variety of sights and sounds and incidents they afford. Even in winter, the coppices are beautiful to the eye. In spring they change their hue from day to day during two whole months, which is about the time from the first appearance of the delicate leaves of the birch to the full expansion of those of the ash. And even before the leaves come at all to intercept the view, what in the vegetable creation is so delightful to behold as the bed of a coppice bespangled with primroses and bluebells?

The opening of the birch leaves is the signal for the pheasant to begin to crow, for the blackbird to whistle and the thrush to sing. And just when the oak buds look reddish, and not a day before, the whole tribe of finches burst forth in songs from every bough while the lark, imitating them all, carries the joyous sound to the sky. These are among the means which Providence has benignantly appointed to sweeten the toils by which food and raiment is produced. These the English Ploughman could once hear without the sorrowful reflection that he himself was *a pauper* and that the bounties of nature had, for him, been scattered in vain. And shall he never see an end to this state of things? Shall unsparing taxation never cease to make him a miserable, dejected being famishing in the midst of abundance, fainting, expiring with hunger's feeble moans, surrounded by a carolling creation? O! accursed paper money! Has hell a torment surpassing the wickedness of the inventor!

SUSSEX JOURNAL
Lewes
[Tuesday, 8 Jan., 1822]
Came here today, from home, to see what passes tomorrow at a meeting to be held here of the owners and occupiers of land at the rapes of Lewes and Pevensey.

In quitting the great Wen we go through Surrey more than half the way to Lewes. From *Saint George's Fields*, which are now covered with houses, we go towards Croydon, between rows of houses nearly half the way, and the whole way is nine miles. There are, erected within these four years, two entire miles of stock-jobbers' houses on this one road, and the work goes on with accelerated force!

From London to Croydon is as ugly a bit of country as any in England. A poor spewy gravel with some clay. Few trees but elms, and those stripped up and villainously ugly. Croydon is a good market town but is, by the funds, swelled out into a Wen.

Upon quitting Croydon for Godstone, you come to the chalk hills, the juniper shrubs and the yew trees. To the westward lie Epsom Downs, which lead on to Merrow Downs and St Margaret's Hill, then, skipping over Guildford, you come to the Hog's Back, which is still of chalk and at the west end of which lies Farnham. With the Hog's Back this vein of chalk seems to end, for then the valleys become rich loam, and the hills sandy and gravel till you approach the Winchester Downs by the way of Alresford.

Godstone, which is in Surrey also, is a beautiful village, chiefly of one street with a fine large green before it and with a pond in the green. A little way to the right (going from London) lies the vile rotten borough of *Bletchingley*, but, happily for Godstone, out of sight. At and near Godstone the gardens are all very neat and, at the inn, there is a nice garden well stocked with beautiful flowers in the season. I saw here, last summer, some double violets as large as small pinks, and the lady of the house was kind enough to give me some roots.

At East Grinstead, which is a rotten borough and a very shabby place, you come to stiff loam at top with sand-stone underneath. To the south of the place the land is fine and the vale on both sides a very beautiful intermixture of woodland and cornfields and pastures. At about three miles from Grinstead you come to a pretty village called Forest Row and then, on the road to Uckfield, you cross Ashurst Forest, which is a heath with here and there a few birch scrubs upon it, verily the most villainously ugly spot I ever saw in England. This lasts you for five miles, getting if possible uglier and uglier, till at last, as if barren soil, nasty spewy gravel, heath and even that stunted were not enough, you see some rising spots which, instead of trees, present you with black, hideous, ragged rocks. There may be Englishmen who wish to see the coast of Nova Scotia. They need not go to see, for here it is to the life. If I had been in a long trance (as our nobility seem to have been) and had been waked up here, I should have begun to look about for the Indians and the squaws, and to have heaved a sigh at the thought of being so far from England.

LEWES

[Wednesday, 9 Jan., 1822]

The meeting and the dinner are now over. Mr Davies Giddy was in the chair: the place the County Hall. A Mr Partington, a pretty little oldish smart truss nice cockney-looking gentleman, with a yellow and red handkerchief around his neck, moved the petition, which was seconded by Lord Chichester who lives in the neighbourhood. Mr Blackman (of Lewes, I believe) disapproved of the petition, and in a speech of considerable length, and also of considerable ability, stated to the meeting that the evils complained of arose from the *currency*, and not from the importation of corn. A Mr Donovan, an Irish gentleman who, it seems, is a magistrate in this 'disturbed county', disapproved of discussing anything at such a meeting, and thought that the meeting should merely state its distresses, leaving it to the wisdom of parliament to discover the remedy. A Mr Woodward, who said he was a farmer, carried us back to the necessity of the war against France, and told us of the horrors of plunder and murder and rape that the war prevented. This gentleman put an end to my patience, which Donovan had put to an extremely severe test, and so I withdrew.

There was a *dinner* after the meeting at the *Star Inn*, at which there occured something rather curious regarding myself. When at Battle, I had no intention of going to Lewes, till on the evening of my arrival at Battle, a gentleman observed to me that I would do well not to go to Lewes. That very observation made me resolve to go. I went, as a spectator, to the meeting, and I left no one ignorant of the place where I was to be found. I did not covet the noise of a dinner of from 200 to 300 persons and I did not intend to go to it, but being pressed to go, I finally went.

After some previous commonplace occurrences, Mr Kemp, formerly a member for Lewes, was called to the chair, and he, having given as toast 'the speedy discovery of a remedy for our distresses', Mr Ebenezer Johnston, a gentleman of Lewes whom I had never seen or heard of until that day, but who, I understand, is a very opulent and most respected man, proposed *my health* as that of a person likely to point out the wished-for remedy.

This was the signal for the onset. Immediately upon the toast being given, a Mr Hitchins, a farmer of Seaford, duly prepared for the purpose, got upon the table and, with candle in one hand and Register in the other read (a) garbled passage. I had not the *Register* with me, and could not detect the garbling. No sooner had Hitchins done, than up started Mr Ingram, a farmer of *Rottendean*, who was the second person in the drama (for all had been duly prepared), and moved that I should be *put out of the room*! Some few of the Webb Hallites, joined by about six or eight of the dark, dirty-faced, half-whiskered tax-eaters from Brighton (which is only eight miles off) joined in the cry. I rose, that they might see the man they had to put out. Fortunately *for themselves*, not one of them attempted to approach me. They were like the mice that resolved that a bell should be put around the cat's neck! At last, however, the chairman, whose conduct was fair and manly, having given my health, I proceeded to address the company, and it is curious enough that even those who, upon my health being given, had taken their hats and gone out of the room, came back, formed a crowd and were just as silent and attentive as the rest of the company!

BRIGHTON
[Thursday, 10 Jan., 1822]
Lewes is in a valley of the South Downs; this town is at eight
miles distance to the south-south-west or therabouts. There is a
great extent of rich meadows above and below Lewes. The town
itself is a model of solidity and neatness. The buildings all
substantial to the very outskirts. The pavements good and
complete, the shops nice and clean, the people well dressed, and,
though last but not least, the girls remarkably pretty, as indeed,
they are in most parts of Sussex. The Sussex men, too, are
remarkable for their good looks. The inns are good as Lewes, the
people civil and not servile and the charges really (considering
the taxes) far below what one could reasonably expect.

From Lewes to Brighton the road winds along between the
hills of the South Downs which, in this mild weather, are most
beautifully green even in this season, with flocks of sheep feeding
on them.

Brighton itself lies in a valley cut across at one end by the sea,
and its extension, or Wen, has swelled up the sides of the hills
and has run some distance up the valley.

Brighton is a very pleasant place, for a *wen* remarkably so. The
Kremlin, the very name of which has long been a subject of
laughter all over the country, lies in the gorge of the valley and
amongst the old houses of the town. The grounds, which cannot
I think exceed a couple or three acres, are surrounded by a wall
neither lofty nor good looking. Above this rise some trees, bad in
sorts, stunted in growth.

As to the *palace*, as the Brighton newspapers call it . . . Take a
square box the sides of which are three and a half feet, and the
height a foot and a half. Take a large Norfolk-turnip, cut off the
green of the leaves, leave the stalks 9 inches long, tie these round
with a string three inches from the top, and put the turnip on the
middle of the top of the box. Then take four turnips of half the
size, treat them in the same way, and put them on the corners of
the box. Then take a considerable number of bulbs of the crown-
imperial, the narcissus, the hyacinth, the tulip, the crocus and
others: let the leaves of each have sprouted to about an inch,
more or less according to the size of the bulb; put all these, pretty
promiscuously but pretty thickly, on the top of the box. Then

stand off and look at your architecture. There! That's '*a Kremlin*'! Only you must cut some church-looking windows in the side of the box. As to what you ought to put *in* the box, that is a subject far above my cut.

Brighton is naturally a place of resort for *expectants*, and a shifty, ugly-looking swarm is, of course, assembled here. Some of the fellows, who had endeavoured to disturb our harmony at the dinner at Lewes, paraded, among this swarm, on the cliff. You may always know them by their lank jaws, the stiffeners round their necks, their hidden or *no* shirts, their stays, their false shoulders, hips and haunches, their half-whiskers and by their skins the colour of veal kidney-suet, warmed a little then powdered with dirty dust. These vermin excepted, the people at Brighton make a very fine figure. The houses are excellent, built chiefly with a blue or purple brick, and bow-windows appear to be the general taste. I can easily believe this to be a very healthy place, the open downs on one side and the open sea on the other. No inlet, cove, or river, and, of course, no swamps.

KENSINGTON
[Friday, 11 January, 1822]
Came home by way of Cuckfield, Worth, and Red-Hill instead of by Uckfield, Grinstead and Godstone, and got into the same road again at Croydon. I see (Jan. 15) that Mr Curteis has thought it necessary to state in the public papers that *he* had *nothing to do* with my being at the dinner at Battle. Who the Devil thought he had? Why, was it not an ordinary, and had I not as much right there as he? He has said, too, that he *did not know* that I was to be at the dinner. Why was it necessary to apprise him of

it any more than the porter at the inn? He has said, that he did not hear of any deputation to invite me to the dinner. Have I said there was any invitation at all? I went to the dinner for my half-crown like another man. But if Mr Curteis thought it necessary to say so much (he) might have said too that, unless I had gone to the dinner, the party would, according to appearances, have been very *select*; that I found him at the head of one of the tables with less than thirty persons in the room, that the number swelled up to about one hundred and thirty; that no person was at the other table; that I took my seat at it and that that table became almost immediately crowded from one end to the other.

The editors of the *Brighton Chronicle and Lewes Express* have, out of mere modesty I dare say, fallen a little into Mr Curteis's strain. In closing their account of the Lewes meeting, they think it necessary to add: 'For ourselves, we can say that we never saw Mr Cobbett until the meeting at Battle.' Now had it not been for pure, maiden-like bashfulness they would doubtless have added that when they did see me, they were profuse in expressions of their gratitude for having merely *named their paper* in my *Register*, a thing which, as I told them, I myself had forgotten. It was, without doubt, out of pure compassion for the perverted taste of their Lewes readers that they suppressed the fact that the agent of the paper at Lewes sent them word that it was useless for them to send any account of the meeting unless that account contained Mr Cobbett's speech; that he, the agent, could have sold a hundred papers that morning if they had contained Mr Cobbett's speech, but could not sell one without it.

HUNTINGDON JOURNAL
Royston
[Monday morning, 21st Jan., 1822]
Came from London, yesterday noon, to this town on my way to Huntingdon. My road through Ware. Royston is just within the line (on the Cambridgeshire side) which divides Hertfordshire from Cambridgeshire. On this road, as on almost all the others going from it, the enormous Wen has swelled out to the distance of about six or seven miles.

After you quit Ware, which is a mere market town, the land grows by degrees poorer. Royston is at the foot of this high, poor land, or rather in a dell the open side of which looks towards the North. It is a common market town. Not mean, but having nothing of beauty about it, and having on it, on three of the sides out of four, those very ugly things, common-fields, which have all the nakedness without any of the smoothness of the Downs.

HUNTINGDON
[Tuesday morning, 22 Jan., 1822]

Immediately upon quitting Royston you come along, for a considerable distance, with enclosed fields on the left and open common fields on the right. Here the land is excellent, a dark rich loam free from stones, on chalk beneath at a great distance.

About four miles, I think it is, from Royston you come to the estate of Lord Hardwicke. You see the house at the end of an avenue about two miles long which, however, wants the main thing, namely fine and lofty trees. A grove, such as I saw at Weston in Herefordshire, would be, here, a thing to attract the attention of all ranks and ages. Lord Hardwicke's avenue appears to be lined with elms chiefly. They are shabby. He might have had *ash*, for ash will grow *anywhere*. It is surprising that those who planted these rows of trees did not observe how well the ash grows here. Its timber is one of the most useful, and as underwood and firewood it exceeds all others of English growth. From the trees of an avenue like that of Lord Hardwicke a hundred pounds' worth of fuel might, if the trees were ash, be cut every year in prunings. Can beggarly stuff like larch and firs ever be profitable to this extent? Ash is timber, fit for the wheelwright, at the age of twenty years or less. What can you do with a rotten fir thing at that age?

Between this place and Huntingdon is the village of Caxton, which very much resembles a village of the same size in *Picardy*, where I saw the women dragging harrows to harrow the corn. Certainly this village resembles nothing English, except some of the rascally rotten boroughs in Cornwall and Devonshire, on which a just Providence seems to have entailed its curse. The land just about here does seem to be really bad. The face of the country is naked. All is bleak and comfortless and, just on the most dreary part of this dreary scene, stands almost opportunely '*Caxton Gibbet*', tendering its friendly one arm to the passers by. It has recently been fresh painted and written on in conspicuous characters for the benefit, I suppose, of those who cannot exist under the thought of wheat at four shillings a bushel.

The country changes but little till you get to Huntingdon itself. Few trees, and those scrubbed: few woods and those small: few hills, and those hardly worthy of the name. All which, when we see them, makes us cease to wonder that this country is so famous for its fox-hunting. Such it has doubtless been from all times, and through this circumstance Huntingdon, that is to say, Huntingdun or Huntingdown, unquestionably owes its name, because *down* does not mean *unploughed* land but open and *unsheltered* land, and the Saxon word is *dun*.

When you come down near to the town itself, the scene suddenly, totally and most agreeably, changes. The *River Ouse* separates Godmanchester from Huntingdown, and there is, I think, no great difference in the population of the two. Both together do not make up a population of more than five thousand souls. Huntingdon is a slightly built town, compared with Lewes, for instance. The houses are not in general so high, nor made of such solid and costly materials. The shops are not so large and their contents not so costly. There is not a show of so much business and so much opulence. But Huntingdon is a very clean and nice place, contains many elegant houses, and the environs are beautiful. Above and below the bridge, under which the Ouse passes, are the most beautiful, and by far the most beautiful, meadows that I ever saw in my life. Here are no reeds, here is no sedge, no unevenness of any sort. Here are *bowling-greens* of hundreds of acres in extent, with a river winding through them, full to the brink. *One* of these meadows is the *race-course*, and so pretty a spot, so level, so smooth, so green and of such an extent I never saw, and never expected to see.

From the bridge you look across the valleys, first to the west and then to the east. The valleys terminate at the foot of rising ground, well set with trees, from amongst which church spires raise their heads here and there. I think it would be very difficult to find a more delightful spot than this in the world. To my fancy (and every one to his taste), the prospect from this bridge far surpasses that from Richmond Hill. All that I have seen of Huntingdon, I like exceedingly. It is one of those pretty, clean, unstenched, unconfined places that tend to lengthen life and make it happy.

JOURNAL: Hertfordshire and Buckinghamshire
Saint Albans
[19 June, 1822]
From Kensington to this place, through Edgeware, Stanmore and Watford, the crop is almost entirely hay from fields of permanent grass manured by dung and other matter brought from the *Wen*. Near the Wen, where they have had the *first haul* of the Irish and other perambulating labourers, the hay is all in rick. Some miles further down it is nearly all in. Towards Stanmore and Watford, a third, perhaps, of the grass remains to be cut. It is curious to see how the thing regulates itself. We saw, all the way down, squads of labourers of different departments migrating from tract to tract, leaving the cleared fields behind them and proceeding on towards the work yet to be performed. And then, as to the classes of labourers, the *mowers*, with their scythes on their shoulders, were in front, going on towards the standing crops, while the *hay-makers* were coming on behind towards the grass already cut or cutting.

The weather is fair and warm so that the public houses on the road are pouring out their beer pretty fast and are getting a good share of the wages of these thirsty souls. It is an exchange of beer for sweat, but the tax-eaters get, after all, the far greater part of the sweat, for if it were not for the tax, the beer would sell for three-halfpence a pot instead of fivepence. Of this threepence halfpenny the jews and jobbers get about twopence halfpenny.

It is curious to observe how the different labours are divided as to the *nations*. The mowers are all *English*, the hay-makers all *Irish*. Scotchmen toil hard enough in Scotland, but when they go from home it is not to *work*, if you please. They are found in gardens, and especially gentlemen's gardens. Tying up flowers, picking dead leaves off exotics, peeping, into melon frames, publishing the banns of marriage between the '*male*' and '*female*' blossoms, tap-tap-tapping against a wall with a hammer that weighs half an ounce. They have backs as straight and shoulders as square as heroes of Waterloo. And who can blame them? The digging, the mowing, the carrying of loads, all the break-back and sweat-extracting work they leave to be performed by those who have less prudence than they have. The great purpose of human art, the great end of human study, is to obtain *ease*, to throw the burden of labour from our own shoulders and fix it on those of others. This is all along here, and especially as far as Stanmore, a very dull and ugly country: flat, and all grass-fields and elms.

KENSINGTON
[24 June, 1822]
Set out at four this morning for Redbourn, and then turned off to the westward to go to High Wycombe, through Hempstead and Chesham. The custom is in this part of Hertfordshire (and I am told it continues into Bedfordshire), to leave a *border* round the ploughed part of the fields to bear grass and to make hay from, so that, the grass being now made into hay, every corn field has a closely mowed grass walk about ten feet wide all round it, between the corn and the hedge. This is most beautiful! The hedges are now full of the shepherd's rose, honeysuckles, and all sorts of wild flowers, so that you are on a grass walk, with this most beautiful of all flower gardens and shrubberies on your one hand, and with the corn on the other. And thus you go from field to field. Talk of *pleasure-grounds* indeed! What that man ever invented, under the name of pleasure-grounds, can equal these fields in Hertfordshire? This is a profitable system, too, for the ground under hedges bears little corn and it bears good grass.

Mr Tull has observed upon the great use of headlands. It is curious enough that these headlands cease soon after you get into Buckinghamshire. Hempstead is a very pretty town, with beautiful environs, and there is a canal that comes near it and that goes on to London. It lies at the foot of a hill. It is clean, substantially built and a very pretty place altogether.

Chesham is a nice little town, lying in a deep and narrow

valley with a stream of water running through it. All along the country that I have come, the labourers' dwellings are good. They are made of what they call *brick-nog*, that is to say, a frame of wood, and a single brick thick, filling up the space between the timbers. They are generally covered with tile.

The orchards all along this country are by no means bad. Not like those of Herefordshire and the north of Kent, but a great deal better than in many other parts of the kingdom. The cherry-trees are pretty abundant and particularly good. There are not many of the *merries*, as they call them in Kent and Hampshire, that is to say, the little black cherry, the name of which is a corruption from the French *merise* in the singular and *merises* in the plural.

I saw the little boys in many places set to keep the birds off the cherries, which reminded me of the time when I followed the same occupation, and also of the toll I used to take in payment. The children are all along here, I mean the little children, locked out of the doors while their fathers and mothers are at work in the fields. I never saw the country children better clad, or look cleaner or fatter than they look here, and I have the very great pleasure to add that I do not think I saw three acres of *potatoes* in this whole tract of fine country. In all the houses where I have been, they use the roasted rye instead of coffee or tea, and I saw one gentleman who had sown a piece of rye (a grain not common in this part of the country) for the express purpose. It costs about three farthings a pound, roasted and ground into powder. The pay of the labourers varies from eight to twelve shillings a week. Grass mowers get two shillings a day, two quarts of what they call strong beer and as much small beer as they can drink.

When I got to High Wycombe, I found everything a week earlier than in the rich part of Hertfordshire. High Wycombe, as if the name was ironical, lies along the bottom of a narrow and deep valley, the hills on each side being very steep indeed. The valley runs somewhere from about east to west, and the wheat on the hills facing south will, if this weather continue, be fit to reap in ten days. I saw one field of oats that a bold farmer would cut next Monday.

Wycombe is a very fine and very clean market town, the

people all looking extremely well, the girls somewhat larger featured and larger boned than those in Sussex and not so fresh coloured and bright-eyed. More like the girls of America, and that is saying quite as much as any reasonable woman can expect or wish for. The hills on the south side of Wycombe form a part and estate now the property of Smith, who was a banker or stocking-maker at Nottingham, who was made a lord in the time of Pitt and who purchased this estate of the late Marquis of Landsdowne, one of whose titles is Baron Wycombe. Wycombe is one of those famous things called boroughs, and 34 votes in this borough send Sir John Dashwood and Sir Thomas Baring to the 'collective wisdom'. After quitting High Wycombe I derived (diversion) from meeting, in all the various modes of conveyance, the cockneys going to *Ealing Fair*, which is one of those things which nature herself would almost seem to have provided for drawing off the matter and giving occasional relief to the overcharged Wen.

This fine summer has already put safe into store such a crop of hay as I believe England never saw before. Looking out of the window, I see the harness of the Wiltshire wagon-horses (at this moment going by) covered with the chalk dust of that county; so that the fine weather continues in the west. The saintfoin hay has all been got in, in the chalk countries, without a drop of wet, and when that is the case the farmers stand in no need of oats. In short, this is one of the finest years that I ever knew.

FROM KENSINGTON TO UPHUSBAND
Chilworth, near Guildford:
[Wednesday, 25th Sept., 1822]
This morning I set off, in rather a drizzling rain, from Kensington on horseback, accompanied by my son, with an intention of going to Uphusband near Andover, which is situated in the north-west corner of Hampshire. It is very true that I could have gone to Uphusband by travelling only about 66 miles, and in the space of about eight hours. But my object was not to see inns and turnpike roads, but to see the *country*, to see the farmers at home and to see the labourers in the fields, and to do this you must either go on foot or on horseback. With a gig

you cannot get about amongst the bye-lanes and across fields, through bridle-ways and hunting gates, and to *trampt it,* is too slow, leaving the labour out of the question, and that is not a trifle.

We went through the turnpike at Kensington, and immediately turned down the lane to our left, proceeded on to Fulham, crossed Putney Bridge into Surrey, went over Barnes Common and then, going on the upper side of Richmond, got again into Middlesex by crossing Richmond-bridge. All Middlesex is *ugly*, notwithstanding the millions upon millions which it is continually sucking up from the rest of the kingdom, and, though the Thames and its meadows now and then are seen from the road, the country is not less ugly from Richmond to Chertsey-bridge, through Twickenham, Hampton, Sunbury and Shepperton, than it is elsewhere. The buildings consist generally of tax-eaters' showy, tea-garden-like boxes, and of shabby dwellings of labouring people who, in this part of the country, look to be about half *Saint Giles,* dirty and having every appearance of drinking gin.

At Chertsey, where we came into Surrey again, there was a fair for horses, cattle and pigs. This county of Surrey presents to the eye of the traveller a greater contrast than any other county in England. It has some of the very best and some of the very worst lands, not only in England but in the world. We were here upon those of the latter description. For five miles on the road towards Guildford the land is a rascally common covered with poor heath. Here we entered the enclosed lands which have the gravel at the bottom, but a nice light mould at top. Through bye-lanes and bridle-ways we came out into the London Road between Ripley and Guildford and, immediately crossing that road, came on towards a village called Merrow.

Lord Onslow lives near Merrow. This is the man that was, for many years, so famous as a driver of four-in-hand. He used to be called Tommy Onslow. He has the character of being a very good landlord. I know he called me 'a d--d *Jacobin*' several years ago only, I presume, because I was labouring to preserve to him the means of still driving four-in-hand while he, and others like him, and their yeoman cavalry were working as hard to defeat my wishes and endeavours.

To come to Chilworth, which lies on the south side of St Martha's Hill, most people would have gone on the level road to Guildford, and come round through Shawford under the hills. But we, having seen enough of streets and turnpikes, took across over Merrow Down where the Guildford race-course is, and then mounted the 'Surrey Hills', so famous for the prospects they afford. We steered for St Martha's chapel, and went round at the foot of the lofty hill on which it stands. This brought us down the side of a steep hill, along a bridle-way, into the narrow and exquisitely beautiful vale of Chilworth, where we were to stop for the night. Down the middle of the vale there is a series of ponds, or small lakes, which meet your eye, here and there, through the trees. Here are some very fine farms, a little strip of meadows, some hop-gardens; and the lakes have given rise to the establishment of powder-mills and paper mills. The trees of all sorts grow well here, and coppices yield poles for the hop-gardens and wood to make charcoal for the powder-mills.

LEA, NEAR GODALMING, SURREY
[Thursday, 26 Sept.]
We started from Chilworth this morning, came down the vale, left the village of Shalford to our right and that of Wonersh to our left and, crossing the river Wey, got into the turnpike road between Guildford and Godalming, went on through Godalming and got to Lea, which lies to the north-east snugly under Hind-Head, about 11 o'clock. This was coming only about eight miles, a sort of rest after the 32 miles of the day before.

Coming along the road, a farmer overtook us, and as he had known me from seeing me at the meeting at Epsom last year, I had a part of my main business to perform, namely to talk politics. He was going to *Haslemere* Fair. Upon the mention of that *sinkhole* of a borough we began to talk, as it were spontaneously, about Lord Londsdale and the Lowthers. The farmer wondered why the Lowthers, that were the owners of so many farms, should be for a system which was so manifestly taking away the estates of the landlords and the capital of the farmers, and giving them to jews, loan-jobbers, stock-jobbers, placemen, pensioners, sinecure people. But his wonder ceased, his eyes were opened and 'his heart seemed to burn within him as I talked to him on the way' when I explained him the nature of *Crown lands* and *Crown tenants*.

I have once before mentioned, but I will repeat it, that Marlborough House in Pall Mall, for which the Prince of Saxe Coburg pays a rent to the Duke of Marlborough of three thousand pounds a year, is rented of this generous public by that most noble duke at the rate of less than *forty pounds* a year. There are three houses in Pall Mall the whole of which pay a rent *to the public* of about fifteen pounds a year, I think it is. I myself, twenty-two years ago, paid three hundred pounds a year for one of them to a man I thought was the owner of them, but I now find that these houses belong to the public. The Duke of Buckingham's house in Pall Mall, which is one of the grandest in all London and which is worth not less than seven or eight hundred pounds a year, belongs to the public. The duke is the tenant, and I think he pays for it much less than twenty pounds a year.

We got into free quarters again at Lea, and there is nothing like free-quarter, as soldiers well know. Lea is situated on the edge of that immense heath which sweeps down from the summit of Hind-Head, across to the north over innumerable hills of minor altitude and of an infinite variety of shapes towards Farnham, to the north-east, towards the Hog's Back leading from Farnham to Guildford, and to the east, or nearly so, towards Godalming. Nevertheless, the inclosed lands at Lea are very good and singularly beautiful. If you go southward from Lea about a mile you get down into what is called, in the old Acts of Parliament, the *Weald* of Surrey.

ODIHAM, HAMPSHIRE
[Friday, 27 Sept.]
From Lea we set off this morning about six o'clock to get free-quarter again at a worthy old friend's at this nice little plain market town. Our direct road was right over the heath through Tilford to Farnham, but we veered a little to the left after we came to Tilford, at which place on the green we stopped to look at an *oak tree* which, when I was a little boy, was but a very little tree, comparatively, and which is now, take it altogether, by far the finest tree I ever saw in my life. The stem, or shaft, is short, but it is full *thirty feet round* at about eight or ten feet from the ground. My son stepped the ground, and nearly as we could judge, the diameter of the extent of the branches was upwards of ninety feet, which would make a circumference of about three hundred feet. The tree is in full growth at this moment. There is a little hole in one of the limbs but, with that exception, there appears not the smallest sign of decay.

In quitting Tilford, we went a little out of the way to go to a place called Bourne, which lies in the heath about a mile from Farnham. It is a winding narrow valley, down which during the wet season of the year there runs a stream beginning at the *Holt Forest*, and emptying itself into the *Wey* just below Moor-Park, which was the seat of Sir William Temple when Swift was residing with him.

We went to this bourn in order that I might show my son the spot where I received the rudiments of my education. There is a little hop-garden in which I used to work from eight to ten years old, from which I have scores of times run to follow the hounds, leaving the hoe to do the best it could to destroy the weed. But the most interesting thing was a *sand-hill* which goes from a part of the heath down to the rivulet. As a due mixture of pleasure with toil, I with my two brothers used occasionally to *desport* ourselves, as the lawyers call it, at this sand-hill. Our diversion was this: we used to go to the top of the hill, which was steeper than the roof of a house. One used to draw his arms out of the sleeves of his smock-frock, and lay himself down with his arms by his sides. And then the others, one at head and the other at feet, sent him rolling down the hill like a barrel or log of wood. By the time he got to the bottom his hair, eyes, nose, and mouth were all full of loose sand. Then the others took their turn and at every roll there was a monstrous spell of laughter.

But that was not all. This was the spot where I was receiving my education, and this was the sort of education; and I am perfectly satisfied that if I had not received such an education, or something very much like it: that, if I had been brought up a milksop with a nursery-maid everlastingly at my heels, I should have been at this day as great a fool, as inefficient a mortal as any of those frivolous idiots that are turned out from Winchester and Westminster School, or from any of those dens of dunces called universities. It is impossible to say how much I owe to that sand-hill.

From the Bourne we proceeded on to Wrecklesham, at the end of which we crossed what is called the river Wey. Here we found a parcel of labourers at parish-work. Amongst them was an old playmate of mine. The account they gave of their situation was very dismal. The harvest was over early. The hop-picking is now over, and now they are employed by the *parish* – that is to say, not absolutely digging holes one day and filling them up the next, but, at the expense of half-ruined farmers and tradesmen and landlords, to break stones into very small pieces to make nice smooth roads lest the jolting, on going along them, should create bile in the stomach of the over-fed tax-eaters.

We left these poor fellows, after having given them not 'religious tracts', which would, if they could, make the labourer content with half-starvation, but something to get them some bread and cheese and beer. However, in speaking of their low wages, I told them that the farmers and hop-planters were as much objects of compassion as themselves, which they acknowledged.

[Saturday, 28th September]
Just after daylight we started for this place. From Wrecklesham to Winchester we have come over roads and lanes of flint and chalk. The weather being dry again, the ground under you, as solid as iron, makes a great rattling with the horses' feet.

Chalk is the favourite soil of the *yew-tree*, and at Preston Candover there is an avenue of yew-trees, probably a mile long. They have probably been a century or two in growing but, in any way that timber can be used, the timber of the yew will last, perhaps, ten times as long as the timber of any other tree that we can grow in England.

Quitting the Candovers, we came along between the two estates of the two Barings. Sir Thomas was to our right while Alexander was on our left. I do not like to be a spy in any man's neighbourhood, but I will tell Sir Thomas Baring what I heard. And if he be a man of sense, I shall have his thanks rather than his reproaches for doing so. I may have been misinformed, but this is what I heard, that he and Lady Baring are very charitable, but that they tack a condition to their charity, that they insist upon the objects of it adopting their notions with regard to religion. I do not say that they are not perfectly pious themselves, but of this I am very certain, that, by pursuing this principle of action, where they make one good man or woman, they will make one hundred hypocrits. Sir Thomas Baring would do better, by using the influence he must naturally have in the neighbourhood, to prevent a diminution in the wages of labour.

[Sunday morning, 29 Sept.]
Yesterday was market-day here. Proceeding on the true military principle, I looked out for free quarter, which the reader will

naturally think difficult for *me* to find in a town containing a *cathedral*. Having done this, I went to the Swan Inn to dine with the farmers. This is the manner I like best of doing the thing. I do not like dinner-meetings on *my* account. I like much better to go and fall in with the lads of the land. At the dinner at Winchester, we had a good number of opulent yeomen and many gentlemen joined us after the dinner and during the session I made the following RUSTIC HARANGUE*.

(UPHUSBAND)
[7 to 10 October, 1822]
Went to Weyhill Fair, at which I was about 46 years ago when I rode a little pony and remember how proud I was on that occasion. But I also remember that my brothers, two out of three of whom were older than I, thought it unfair that my father selected me, and my own reflections upon the occasion have never been forgotten by me.

The 11th October is the Sheep-fair. About £300,000 used, some few years ago, to be carried home by the sheep-sellers. Today, less perhaps than £70,000, and yet the *rents* of these sheep-sellers are, perhaps, as high on an average as they were then. The countenances of the farmers were descriptive of their ruinous state. I never, in all my life, beheld a more mournful scene.

[12–16 October]
The fair was too dismal for me to go to it again. My sons went two of the days, and their account of the hop-fair was enough to make one gloomy for a month, particularly as my townsmen of Farnham were, in this case, among the sufferers. On the 12th I went to dine with, and harangue, the farmers at Andover. Great attention was paid to what I had to say.

[17 October]
Went to Newbury to dine with and harangue the farmers. It was

* Here Cobbett inserts a lengthy speech on the subject of tithes, ending: 'I will give you a toast, leaving you to drink it or not, as you please: *A large reduction of Tithes*'.

a fair day. It rained so hard that I had to stop at Burghclere to dry my clothes, and to borrow a greatcoat to keep me dry the rest of the way, so as not to have to sit in wet clothes. At Newbury, the company was not less attentive than at Andover. Some one of the tax-eating crew had, I understand, called me an 'incendiary'. After the dinner was over I went back to Burghclere.

[18–20 October]
At Burghclere, one half the time writing, and the other half hare-hunting.

[22 October]
Went to dine with the farmers at Salisbury, and got back to Uphusband by ten o'clock at night, two hours later than I have been out of bed for a great many months.

In quitting Andover to go to Salisbury you cross the beautiful valley that goes winding down the hills to Stockbridge. You then rise into the open country that very soon becomes a part of that large tract of downs called Salisbury Plain. You leave Tidworth away to your right. This is the seat of Asheton Smith, and the fine *coursing* I once saw there I should have called to recollection with pleasure, if I could have forgotten the hanging of the men at Winchester last spring for resisting one of this Smith's gamekeepers! This Smith's son and a Sir John Pollen are the members for Andover.

Before you get to Salisbury, you cross the valley that brings down a little river from Amesbury. Not far above Amesbury is a little village called Netherhaven, where I once saw an *acre of hares*. We were coursing at Everly, a few miles off, and one of the party happening to say that he had seen 'an acre of hares' at Mr Hick Beech's at Netherhaven, we, who wanted to see the same, or to detect our informant, sent a messenger to beg a day's coursing, which, being granted, we went over the next day. Mr Beech received us very politely. He took us into a wheat stubble close by his paddock; his son took a gallop round, cracking his whip at the same time. The hares (which were very thickly in sight before) started all over the field, ran into a *flock* like sheep, and we all agreed that the flock did cover *an acre of ground*.

In crossing this valley to go to Salisbury, I thought of Mr
Beech's hares, but I really have neither thought or nor seen any
game with pleasure, since the hanging of the two men at
Winchester. If no other man will petition for the repeal of the
law under which these two poor fellows suffered, I will. But let us
hope there will be no need for petitioning.

The company at Salisbury was very numerous; not less than
500 farmers were present. They received very docilely what I
said against squeezing the labourers. A fire, in a farm-yard, had
lately taken place near Salisbury, so that the subject was a
ticklish one. But it was my very first duty to treat of it and I was
resolved, be the consequence what it might, not to neglect that
duty.

[27 to 29 October]
At Burghclere. Very nasty weather. On the 28th the fox hounds
came to throw off at *Pendwood*. Having heard that *Dundas**
would be out with the hounds, I rode to the place of meeting in
order to look him in the face and to give him an opportunity to
notice, on his own peculiar dung-hill, what I had said of him at
Newbury. He came. I rode up to him and about him, but he said
not a word.

[31 October]
Set off for London and slept at Oakingham. Set off at daylight
and got to Kensington about noon. On leaving Oakingham for
London, you get upon what is called *Windsor Forest*, that is to say

* He had earlier called Cobbett 'an incendiary'. See October 17.

upon as bleak, as barren and as villainous a heath as ever man set his eyes on. However, here are new enclosures without end. These new enclosures and houses arise out of the beggaring of the parts of the country distant from the vortex of the funds. The farm-houses have long been growing fewer and fewer, the labourers' houses fewer and fewer, and it is manifest to every man who has eyes to see with that the villages are regularly wasting away. This is the case all over the parts of England where the tax-eaters do not haunt. As to this rascally heath, that which has ornamented it has brought misery on millions. The spot is not distant from the stock-jobbing crew. The roads to it are level. They are smooth. The wretches can go to it from the 'Change without any danger to their worthless necks.

At the end of this blackguard heath you come (on the road to Egham) to a little place called *Sunning Hill*. It is a spot all made into 'grounds' and gardens by tax-eaters. The inhabitants of it have beggared twenty agricultural villages and hamlets.

[8 November]
From London to Egham in the evening.

[9 November]
Started at daybreak in a hazy frost, for Reading. The horses' manes and ears covered with the hoar before we got across Windsor Park. A very large part of the Park is covered with heath or rushes, a sure sign of execrable soil. But the roads are such as might have been made by Solomon. 'O, greater than Solomon is here,' some one may exclaim. Of that I know nothing. I am but a traveller and the roads in this park are beautiful indeed. My servant, whom I had brought with me from amongst the hills and flints of Uphusband, must certainly have thought himself in Paradise as he was going through the Park. If I had told him that the buildings and labourers' clothes and meals at Uphusband were the *worse* for these pretty roads with edgings cut to line, he would have wondered at me, I dare say.

At Binfield, I stopped to breakfast at a very nice country inn called the *Stag and Hounds*. A road as smooth as a die, a real stock-jobber's road, brought us to Reading by eleven o'clock. We dined at one, and very much pleased I was with the company.

I came on horseback 40 miles, slept on the road and finished my harangue at the end of *twenty-two hours* from leaving Kensington, and I cannot help saying that is pretty well for 'Old Cobbett'. I am delighted with the people I have seen at Reading. Their kindness to me is nothing in my estimation with the sense and spirit which they appear to possess.

[11 November]
Uphusband once more, and for the sixth time this year over the North Hampshire Hills which, notwithstanding their everlasting flints, I like very much. As you ride along, even in a *green lane*, the horses' feet make a noise like *hammering*. Yet the soil is good, and bears some of the best wheat in England. They manure the land here by digging *wells* in the field and bringing up the chalk, which they spread on the land and which, being free-chalk, is reduced to powder by the frosts.

[17 November]
Set off from Uphusband for Hambledon. The first place I had to get to was Whitchurch . . a small town, but famous for being the place where the paper has been made for the *Borough-Bank*! I passed by the *mill* on my way to get out upon the downs to go to Alresford, where I intended to sleep. I hope that the time will come when a monument will be erected where that mill stands and when on the monument will be described *the curse of England*. This spot ought to be held accursed in all time henceforth and for ever more. It has been the spot from which have sprung more and greater mischiefs than ever plagued mankind before.

Quitting Whitchurch, I went off to the left out of the Winchester road, got out upon the highlands, 'took an observation', as the sailors call it, and off I rode, in a straight line, over hedge and ditch towards the rising ground between Stratton Park and Micheldever Wood. A little girl of whom I asked my way down into East Stratton, and who was dressed in a camlet gown, white apron and plaid cloak (it was Sunday) and who had a book in her hand, told me that Lady Baring gave her the clothes, and had her taught to read and to sing hymns and spiritual songs.

As I came through the Strattons I saw not less than a dozen

girls clad in this way. It is impossible not to believe that it is done with good motive, but it is possible not to believe that it is productive of good. It must create hypocrits, and hypocrisy is the great sin of the age. Society is in a *queer* state when the rich think that they must *educate* the poor in order to protect their *own safety*: for this, at the bottom, is the great motive now at work in pushing on the education scheme.

[18 November]
Came from Alresford to Hambledon, through Titchbourne, Cheriton, Beauworth, Kilmston and Exton. At Cheriton, I found a grand camp of *Gipsys*, just upon the move to Alresford. I had met some of the scouts first and afterwards the advance guard, and here the main body was getting into motion. One of the scouts that I met was a young woman who, I am sure, was six feet high. There were two or three more in the camp about the same height, and some most strapping fellows of men. It is curious that this race should have preserved their dark skin and coal-black straight and coarse hair, very much like that of the American Indians. The tall girl that I met at Titchbourne, who had a huckster basket on her arm, had the most beautiful features. I pulled up my horse and said 'Can you tell me my fortune, my dear?' She answered in the negative, giving me a look at the same time that seemed to say it was *too late*, and that if I had been thirty years younger she might have seen a little what she could do with me.

[24 November: Sunday]
Set off from Hambledon to go to Thursley in Surrey, about five miles from Godalming. Here I am at Thursley, after as interesting a day as I ever spent in my life.
   To go to Thursley from Hambledon, the plain way was up the downs to Petersfield, and then along the turnpike road through Liphook, and over Hindhead, at the north-east foot of which Thursley lies. But I had been over that sweet Hindhead, and had seen too much of a turnpike road and of heath, to think of taking another large dose of them. The map of Hampshire showed me the way to Headley, which lies on the west of Hindhead, down upon the flat. I knew it was but about five

miles from Headley to Thursley and I therefore resolved to go to Headley, in spite of the remonstrances of friends who represented to me the danger of breaking my neck at Hawkley and of getting buried in the bogs of Woolmer Forest.

Off we set over the downs from West-End to East Meon. We came down a long and steep hill that led us winding round into the village, that has a rivulet that comes out of the hills near Petersfield. And if I had not seen anything further today, I should have dwelt long on the beauties of this place. Here is a very fine valley, in nearly an elliptical form, sheltered by high hills gradually sloping from it. And not far from the middle of this valley there is a hill nearly in the form of a goblet-glass with the foot and stem broken off and turned upside down. And this is clapped down upon the level of the valley, just as you would put such a goblet upon a table. The hill is lofty partly covered with wood, and it gives an air of great singularity to the scene.

I am sure that East Meon has been a *large place*. The church has a *Saxon tower* pretty nearly equal, as far as I can recollect, to that of the Cathedral at Winchester. The rest of the church has been rebuilt and, perhaps, several times. But the *tower* is complete; it has a large *steeple* upon it, but it retains all its beauty and shows that the church (which is still large) must at first have been a very large building. Let those who talk so glibly of the increase of population in England go over the country from Highclere to Hambledon. Let them look at the size of the churches, and let them observe those numerous small inclosures on every side of every village which had, to a certainty, *each its house* in former times. But let them go to East Meon and account for that church. Where did the hands come from to make it?

From East Meon I did not go on to Froxfield church, but turned off to the left to a place (a couple of houses) called *Bower*. Near this I stopped at a friend's house, which is in about as lonely a position as I ever saw. A very pleasant place, however.

At Bower I got instructions to go to Hawkley, but accompanied with most earnest advice not to go that way, for that it was impossible to get along. The roads were represented as so bad: the floods so much out, the hills and bogs so dangerous that, really, I began to *doubt*, and, if I had not been brought up among the clays of the Holt Forest and the bogs of the neighbouring heaths, I should certainly have turned off to go to my right, to go over Hindhead, great as was my objection to going that way. 'Well, then,' said my friend at Bower, 'if you *will* go that way, by G-, you must go down *Hawkley Hanger*,' of which he then gave me *such* a description! But even this I found to fall short of the reality. I inquired simply whether *people were in the habit* of going down it. And the answer being in the affirmative, on I went through green lanes and bridle-ways until I came to the turnpike-road from Petersfield to Winchester which I crossed, going into a narrow and almost untrodden green lane, on the

side of which I found a cottage. Upon my asking the way to *Hawkley*, the woman at the cottage said: 'Right up the lane, sir; you'll come to a *hanger* presently; you must take care, sir, you can't ride down; will your horses go alone?'

On we trotted up this pretty green lane. The lane was between highish banks and pretty high stuff growing on the banks, so that we could see no distance from us, and could receive not the smallest hint of what was so near at hand. The lane had a little turn towards the end; so that out we came, all in a moment, at the very edge of the hanger! And never, in all my life, was I so surprised and delighted. I pulled up my horse and sat and looked; and it was like looking from the top of a castle down into the sea, except that the valley was land and not water. I looked at my servant to see what this unexpected sight had upon him. His surprise was as great as mine, though he had been bred among the North Hampshire Hills. Those who had so strenuously dwelt on the dirt and dangers of this route, had said not a word about beauties, the matchless beauties of the scenery. These hangers are woods on the side of very steep hills. The trees and underwood *hang*, in some sort, to the ground instead of *standing on* it. Hence these places are called *Hangers*. From the summit of that which I now had to descend, I looked down upon the villages of Hawkley, Greatham, Selborne and some others.

From the south-east round southward, to the north-west, the main valley has cross-valleys running out of it, the hills on the side of which are very steep and, in many parts, covered with wood. The hills that form these cross-valleys run out, into the main valley, like piers into the sea. Two of these promontories, of very great height, are on the west side of the main valley and were the first objects that struck my sight when I came to the edge of the hanger, which was on the south. The ends of these promontories are nearly perpendicular, and their tops so high in the air, that you cannot look down on the village below without something like a feeling of apprehension. The leaves are all off, the fields have little verdure; but, while the spot is beautiful beyond description even now, I must leave to imagination to suppose what it is when the trees and hangers are in leaf, the corn waving, the meadows bright and the hops on the poles!

Men, however, are not to have such beautiful views as this

without trouble. We had had the view, but we had to get down the hanger. The horses took the lead, and crept partly down upon their feet and partly upon their hocks. It was extremely slippery, too; for the soil is a sort of marl, or, as they call it here, maume or mame, which is, when wet, very like grey soap. In such a case it was likely that I should keep in the rear, which I did, and I descended by taking hold of the branches of the underwood, and so letting myself down.

Our worst, however, was not come yet, nor had we by any means seen the most novel sights. After crossing a little field, and going through a farmyard, we came into a lane which was, at once, road and river. We found a hard bottom, however, and when we got out of the water, we got into a lane with high banks. The banks were quarries of white stone, like Portland-stone, and the bed of the road was of the same stone; and, the rains having been heavy a day or two before, the whole was as clean and white as the steps of a fund-holder or dead weight doorway in one of the squares of the *Wen*. Here were we, then, going along a stone road with stone banks, and yet the underwood and trees grew well upon the tops of the banks. In the solid stone beneath us, there were a horse-track and wheel track, the former about three and the latter about six inches deep. How many ages it must have taken the horses' feet, the wheels, and the water to wear down this stone so as to form a hollow way! The horses seemed alarmed at their situation; they trod with fear, but they took us along very nicely and at last got us safely into the indescribable dirt and mire of the road from Hawkley Green to Greatham.

At Hawkley Green I asked a farmer the way to Thursley. He pointed to one of the two roads going from the Green; but, it appearing to me that that would lead me up the London road and over Hindhead, I gave him to understand that I was resolved to get along, somehow or other, through the 'low countries'. He besought me not to think of it. However, finding me resolved, he got a man to go a little way to put me into the Greatham road. The man came, but the farmer could not let me go off without renewing his entreaties that I would go away to Liphook, in which entreaties the man joined, though he was to be paid very well for his trouble.

Upon leaving Greatham, we came out upon Woolmer Forest.

I asked a man the way to Thursley. 'You *must* go to *Liphook*,' said he. 'But,' I said, 'I will *not* go to Liphook.' These people seemed to be posted at all these stages to turn me aside from my purpose, and to make me go over that Hindhead, which I had resolved to avoid. I went on a little further and asked another man the way to Headley, which, as I have already observed, lies on the western foot of Hindhead, whence I knew there must be a road to Thursley without going over that miserable hill. The man told me I must go across the *forest*. I asked him whether it was a *good* road. 'It is a *sound* road,' said he, laying emphasis upon the word *sound*. 'Do people *go* it?' said I. '*Ye-es*,' said he. 'Oh, then,' said I to my man, 'as it is a *sound* road, keep you close to my heels and do not attempt to go aside, not even for a foot.' Indeed it was a *sound* road. The rain of the night had made the fresh horse-tracks visible. And we got to Headly in a short time, over a sand-road which seemed so delightful after the flints and stone and dirt and sloughs that we had passed over and through since the morning. This road was, if we had been benighted, not without its dangers, this forest being full of quags and quicksands.

We got to Headley, the sign of the Holly Bush, just at dusk and just as it began to rain. I had neither eaten nor drunk since eight o'clock in the morning; and as it was a nice little public-house, I at first intended to stay all night, an intention that I afterwards very indiscreetly gave up. I had *laid my plan*, which included the getting to Thursley that night. When, therefore, I had had some cold bacon and bread and some milk, I began to feel ashamed of stopping short of my *plan*, especially after having so heroically persevered in the 'stern path' and so disdainfully scorned to go over Hindhead. I knew that my road lay through a hamlet called *Churt*, where they grow also fine *bennet-grass* seed. There was a moon, but there was also a hazy rain. I had heaths to go over, and I might go into quags.

Wishing to execute my plan, however, I at last brought myself to quit a very comfortable turf-fire, and to set off in the rain, having bargained to give a man three shillings to guide me out to the northern foot of Hindhead. I took care to ascertain that my guide knew the road perfectly well, that is to say, I took care to ascertain it as far as I could, which was, indeed, no further than his word would go.

Off we set, the guide mounted on his own or his master's horse, and with a white smock frock, which enabled us to see him clearly. We trotted on pretty fast for about half an hour; and I perceived, not without some surprise, that the rain, which I knew to be coming from the *south*, met me full in the face, when it ought according to my reckoning to have beat upon my right cheek. I called to the guide repeatedly to ask him if he was *sure that he was right*, to which he always answered, 'Oh, yes, sir. I know the road.' I did not like this '*I know the road.*' At last, after going about six miles in a southern direction, the guide turned short to the left; and after going about a mile in this new direction I began to ask the guide *how much further we had to go*, for I had got a pretty good soaking, and was rather impatient to see the foot of Hindhead. Just at this time, in raising my head and looking forward as I spoke to the guide, what should I see but a long, high and steep *hanger* arising before us. The fact was, we were just getting to the outside of the heath, and were on the brow of a steep hill which faced this hanging wood. The guide had begun to descend and I had called to him to stop, for the hill was so steep that, rain as it did, and wet as my saddle must be, I got off my horse in order to walk down.

But now, behold, the fellow discovered that he *had lost his way*! Where we were I could not even guess. There was but one remedy, and that was to get back, if we could. I became guide now. We went back about half the way we had come, when we saw two men who showed us the way we ought to go. At the end of about a mile, we fortunately found the turnpike road; not indeed at the *foot* but on the tip-top of that very Hindhead on which I had repeatedly vowed I would not go! We came out on the turnpike some hundred yards on the Liphook side of the buildings called *the Hut*; so that we had the whole of three miles of hill to come down at not much better than a foot pace, with a good rain pelting at our backs.

It is odd how differently one is affected by the same sight, under different circumstances. At the '*Holly Bush*' at Headley there was a room full of fellows in white smock frocks, drinking and smoking and talking, and I, who was then dry and warm, moralised within myself on their *folly* in spending their time in such a way. But when I got down from Hindhead to the public house at Road Lane, with my skin soaking and my teeth chattering, I thought just such another group, whom I saw through the window sitting round a good fire with pipes in their mouths, the *wisest assembly* I have ever set my eyes on. A real *Collective Wisdom*.

It was now but a step to my friend's house, where a good fire and a change of clothes soon put all to rights, save and except the having come over Hindhead after all my resolutions. This mortifying circumstance; this having been *beaten*, lost the guide the three shillings that I had agreed to give him. 'Either,' said I, 'you did not know the way well, or you did. If the former, it was dishonest in you to undertake to guide me; if the latter, you have wilfully led me miles out of my way.' He grumbled, but off he went. He certainly deserved nothing, for he did not know the way, and he prevented some other man from earning and receiving the money. But had he not caused me to *get upon Hindhead* he would have had the three shillings. I had, at one time, got my hand in my pocket; but the thought of having been beaten pulled it out again.

Thus ended the most interesting day, as far as I know, that I ever passed in all my life. Hawkley-hangers, promontories and stone-roads will always come into my mind when I see, or hear, of picturesque views. I forgot to mention that, in going from Hawkley to Greatham, the man who went to show me the way told me at a certain fork: 'that road goes to *Selborne*'. This put me in mind of a book, which was once recommended to me but which I never saw, entitled *The History and Antiquities of Selborne* (or something of that sort) written, I think, by a parson of the name of *White*, brother of Mr *White* so long a bookseller in Fleet Street. This parson had, I think, the living of Selborne. The book was mentioned to me as a work of great curiosity and interest. But at that time the THING was biting *so very sharply* that one had no attention to bestow on antiquarian researches. Wheat at 39*s*. a quarter, and South-Down ewes at 12*s*. 6*d*., have so weakened the THING's jaws and so filed down its teeth, that I shall now certainly read this book if I can get it. By the by, if *all the parsons* had, for the last thirty years or so, employed their leisure in writing the histories of their several parishes, instead of living, as so many of them have, engaged in pursuits that I need not here name, neither their situation nor that of their flocks would, perhaps, have been the worse for it at this day.

[26–28 November, Godalming]
I came here to meet my son, who was to return to London when
we had done our business.

[November 29]
Went on to Guildford, where I slept.

[Dorking, November 30]
I came over the high hill on the south of Guildford, and came
down to Chilworth and up the valley to Albury. I noticed, in my
first Rural Ride, this beautiful valley, its hangers, its meadows,
its hop-gardens, and its ponds. This valley of Chilworth has
great variety and is very pretty, but after seeing Hawkley every
other place loses in point of beauty and interest.

This pretty valley of Chilworth has a run of water which
comes out of the high hills and which, occasionally, spreads into
ponds. This valley, which seems to have been created by a
bountiful providence as one of the choicest retreats of man;
which seems formed for a scene of happiness and innocence, has
been, by ungrateful man, so perverted as to make it instru-
mental in effecting two of the most damnable of purposes,
namely the making of *gunpowder* and *banknotes*! Here, in this
tranquil spot, where the nightingales are to be heard earlier and
later in the year than in any other part of England; where the
first bursting of the buds is seen in spring, where no rigour of
season can ever be felt; where everything seems formed for
precluding the very thought of wickedness; here has the devil
fixed as one of the seats of his grand manufactory; and perverse
and ungrateful man not only lends him his aid, but lends it
cheerfully!

As to the gunpowder, indeed, we might get over that. In some
cases that may be innocently and, when it sends the lead at the
hordes that support a tyrant, meritoriously employed. The
alders and the willows, therefore, one can see, without so much
regret, turned into powder by the waters of this valley. But the
bank-notes! To think that the springs which God has commanded
to flow from the sides of these happy hills, for the comfort and
delight of man; to think that these springs should be perverted
into means of spreading misery over a whole nation; and that,

too, under the base and hypocritical pretence of promoting its *credit* and maintaining its *honour* and *faith*! There was one circumstance, indeed, that served to mitigate the melancholy excited by these reflections; namely, that a part of these springs have, at times, assisted in turning rags into *Registers*!

Somewhat cheered by the thought of this, but still in a more melancholy mood than I had been for a long while, I rode on with my friend towards Albury, up the valley, the sand-hills on one side of us and the chalk hills on the other. Albury is a little village consisting of a few houses, with a large house or park or two near it. At the end of the village we came to a park, which is the residence of Mr Drummond. Having heard a great deal of this park, and of the gardens, I wished very much to see them. My way to Dorking lay through Shire, and it went along on the outside of the park. I *guessed*, as the Yankees say, that there must be a way through the park to Shire; and I fell upon the scheme of going through the park as far as Mr Drummond's house, and then asking his leave to go out the other end of it. This scheme, though pretty bare-faced, succeeded very well. I sent in word that, having got into the park, I should be exceedingly obliged to Mr Drummond if he would let me go out of it on the side next to Shire. He not only granted this request but, in the most obliging manner, permitted us to ride all about the park and to see his gardens, which, without any exception, are to my fancy the prettiest in England, that is to say, that I ever saw in England.

They say that these gardens were laid out for one of the Howards, in the reign of Charles II, by Mr Evelyn, who wrote the *Sylva*. The mansion-house, which is by no means magnificent, stands on a little flat by the side of the parish church, having a steep but not lofty hill rising up the south side of it. It looks right across the gardens, which lie on the slope of a hill which runs along about a quarter of a mile distant from the front of the house. Between the house and gardens there is a very beautiful run of water. At the back of the garden is a wall probably ten feet high which forms the breastwork of a terrace. And it is this terrace which is the most beautiful thing that I ever saw in the gardening way. It is a quarter of a mile long and, I believe, between thirty and forty feet wide; of the finest greensward and as level as a die. The whole thing is a great compliment to the taste of the times in which it was formed. I know there are ill-natured persons who will say that I want a revolution that would turn Mr Drummond out of this place and put me into it. Such persons will hardly believe me, but upon my word I do not. From everything that I hear, Mr Drummond is very worthy of possessing it himself, seeing that he is famed for his justice and kindness *towards the labouring classes*, who, God knows, have very few friends among the rich.

I saw in the gardens of Albury Park what I never saw before in all my life; that is, some plants of American Cranberries. I never saw them in America, for there they grow in those swamps into which I never happened to go at the time of their bearing fruit. They grew in a long bed near the stream of water which I have spoken about, and therefore it is clear that they may be cultivated with great ease in this country.

[Reigate, December]

I set off this morning with an intention to go across the weald to Worth; but the red rising of the sun and the other appearances of the morning admonished me to keep upon *high ground*. In one rotten borough, one of the most rotten too, and with another still more rotten *up upon the hill*, in Reigate, and close by Gatton, how can I help reflecting on the marvellous deeds of the Collective Wisdom of the nation! At present, however (for I want to get to bed), I will notice only one of those deeds, the new Turnpike Act. This Act makes *chalk* and *lime* everywhere liable to turnpike duty, which in many cases there were not before. This is a monstrous oppression upon the owners and occupiers of clay lands; and comes just at the time, too, when they are on the point, many of them, of being driven out of cultivation, or thrown upon the parish, by other burdens. But it is the provision with regard to the *wheels* which will create the greatest injury, distress and confusion. The wheels which this law orders to be used on turnpike roads, on pain of enormous toll, cannot be used on the *cross-roads* throughout more than nine-tenths of the kingdom. To make these roads and the *drove lanes* (the private roads of farms) fair for the cylindrical wheels described in this Bill would cost a pound an acre. And this is enacted, too, when all is perishing for want of means in the farmer to keep it in repair.

[Worth (Sussex), December 2]
I set off from Reigate this morning and after a pleasant ride of ten miles, got here to breakfast. Thus, sir, have I led you about the country. All sorts of things I have talked of, to be sure, but there are very few of these things which have not their interest of one sort or another. At the end of a hundred miles or two of travelling, stopping here and there; talking freely with everybody; hearing what gentlemen, farmers, tradesmen, journeymen, labourers, women, girls, boys and all have to say; reasoning with some, laughing with others, and observing all that passes; at the end of a tramp like this you get impressed upon your mind a true picture, not only of the state of the country, but of the state of the people's minds throughout the country.

RIDE FROM KENSINGTON TO WORTH, IN SUSSEX
[Monday, May 5 1823]
From London to Reigate, through Sutton, is about as villainous a tract as England contains. At Reigate they are (in order to save a few hundred yards length of road) cutting through a hill. They have lowered a little hill on the London side of Sutton. Thus is the money of the country actually thrown away. Mark the process: the town of Brighton, in Sussex, 50 miles from the Wen, is on the seaside, and is thought by the stock-jobbers to have a *salubrious* air. It is so situated that a coach, which leaves it not very early in the morning, reaches London by noon; and, starting to go back in two hours and a half afterwards, reaches Brighton not very late at night. Great parcels of stock-jobbers stay at Brighton with the women and children. They skip backward and forward on the coaches and actually carry on stock-jobbing, in 'Change Alley', though they reside in Brighton. There are not less than about 20 coaches that leave the Wen every day for this place; and there being three or four different roads, there is a great rivalship for the custom. This sets the people to work to shorten and to level the roads; and here you see

hundreds of men and horses constantly at work to make quick
and pleasant travelling for the jews and jobbers. The jews and
jobbers pay the turnpikes, to be sure; but they get the money
from the land and labourers. They drain these, from John-a-
Groats to Land's End, and they lay out some of the money on the
Brighton road!

[Worth, 30 July]

I met at Worth a beggar who told me, in consequence of my
asking where he belonged, that he was born in South Carolina. I
found, at last, that he was born in the English army, during the
American rebel-war; that he became a soldier himself; and that
it had been his fate to serve under the Duke of York, in Holland;
under General Whitelock, at Buenos Ayres; under Sir John
Moore, at Corunna; and under 'the Greatest Captain' at
Talavera! This poor fellow did not seem to be at all aware that,
in the last case, he partook in a *victory*! He had never before heard
of its being a victory. He, poor fool, thought it was a defeat!
'Why,' said he, 'we *ran away*, sir.' Oh, yes, said I, and so you did
afterwards in Portugal, when Massena was at your heels. But it
is only in certain cases that running away is a mark of being
defeated; or rather, it is only with certain commanders.

[Horsham (Sussex) Thursday, July 31]

I left Worth this afternoon about 5 o'clock, and am got here to
sleep, intending to set off for Petworth in the morning. This is a
very nice, solid country town. Very clean, as all the towns in
Sussex are. The people very clean. The Sussex women are very
nice in their dress and in their houses. The men and boys wear
smock-frocks more than they do in some counties. When people
do not, they always look dirty and comfortless.

Billingshurst (Sussex)
[Friday, Morning, 1 Aug.]

This village is 7 miles from Horsham, and I got here to breakfast
about seven o'clock. A very pretty village, and a very nice
breakfast, in a very neat little parlour of a very decent public-
house. The landlady sent her son to get me some cream, and he
was just such a chap as I was at his age, and dressed just in the

same sort of way, his main garment being a blue smock-frock, faded from wear and mended with pieces of *new* stuff and, of course, not faded. This boy will, I dare say, perform his part at Billingshurst, or at some place not far from it. If accident had not taken me from a similar scene, how many villains and fools, who have been well teased and tormented, would have slept in peace at night and fearlessly swaggered about by day. When I look at this little chap, at his smock-frock, his nailed shoes, his clean, plain and coarse shirt, I ask myself will anything, I wonder, ever send this chap across the ocean to tackle the base, corrupt perjured Republican judges of Pennsylvania? Will this lively, but at the same time, simple boy ever become the terror of villains and hypocrits across the Atlantic?

I was afraid of rain, and got on as fast as I could. However, I had no rain; and got to Petworth nine miles further, by about ten o'clock.

Petworth (Sussex)
[Friday evening, 1 Aug.]
Today, near a place called Westborough Green, I saw a woman bleaching her home-spun and home-woven linen. I have not seen such a thing before, since I left Long Island. Almost the whole of both linen and woollen used in the country, and a large part of that used in towns, is made in the farm-houses. All but the weaving is done by the family. There is a loom in the house, and the weaver goes from house to house. I once saw about three thousand farmers, or rather country people, at a horse race in Long Island and in my opinion there were not five hundred who were not dressed in home-spun coats. As to linen, no family thinks of buying linen.

Petworth is a nice market town, but solid and clean. The great abundance of *stone* in the land hereabouts has caused a corresponding liberality in paving and wall-building, so that everything of the building kind has an air of great strength, and produces the agreeable idea of durability. Lord Egremont's house is close to the town, and with its outbuildings, garden walls and other erections is, perhaps, nearly as big as the town; though the town is not a very small one. It is, upon the whole, a most magnificent seat, and the jews will not be able to get it from the *present* owner, though, if he lives many years, they will give even him a twist. If I had time, I would make an actual survey of one whole county and find out how many of the old gentry have lost their estates, and have been supplanted by the jews, since Pitt began his reign. I am sure I should prove that, in number, they are one-half extinguished.

Singleton (Sussex)
[Saturday 2, Aug.]

Even since the middle of March, I have been trying remedies for the *hooping-cough* and have, I believe, tried everything except riding, wet to the skin, two or three hours among the clouds on the South Downs. This remedy is now under trial.

I had resolved to come to this place for breakfast. I quitted the turnpike road (from Petworth to Chichester) at a village called Upwaltham, and came down a lane which led me first to a village called Eastdean and then to this village of Singleton. In cases like mine you are pestered to death to find out the way to *set out* to get from place to place. The people you have to deal with are innkeepers, ostlers, and post-boys; and they think you mad if you express your wish to avoid turnpike roads. They think you a strange fellow if you will not ride six miles on a turnpike road rather than two on any other road.

There is an appearance of comfort about the dwellings of the labourers all along here, that is very pleasant to behold. The

gardens are neat, and full of vegetables of the best kind. I see very few of 'Ireland's lazy root'. As I came along between Upwaltham and Eastdean I called to me a young man who, along with other turnip-hoers, was sitting under the shelter of a hedge at breakfast. He came running to me with his victuals in his hand, and I was glad to see that his food consisted of a good lump of household bread and not a very small piece of *bacon*. I did not envy him his appetite, for I had at that moment a very good one of my own. But I wanted to know the distance I had to go before I should get to a good public house. In parting with him I said, 'You do get some *bacon* then?' 'Oh, yes, sir,' said he, and with an emphasis and a swag of the head which seemed to say, 'We *must* and *will* have that.' I saw, and with great delight, a pig at almost every labourer's house. The houses are good and warm; and the gardens some of the best I have seen in England.

At Upwaltham is a toll gate, and when the woman opened the door of the house to come and let me through I saw some *straw plat* lying in a chair. She showed it me, and I found that it was made by her husband, in the evenings, after he came home from work, in order to make him a hat for the harvest. I told her how to get better straw for the purpose, and when I told her she must cut the grass, or the grain, *green* she said, 'Aye, I dare say it is so; and I wonder we never thought of that before; for we sometimes make hats out of rushes, cut green and dried, and the hats are very durable.' This woman ought to have my *Cottage Economy*. She keeps the tollgate at Upwaltham, which is on the turnpike road from Petworth to Chichester. Now if any gentleman who lives at Chichester will call upon my son, at the office of the *Register* in Fleet Street, and ask for a copy of *Cottage Economy*, to be given to this woman, he will receive the copy and my thanks, if he will have the goodness to give it to her, and point to her the Essay on Straw Plat.

Botley (Hampshire)
[5 August 1823]

I got to Fareham on Saturday night, after having got a soaking on the South Downs on the morning of that day. On the Sunday morning, I got up, struck a bustle, got up the ostler, set up and got to my destined point before seven o'clock in the morning.

And here I experienced the benefits of early rising; for I had scarcely got well and safely under cover, when St Swithin began to pour down again. I got to Botley about 9 o'clock, having stopped two or three times to look about me as I went along.

Botley lies in a valley, the soil of which is a deep and stiff clay. Oak trees grow well; and this year the wheat grows well, as it does upon all the clays that I have seen.

The best news that I have learned here is that the Botley parson is become quite a gentle creature, compared to what he used to be. The people in the village have told me the most ridiculous stories about his having been hoaxed in London! It seems that somebody danced him up from Botley to London by telling him that a legacy had been left to him, or some such story. Up went the parson on horseback, being in too great a hurry to run the risk of a coach. The hoaxers, it appears, got him to some hotel, and there set upon him a whole tribe of applicants, wet-nurses, dry-nurses, lawyers with deeds of conveyance for borrowed money, curates in want of churches, coffin-makers, travelling companions, ladies' maids, dealers in Yorkshire hams, Newcastle coals, and dealers in dried night-soil at Islington. In short, if I am rightly informed, they kept the parson in town for several days, bothered him three parts out of his senses, compelled him to escape as it were from a fire and then, when he got home, he found the village posted all over with handbills giving an account of his adventure, under pretence of offering £500 reward for a discovery of the hoaxers. The good of it was, the parson ascribed his disgrace *to me*, and they say that he perseveres to this hour in accusing me of it.* Upon my word, I had nothing to do with the matter, and this affair only shows that I am not the only friend that the parson has in the world.

EASTON [HAMPSHIRE]
[Wednesday evening, 6 August]
This village of Easton lies a few miles towards the north-east from Winchester. It is distant from Botley by the way which I came about fifteen or sixteen miles. I came through Durley,

* Cobbett's home was at Botley from 1805–1820.

where I went to the house of farmer Mears. I was very much pleased with what I saw at Durley. Mrs Mears, the farmer's wife, had made, of the crested dog's-tail grass, a bonnet which she wears herself. I there saw girls platting the straw. They had made plat of several degrees of fineness and they sell it to some person or persons at Fareham who, I suppose, makes it into bonnets. Mrs Mears, who is a very intelligent and clever woman, has two girls at work each of whom earns per week (within a shilling) as much as her father, who is a labouring man, earns per week. The father has at this time only 7s. per week. These two girls (and not very stout girls) earn six shillings a week, each; thus the income of this family is, from seven shillings a week, raised to nineteen shillings a week. Very little, indeed, could these poor things have done in the field during the last forty days. The farmer, who is also a very intelligent person, told me that he should endeavour to introduce the manufacture as a thing to assist the obtaining of employment, in order to lessen the amount of the poor rates. From the very first; from the first moment of my thinking about this straw affair, I regarded it as likely to assist in bettering the lot of the labouring people.

From Durley I came on in company with farmer Mears through Upham. This Upham is the place where Young, who wrote that bombastical stuff called *Night Thoughts*, was once the parson and where, I believe, he was born. At the end of this tract we came to a spot called Whiteflood, and here we crossed the old turnpike road which leads from Winchester to Gosport through Bishop's Waltham. Whiteflood is at the foot of the first of a series of hills over which you come to get to the top of that lofty ridge called Morning Hill. From the top of this high land, the real name of which is Magdalen Hill, from a chapel which once stood there dedicated to Mary Magdalen; from the top of this land you have a view of a circle which is upon an average seventy miles in diameter. You see the Isle of Wight in one direction, and in the other direction you see the high lands in Berkshire. Descending this hill, you cross the turnpike road leading from Winchester to London. As soon as you cross the road, you enter the estate of Rollo, Duke of Buckingham. In this estate, the duke has a farm, not very good land. On this farm of the duke I saw (in a little close by the farm-house) several hens in coops with broods of pheasants instead of chickens. It seems that a game-keeper lives in the farmhouse, and I dare say the duke thinks much more of the pheasants than of the corn.

The turnips upon this farm are by no means good. But I was in some measure compensated for the bad turnips by the sight of the duke's turnip-hoers, about a dozen females amongst whom there were several pretty girls, and they were as merry as larks. There had been a shower that had brought them into a sort of huddle on the road side. When I came up to them, they all fixed their eyes upon me, and upon my smiling, they bursted into laughter. I observed to them that the Duke of Buckingham was a very happy man to have such turnip-hoers, and really they seemed happier and better off than any work-people that I saw in the fields all the way from London to this spot. It is curious enough, but I have always observed that the women along this part of the country are usually tall. These girls were all tall, straight, fair, round-faced, excellent complexions and uncommonly gay. They were well-dressed, too, and I observed the same of all the men that I saw. This could not be the case if the duke were a cruel or hard master; and this is an act of justice due from me to the descendants of Rollo.

SELBORNE (HANTS)
[Thursday, 7 August, noon]
I came through Alresford about eight o'clock, having loitered a good deal coming up the valley. After having quitted Alresford you come (on the road towards Alton) to the village of Bishop's Sutton, and then to a place called Ropley Dean where there is a house or two. Just before you come to Ropley Dean, you see the beginning of the Valley of the Itchen. The *Itchen* river falls into the salt water at Southampton. It rises, or rather has its first rise, just by the roadside at Ropley Dean. All along by the Itchen river, up to its very source, there are meadows. And this vale of meadows, which is about 25 miles in length and is, in some places a mile wide, is, at the point of which I am now speaking, only about twice as wide as my horse is long! The fertility of this vale, and of the surrounding country, is best proved by the fact that, besides the town of Alresford and that of Southampton,

there are seventeen villages, each having its parish church, upon its borders. When we consider these things we are surprised that a spot situated about half way down the vale should have been chosen for the building of a city, or that that city should have been for a number of years a place of residence for the kings of England.

Winchester, which is at present a mere nothing to what it was, stands across the vale at a place where the vale is made very narrow by the jutting forward of two immense hills. The city is, of course, in one of the deepest holes that can be imagined. It never could have been thought of as a place to be defended since the discovery of gunpowder and, indeed, one would think that very considerable annoyance might be given to the inhabitants even by flinging of the flintstones from the hills down into the city.

At Tisted I crossed the turnpike road and entered a lane which, at the end of about four miles, brought me to this village of Selborne. My readers will recollect that I mentioned this Selborne when I was giving an account of Hawkley hanger, last fall. I was desirous of seeing this village about which I have read in the book of Mr White, which a reader has been so good as to send me.

The village of Selborne is precisely what is described by Mr White. A straggling irregular street, bearing all the marks of great antiquity, and showing from its lanes and its vicinage that it was once a very considerable place. I went to look at the spot where Mr White supposes the convent formerly stood. It is very beautiful. Nothing can surpass in beauty these dells and hillocks and hangers, which last are so steep that it is impossible to ascend them, except by means of a serpentine path. The churchyard of Selborne is most beautifully situated. The land is good, all about it. The trees are luxuriant and prone to be lofty and large. I measured the yew tree in the churchyard, and found the trunk to be, according to my measurement, twenty-three feet, eight inches in circumference. The trunk is very short, as is generally the case with yew trees. But the head spreads to a very great extent and the whole tree, though probably several centuries old, appears to be in perfect health.

I have never seen such quantities of grapes as I have seen upon the vines of this village, badly pruned though all the vines have been. To be sure, this is a year for grapes, such, I believe, as has seldom been known in England, and the cause is, the perfect ripening of the wood by the last beautiful summer. I am afraid, however, that the grapes come in vain, for this summer has been so cold, and is now so wet, that we can hardly expect grapes, which are not under glass, to ripen. As I was coming into this village, I observed to a farmer standing at his gateway that people ought to be happy here, for that God has done everything for them. His answer was, that he did not believe there was a more unhappy place in England, for there were always quarrels of some sort or other going on. This made me call to mind the king's proclamation relative to a reward for discovering the person who had recently *shot at the parson of this village*. This parson's name is Cobbold, and it really appears that there was a shot fired through his window. He has had law-suits with the people, and I imagine that it was these to which the farmer alluded.

THURSLEY (SURREY)
[Thursday, 7 August]
I got a boy at Selborne to show me along the lanes out into Woolmer Forest on the way to Headley. From Selborne, I had first to come to Headley, about five miles. I came to the identical public house where I took my blind guide last year, who took me such a dance to the southward and led me up to the top of Hindhead at last. At Churt I had, upon my left, three hills out upon the common called the *Devil's Jumps*. The Unitarians will not believe in the Trinity, because they cannot account for it. Will they come here to Churt, go and look at these 'Devil's Jumps', and account to me for the placing of these three hills, in the shape of three rather squat sugar-loaves, along in a line upon this heath, or the placing of a rock stone upon the top of one of them as big as a church tower? For my part, I cannot account for the placing of these hills. That they should have been formed by mere chance is hardly to be believed. How could waters rolling about have formed such hills? How could such hills have bubbled up from underneath?

It is a strange taste which our ancestors had to ascribe no

inconsiderable part of these wonders of nature to the Devil. Not far from the Devil's Jumps is that singular place which resembles a sugar-loaf inverted, hollowed out and an outside rim only left. This is called the '*Devil's Punch Bowl*'; and it is very well known in Wiltshire that the forming, or perhaps the breaking up of Stonehenge is ascribed to the Devil, and that the mark of one of his feet is now said to be seen in one of the stones.

REIGATE (SURREY)
[Friday, 8 August]
At the end of a long, twisting-about ride, but a most delightful ride, I got to this place about nine o'clock in the evening. From Thursley I came to Brook, and there crossed the turnpike road from London to Chichester. Thence I came on, turning upon the left upon the sandhills of Hambledon. On one of these hills is one of those precious jobs called '*Semaphores.*' For what reason this pretty name is given to a sort of telegraph house, stuck up at public expense upon a high hill; for what reason this pretty name is given to the thing, I must leave the reader to guess.

WEN
[Sunday 10 August]
I stayed at Reigate yesterday, and came to the Wen today, every step of the way in a rain. I promised that I would give an account of the effect which the soaking on the South Downs had upon the hooping-cough. I do not recommend the remedy to others, but this I will say, that I had a spell of the hooping cough the day before I got that soaking, and that I have not had a single spell since, though I have slept in several different beds and got a second soaking. The truth is, I believe that rain upon the South Downs, or at any place near the sea, is by no means the same thing with rain in the interior. No man every catches cold with getting wet with sea water; and indeed I have never known an instance of a man catching cold at sea. The air upon the South Downs is saltish, I dare say; and the clouds may bring something a little partaking of the nature of sea water.

Between Sutton and the Wen there is little besides houses, gardens, grass plats and other matters to accommodate the jews and jobbers and the mistresses and bastards that are put out a-keeping. There is no corn, as I recollect, to almost the street of Kensington. I came up by Earl's Court where there is, among the market gardens, a field of wheat.

Thus I have concluded this 'rural ride' from the Wen and back again to the Wen, taking in all the turnings and windings, as near as can be, two hundred miles in length. The state of the farmers is much worse than it was last year, notwithstanding the ridiculous falsehoods of the London newspapers, and the more ridiculous delusions of the jolterheads. The delusion caused by the rise in price of corn has pretty nearly vanished already. The quantity of the harvest will be great. If the quality be bad, owing to wet weather, the price will be still lower than it would have been in the case of dry weather.

RIDE THROUGH THE NORTH-EAST PART OF SUSSEX AND ALL
ACROSS KENT FROM THE WEALD OF SUSSEX TO DOVER
Worth (Sussex)
[Friday, 29 August, 1823]
I have so often described the soil and other matters appertaining to the country between the Wen and this place that my readers will rejoice at being spared the repetition here.

At Walton Heath I saw a man who had suffered most horribly from the *game-laws*. He saw me going by, and came out to tell me his story; and a horrible story it is; as the public will find when it shall come regularly and fully before them. Sir James Mackintosh, after years of incessant toil, has, I believe, succeeded in getting a repeal of the laws for the punishment of 'witchcraft', of the very existence of which laws the nation was unacquainted. But the devil a word he has said about the *game-laws*, which put into the gaols a full third part of the prisoners, and to hold which prisoners the gaols have actually been enlarged in all parts of the country!

TUNBRIDGE WELLS (KENT)
[Saturday, 30 August]
I came from Worth about seven this morning, passed through

East Grinstead, through Ashurst and thence to this place. The morning was very fine, and I left them at Worth making a rick. The buildings at Ashurst (which is the first parish in Kent on quitting Sussex) are a mill, an alehouse, a church and about six or seven other houses. I stopped at the alehouse to bait my horse, and, for want of bacon, was compelled to put up with bread and cheese for myself. While I was at the alehouse, I heard some labouring men talking about the roads, and they having observed that the parish roads had become so wonderfully better within the last seven or eight years, I put in my word and said, 'It is odd enough, too, that the parish roads should become *better and better* as the farmers become *poorer and poorer!*' They looked at one another, and put on a sort of *expecting* look, for my observation seemed to *ask for information*. At last one of them said, 'Why, it is because the farmers *have not the money to employ men* and so they are put on the roads.' 'Yes,' said I, 'But they must pay them there.' They said no more, and only *looked hard at one another*. They had probably never thought about this before.

This is a great *nut* year. I saw them hanging very thick on the way-side during a great part of this day's ride and they put me in mind of the old saying 'That a great *nut* year is a great year for

that class whom the lawyers, in their Latin phrase, call the "sons and daughters of nobody."' I once asked a farmer, who had often been overseer of the poor, whether he really thought there was any ground for this old saying, or whether he thought it was mere banter? He said that he was sure that there were good grounds for it, and he even cited instances in proof and mentioned one particular year when there were four times as many of this class as ever had been born in the parish before, an effect which he ascribed solely to the crop of nuts the year before. Now, if this be the case, ought not Parson Malthus and the rest of that tribe, to turn their attention to the nut-tree? The *Vice* Society, too, with that holy man Wilberforce at its head, ought to look out sharp after these mischievous nut-trees. A law to cause them all to be grubbed up, and thrown into the fire, would certainly be far less unreasonable than many things which we have seen and heard of.

TENTERDEN (KENT)
[Sunday, 31 August]

Here I am after a most delightful ride of twenty-four miles, through Frant, Lamberhurst, Goudhurst, Milkhouse Street, Benenden and Rolvenden. By making a great stir in rousing waiters and 'boots' and maids, and by leaving behind me the name of 'a d-d noisy, troublesome fellow', I got clear of '*the Wells*', and out of the contagion of its Wen-engendered inhabitants, in time enough to meet the first rays of the sun, on the hill that you come up in order to get to Frant, which is a most beautiful little village at about two miles from '*the Wells*'. Here the land belongs, I suppose, to Lord Abergavenny, who has a mansion and park here. A very pretty place and kept seemingly in very nice order. I saw here what I never saw before; the bloom of the *common heath* we wholly overlook; but it is a very pretty thing; and here, when the plantations were made, and as they grew up, heath was *left to grow* on the sides of the roads in the plantations. The heath is not so much a dwarf as we suppose. This is four feet high; and being in full bloom, it makes the prettiest border that can be imagined.

I got to Goudhurst to breakfast, and as I heard that the Dean of Rochester was to preach a sermon on behalf of the *National Schools* I stopped to hear him. In waiting for his reverence I went to the Methodist Meeting-House, where I found the Sunday School boys and girls assembled to the almost filling of the place. The 'minister' was not come, and the schoolmaster was reading to the children out of a *tract-book*, and shaking the brimstone bag at them most furiously. This schoolmaster was a *sleek*-looking young fellow; his skin perfectly tight; well fed, I'll warrant him; and he has discovered the way of living, without work, on the labours of those who do work. There were 30 little fellows in smock frocks, and about as many little girls listening to him, and I daresay he eats as much meat as any ten of them. By this time, the dean I thought would be coming on, and therefore to the church I went. But to my great disappointment, I found that the parson was operating preparatory to the appearance of the dean, who was to come on in the afternoon, when I, agreeably to my plan, must be off. The sermon was from 2 Chronicles, xxxi, 21, and the words of this text described King Hezekiah as a most *zealous man*, doing whatever he did *with all his heart*. The object of the preacher was to hold up to his hearers the example of Hezekiah and particularly in the case of the school affair. He called upon them to subscribe with all their hearts, but alas! how little of persuasive power was there in what he said! All was general, commonplace, cold, and that, too, in a language which the far greater part of his hearers could not understand. This church would hold *three thousand people*, and it had in it 214, besides 53 Sunday School or National School boys. It is very true that the *labouring* people have, in a great measure, ceased to go to church. There were scarcely any of that class in this great country church today. I do not believe there were *ten*. I can remember when they were so numerous that the parson could not attempt to begin till the rattling of their nailed shoes ceased.

After 'service' I mounted my horse and jogged on through Milkhouse Street to Benenden. Coming through the village, I heard a man at my right talking very loud about *houses*! *houses*! *houses*! It was a Methodist parson, in a house close by the road side. I pulled up and stood still, in the middle of the road but looking, in silent soberness, into the window (which was open) of the room in which the preacher was at work. I believe my stopping there disconcerted him, for he got into shocking repetition. 'Do you *know*,' he said, laying great stress on the word *know*; 'do you *know*, that you have ready for you houses, houses I say; I say, do you know? Do you know that you have houses in the heavens not made with hands? Do you know this from *experience*? Has the Blessed Jesus *told you so*?' And on he went to say that, if Jesus had told them so, they would be saved, and that if he had not, and did not, they would be damned. Some girls whom I saw in the room, plump and rosy as could be, did not seem at all daunted by these menaces, and indeed they appeared to be thinking much more about getting houses *in this world first*, just to *see a little* before they entered, or endeavoured to enter or even thought much about those *houses* of which the parson was speaking; houses with pig-styes and little snug gardens attached to them, together with all the other domestic and conjugal circumstances, these girls seem to me to be preparing themselves for. The truth is, these fellows have no power on the minds of any but the miserable.

Scarcely had I proceeded a hundred yards from the place where this fellow was bawling, when I came to the very situation which he ought to have occupied, I mean the *stocks*, which the people of Benenden have, with singular humanity, fitted up with a *bench*, so that the patient, while he is receiving the benefit of the remedy, is not exposed to the danger of catching cold by sitting, as in other places, upon the ground, always damp and sometimes actually wet. But I would ask the people of Benenden what is the *use* of this humane precaution, and indeed what is the use of the stocks themselves if, while a fellow is ranting and bawling in the manner just described, at the distance of a hundred yards from the stocks, the stocks (as is here actually the case) are almost hidden by grass and nettles? This, however is the case all over the country; not nettles and grass indeed smothering the stocks, but I never see any feet peeping through the holes, anywhere, though I find Methodist parsons every-where, and though *the law compels the parishes to keep up* all the pairs of stocks that exist in all parts of them; and in some parishes they have to keep up several pairs. I am aware that a good part of the use of the stocks is the terror they ought to produce. It is clear that a fellow, who has had the stocks under his eye all his lifetime and has *never* seen a pair of feet peeping out of them, will stand not more in awe of the stocks than rooks do of the old shoy-hoy. Stocks that never pinch a pair of ankles are like ministerial responsibility, a thing to talk about but for no other use. It is time that the stocks were again in *use*, or that the expense of keeping them up were put an end to.

Just after I quitted Benenden, I saw some bunches of *straw* lying upon the quickset hedge of a cottage garden. I found, upon inquiry, that they were bunches of the straw of grass. Seeing a face through the window of the cottage I called out and asked what the straw was for. The person within said it was to make *Leghorn*-plat with. I asked him (it was a young man) how he knew how to do it. He said he had got a little book that had been made by Mr Cobbett. I told him that I was the man, and should like to see some of his work; and asked him to bring it out to me, I being afraid to tie my horse. He told me that he was a *cripple*, and that he could not come out. At last I went in, leaving my horse to be tied by a little girl. I found a young man, who has been a cripple for fourteen years. Some ladies in the neighbourhood had got him the book, and his family had got him the grass. He had made some very nice plat, and he had knitted the greater

part of the crown of a bonnet, and had done the whole very nicely, though, as to knitting, he had proceeded in a way to make it very tedious. He was knitting upon a block. However, these little matters will soon be set to rights. There will soon be persons to teach knitting in all parts of the country. I left this unfortunate young man with the pleasing reflection that I had in all likelihood, been the cause of his gaining a good living, by his labour during the rest of his life.

This Tenterden is a market town, and a singularly bright spot. It consists of one street, which is, in some places, more perhaps than two hundred feet wide. On one side of the street the houses have gardens before them, from 20 to 70 feet deep. The town is upon a hill; the afternoon was very fine, and just as I rose the hill and entered the street, the people had come out of church and were moving along towards their houses. It was a very fine sight. *Shabbily-dressed people do not go to church.* I saw, in short, drawn out before me the dress and the beauty of the town, and a great many very, very pretty girls I saw; and saw them, too, in their best attire. I remember the girls in the *Pays de Cauxe* and, really, I think those of Tenterden resembled them. I do not know why they should not, for there is the Pays de Cauxe, just opposite this very place.

The church at this place is a very large and fine old building. Like the church at Goudhurst, it will hold three thousand people. And, let it be observed that, when these churches were built, people had not yet thought of cramming them with *pews*, as a stable is filled with stalls. Those who built these churches had no idea that worshipping God meant going to *sit* to hear a man talk out what he called preaching. By *worship* they meant very different things. And, above all things, when they had made a fine and noble building, they did not dream of disfiguring the inside with large and deep boxes made of deal boards. In short, the floor was the place for the worshippers to stand or kneel. And there was *no distinction*, no *high* place and *low* place. All were upon a level *before God*, at any rate. Some were not stuck into pews lined with green or red cloth, while others were crammed into corners to stand erect, or sit on the floor. These odious distinctions are of Protestant origin and growth. This lazy lolling in pews we owe to what is called the *Reformation*.

A place filled with benches and boxes looks like an eating or a drinking place, but certainly not a place of worship. A Frenchman went to church along with me one Sunday. He had never been in a Protestant place of *worship* before. Upon looking round him and seeing everybody comfortably seated, while a couple of good stoves were keeping the place as warm as a slack over, he exclaimed, '*Pardi! On sert Dieu bien a son aise ici!*' That is 'Egad! They serve God very much at their ease here!'

This evening I have been up to the Methodist Meeting-house. I was attracted, fairly drawn down the street, by the *singing*. When I came to the place the parson was got into prayer. His hands were clenched together and held up, his face turned up and back so as to be nearly parallel with the ceiling, and he was bawling away with his 'do thou' and 'mayest thou' and 'may we' enough to stun one. Noisy, however, as he was, he was unable to fix the attention of a parcel of girls in the gallery whose eyes were all over the place, while his eyes were so devoutly shut up. After a deal of this rigmarole called prayer, came the *preachy*, as the negroes call it. And a preachy it really was. Such a mixture of whining cant and of foppish affectation I scarcely ever heard in

my life. Monstrous it is to think that the clergy of the church really encourage these roving fanatics. The church seems unaware of its loss of credit and power.

FOLKESTONE (KENT)
[Monday (noon), 1 Sept.]
From Tenterden I set off at five o'clock, and got to Appledore after a most delightful ride, the high land upon my right, and the low land on my left. In quitting this Appledore I crossed a canal and entered on Romney Marsh. At Brenzett I with great difficulty got a rasher of bacon for breakfast. The few houses that there are, are miserable in the extreme. At Old Romney there is a church (two miles only from the last one, mind), fit to contain one thousand five hundred people, and there are for the people of the parish to live in twenty-two or twenty-three houses. And yet the vagabonds have the impudence to tell us that the population of England has vastly increased! Curious system that depopulates Romney Marsh and populates Bagshot heath! It is an unnatural system. It is the vagabond's system. It is a system that must be destroyed, or that will destroy the country.

I had baited my horse at New Romney, and was coming jogging along very soberly, now looking at the sea, then looking at the cattle, then the corn, when my eye, in swinging round, lighted upon a great round building. I had scarcely had time to think about it when twenty or thirty others, standing along the coast, caught my eye. And if anyone had been behind me he might have heard me exclaim in a voice that made my horse bound: 'The *Martello Towers*, by—!' Oh, Lord, to think that I should be destined to behold these monuments of the wisdom of Pitt and Dundas and Perceval! Good God! Here they are, piles of bricks in a circular form about three hundred feet (*guess*) circumference at the base, about forty feet high, and about one hundred and fifty feet at the top. There is a doorway, about midway up, in each, and each has two windows. Cannons were to be fired from the top of these things, in order to defend the country against the French Jacobins.

I think I have counted along here upwards of thirty of these ridiculous things which, I dare say, cost five, perhaps ten

thousand pounds each and one of which was, I am told, *sold* the
other day for two hundred pounds. There is, they say, a chain of
these things all the way to Hastings. I dare say they cost millions.
But far indeed are these from being all, or half, or a quarter of the
squanderings along here. Hythe is half *barracks*. Here is a canal
(I crossed it at Appledore) made for the length of thirty miles
(from Hythe in Kent to Rye in Sussex) to *keep out the French*: for
those armies who had so often crossed the Danube and the
Rhine, were to be kept back by a canal, made by Pitt, thirty feet
wide at the most! All along the coast there are works of some sort
or another; incessant sinks of money, masses of stone brought
and put into piles. Then you see some of the walls and buildings
falling down; some that have never been finished. The whole
thing, all taken together, looks as if a spell had been, all of a
sudden, set upon the workmen, or, in the words of the Scripture,
here is the *'desolation of abomination, standing in high places'*.

Between Hythe and Sandgate I first saw the French coast.
The chalk cliffs at Calais are as plain to the view as possible, and
also the land which they tell me is near Boulogne. Folkestone lies
under a hill here, as Reigate does in Surrey, only here the sea is
open to your right as you come along. The corn is very early
here, and very fine.

DOVER
[Monday, 1 September, Evening]
I got here this evening about six o'clock, having come today
about thirty-six miles. What place I shall date from after
Dover I am by no means certain. I am, in real truth, undecided
as yet whether I shall go on to France, or back to the *Wen*. I think
I shall, when I go out of this inn, toss the bridle upon my horse's
neck and let him decide for me. I am sure he is more fit to decide
on such a point than our ministers are to decide on any point
connected with the happiness, greatness and honour of this
kingdom.

FROM DOVER, THROUGH THE ISLE OF THANET, BY CANTER-
BURY AND FAVERSHAM, ACROSS TO MAIDSTONE, UP TO

TONBRIDGE, THROUGH THE WEALD OF KENT, AND OVER THE
HILLS BY WESTERHAM AND HAYS, TO THE WEN.
Dover
[Wednesday, 3 Sept., 1823 (Evening)]
On Monday, I was balancing in my mind whether I should go to
France or not. Today I have decided the question in the
negative, and shall set off this evening for the Isle of Thanet, that
spot so famous for corn.

The town of Dover is like other seaport towns; but really
much more clean and with less blackguard people in it that I
ever observed in any sea-port before. It is a most picturesque
place, to be sure. On one side of it rises, upon the top of a very
steep hill, the Old Castle with all its fortifications. On the other
side of it there is another chalk hill, the side of which is pretty
nearly perpendicular and rises up from sixty to a hundred feet
higher than the tops of the houses, which stand pretty nearly
close to the foot of the hill.

I got into Dover rather late. It was dusk when I was going
down the street towards the quay. I happened to look up and
was quite astonished to perceive cows grazing upon a spot
apparently fifty feet above the tops of houses. On the south side
of the town is that cliff which is described by Shakespear in the
play of *King Lear*. It is fearfully steep, certainly.

It was not, however, these natural curiosities that took me
over *this* hill. I went to see, with my own eyes, something of the
sort of means that have been made use of to squander away
countless millions of money. Here is a hill containing, probably,
a couple of square miles or more, hollowed out like a
honeycomb. Here are line upon line, trench upon trench, cavern
upon cavern, bomb-proof upon bomb-proof – in short, the very
sight of the thing convinces you that either madness the most
humiliating, or profligacy the most scandalous, must have been
at work here for years. The question that every man of sense asks
is: What reason had you to suppose that the *French would ever come
to this hill* to attack it, while the rest of the country was so much
more easy to assail? It is a parcel of holes made in a hill to hide
Englishmen from Frenchmen.

It is impossible to be upon this honeycombed hill upon this
enormous mass of anti-jacobin expenditure without seeing the
chalk hills of Calais and the cornfields of France. At this season,

it is impossible to see those fields without knowing that the farmers are getting in their corn there as well. And it is impossible to think of that fact without reflecting, at the same time, on the example which the farmers of France hold out to the farmers of England. Looking down from this very anti-jacobin hill, I saw the parson's shocks of wheat and barley, left in the field after the farmer had taken his away. Turning my head, and looking across the Channel, 'There,' said I, pointing to France, 'there the spirited and sensible people have ridded themselves of this burden, of which our farmers so bitterly complain.'

SANDWICH
[Wednesday, 3 September, Night]
I got to this place about half an hour after the ringing of the eight o'clock bell, or curfew, which I heard about two miles distance from the place. From the town of Dover you come up Castle Hill, and have a most beautiful view from the top of it.

Deal is a most villainous place. It is full of filthy-looking people. Great desolations of abomination have been going on here; tremendous barracks partly pulled down and partly tumbling down, and partly occupied by soldiers. Everything seems upon the parish. I was glad to hurry along through it.

CANTERBURY
[Thursday afternoon, 4 Sept.]
In quitting Sandwich, you immediately cross a river up which vessels bring coals from the sea. Soon after crossing the river, I

passed by a place for making salt, and could not help reflecting that there are no excisemen in these salt-making places in France: that, before the Revolution, the French were most cruelly oppressed by the duties on salt: that thousands and thousands of men and women were every year sent to the galleys for what was called smuggling salt: that the fathers and even the mothers were imprisoned or whipped if the children were detected in smuggling salt. I could not help reflecting with delight, as I looked at these salt pans in the Isle of Thanet, that in spite of Pitt, Dundas, Perceval and the rest of the crew, the gallant French people had ridden themselves of the tyranny which sent them to the galleys for endeavouring to use without tax the salt which God sent upon their shores. Can any man tell me why we should still be paying five, or six, or seven shillings a bushel for salt instead of one?

I left Ramsgate to my right, about three miles, and went across the island to Margate; but that place is so thickly settled with stock-jobbing cuckholds, at this time of the year, that, having no fancy to get their horns stuck into me, I turned away to my left when I got within half a mile of the town. I got to a little hamlet where I breakfasted but could get no corn for my horse, and no bacon for myself!

The labourers' houses, all along this island, beggarly in the extreme. The people dirty, poor-looking, ragged, but particularly *dirty*. The men and boys with dirty faces, and dirty smock-frocks and dirty shirts; and, Good God! What a difference between the wife of a labouring man here, and the wife of a labouring man in the forests and woodlands of Hampshire and Sussex. Invariably have I observed, that the richer the soil and the more destitute of woods – that is to say, the more purely a corn country – the more miserable the labourers. The cause is this; the great, the big bull-frog grasps all.

At Sarre I began to cross the marsh, and had, after this. to come to Up-street. At Up-street I was struck with the words written upon a board which was fastened upon a pole, which pole was standing in a garden near a neat little box of a house. The words were these 'PARADISE PLACE. *Spring guns and steel traps are set here*'. A pretty idea it must give us of Paradise to know that spring guns and steel traps are set in it! This is doubtless some stock-jobber's place; for, in the first place, the name is likely to have been selected by one of that crew, and, in the next place, whenever any of them go to the country they look upon it that they are to begin a sort of warfare against everything around them. They invariably look upon every labourer as a thief.

This fine old town is remarkable for cleanliness and niceness, notwithstanding it has a cathedral in it. The country round it is very rich and this year, while the hops are so bad in most other parts, they are not so very bad just about Canterbury.

MERRYWORTH
[Friday evening, 5 Sept.]
A friend at Tenterden told me if I had a mind to know Kent, I must go through Romney Marsh to Dover, from Dover to Sandwich, from Sandwich to Margate, from Margate to Canterbury, from Canterbury to Faversham, from Faversham to Maidstone and from Maidstone to Tonbridge. I found this morning that the regular turnpike route was through Sittingbourne. I had been along that road several times and, besides, to be covered with dust was what I could not think of when I had it in my power to get to Maidstone without it. I took the road across the country, quitting the London road. I came through the villages of Newnham, Diddington, Ringlestone, and to that of Hollingbourne. I found fine meadows here: this sort of ground is characterised by an astonishing depth that they have

to go for water. I was just thinking to go up to some house, to ask how far they had to go for water, when I saw a large well-bucket and all the chains and wheels belonging to such a concern; but here was all the tackle for a *horse* to work in drawing up the water. I asked about the depth of the well, and the information I received must have been incorrect because I was told it was three hundred yards. I asked this of a public-house keeper further on, not seeing anybody where the farmhouse was.

TONBRIDGE
[Saturday morning, 6 Sept.]

I came off from Merryworth a little before five o'clock. All along here the villages are not more than two miles distance from each other. They have all large churches, and scarcely anybody to go to them. At a village called Hadlow there is a house belonging to a Mr May, the most singular looking thing I ever saw. An immense house, stuck all over with a parcel of chimneys, or things like chimneys; little brick columns with a sort of caps on them, looking like carnation sticks, with caps at the tops to catch earwigs. The buildings is all of brick and has the oddest appearance of anything I ever saw. This Tonbridge is but a common market town, though very clean, and the people looking very well. The climate must be pretty warm here for, in entering the town, I saw a large Althea Frute in bloom, a thing rare enough, any year, and particularly a year like this.

WESTERHAM
[Saturday, Noon, 6 September]

Instead of going to the Wen along the turnpike road through Sevenoaks, I turned to my left when I got about a mile out of Tonbridge. Not far from Bough-beach, I saw two oak trees, one of which was, they tell me, more than thirty feet round, and the other more than twenty-seven: but they have been hollow for half a century. They are not much bigger than the oak upon Tilford Green, if any. I mean in the trunk, but they are hollow, while that tree is sound in all its parts and growing still. I have had a most beautiful ride through the Weald. The day is very hot, but I have been in the shade and my horse's feet very often in the rivulets and wet lanes. In one place, I rode over a mile completely arched over by the boughs of the underwood, growing in the banks of the lane. What an odd taste that man must have who prefers a turnpike road to a lane like this.

KENSINGTON
[Saturday night, 6 Sept.]
Here I close my day at the end of forty-four miles. I was anxious to make this journey into Kent, in the midst of harvest, in order that I might know the *real* state of the crops. In order to enable others to judge, as well as myself, I took samples from the fields as I went along. I took them very fairly, and as often as I thought there was any material change in the soil or other circumstances. During the ride, I took sixteen samples. These are now at the office of the *Register* in Fleet Street, where they may be seen by any gentleman who thinks the information likely to be useful to him. Now then we shall see how all this tallies with the schemes, with the expectations and intentions of our matchless gentlemen in Whitehall.

PROGRESS OF A PLAINTIVE PILGRIM to pray for Justice at the SHRINE OF THE GREAT UNPAID
North Cray, in Kent (Where Castlereagh cut his own throat)
[Thursday, 28th July, 1825]
During the last spring and the most beautiful summer that has succeeded it I have, with the exception of a mere gallop into Somersetshire, been constantly at Kensington, occupied chiefly in sowing and rearing American trees and shrubs, of which I have now, I think, a *million* of various sorts including about ten thousand apple trees.

Seeing all this matter in a fair way, and having seen the Parliament (thank God and the King) fairly dispersed, I and my little son Richard thought that we would sally forth to see the *farmers, to view the state of the crops* and to philosophise, unchoked by smoke and unstunned by the rattle of the infernal coaches and drays. I had scarcely set foot in this country before I asked a carrier how the *Turnpike fellows behaved now*. He told me *bad enough*, for that the toll-collector at Ruxley Gate made the farmers *pay for manure*, though manure was exempted by *law*. I am taking the necessary steps to have this question decided.

Foot's Cray
[Thursday 28th July, 1825]

Arrived at the public house, the *Red Cross*, kept by Mr Farmer, we put up our horses and were shown into the *parlour*, a little room about ten feet square. We were very thirsty, having had a pretty long ride after a breakfast upon bacon and beer. Mrs Farmer brought us a pint of beer that either was, or seemed to be, some of the best I ever tasted of. I took that opportunity to ask her whether I was in the very room where the Inquest was held of 'Lord' Castlereagh's body. 'Yes, sir,' shaking her head, 'a shocking affair! a sad day for North Cray and indeed all the parishes around here.' 'Why?' said I. 'Oh! Sir, he was so good to the poor, such a good master, so good to tradesmen, laid out so much money amongst us, that he was beloved by everybody.' 'But,' said I, 'you should consider, Ma'am, that the *other gentlefolk* have only their own earning or their *own incomes* to expend, and his money, or a great part of it at least, came out of the taxes raised, in great part upon these very gentlefolks.' 'Yes,' said she. 'I have heard people say that before; I don't know anything about *that*. I know he was good to *all of us* and I shall always speak well of him.' Thus it is that the ancient gentry of England have suffered the tax-eaters to take away their good names as well as their income.

Mrs Farmer's gratitude appeared to be so sincere, she was so zealous and she was, into the bargain, so very pretty a woman, that I pressed my opposition no further. We finished our pint of beer and went out for a walk down to the river, along a lane that runs by the side of CASTLEREAGH's ground and that is well shaded by lofty trees. Over the river, at the bottom of the lane, there is a little wooden footbridge with some alders growing to shade each end of it. I sat down upon one end of this bridge, under the shade of the alders, with my feet hanging down nearly into the water, and, on the crown of my hat, wrote the first part of this account of my pilgrimage. Having finished that, and finding that Mrs Farmer's beer had increased rather than allayed our thirst, Richard made a *glass*, by twisting paper as grocers do to put sugar-plums in, and dipped up water out of CASTLEREAGH's river, of which we drank a good parcel.

I wished, if I could do it with propriety, to see the *inside of the house* and, if possible, the very spot where CASTLEREAGH fell! The sight of the house crowded my mind with subjects of recollection. I remembered the huzzas and shouts and clappings of hands with which this fellow had, upon his return from the Continent, been received by a crew of the most corrupt and villainous that ever disgraced the face of this earth: I remembered the cool statement of the number of 'soldiers wanted to collect the taxes in Ireland': I remembered the '*basest populace*' applied to the virtuous, just and generous people of England who saved from ignominy the hapless and ill-treated Queen: I remembered the two voyages of myself and wife and children across the Atlantic. I remembered how poor little Richard (whose hand I held at this moment) had asked his mother (he being then only three years old) why she cried, and *what it was* that had made his dear papa not come to kiss him before he went away: I remembered all these things and other innumerable and, despising from my soul the hypocritical cant of '*liberality*', I wished to take this very child and, in triumph, show him the spot where *Castlereagh fell*!

With this desire, I went into the gate, which was open, and asked a woman, who was in the porter's lodge, whether I could see the gardens and the inside of the house. She told me that I could not, for that they were never shown to anybody. I thought it would be wrong to tempt her with money, and so I came out into the road, very near to which the house stands, having a high wall before it. I went to the opposite side of the road, whence I could see the upstairs windows of the house, and I was for some time guessing which was the window of the room in which the deed was done. At last I returned to the Red Cross and Mrs Farmer, and again sat down in the room where the famous Inquest was held, not without reflecting on the curious *law* which was passed soon after that Inquest took place. The law of England had, since England was England, always been, that a *self-murderer* should not have Christian burial but should be buried at cross roads, in the public highway, and have a stake or post driven through down the body, to mark the spot and to commemorate the ignominy of the deceased. But, though this law had been maintained for so many hundred years, it was *soon after* CASTLEREAGH *cut his throat* REPEALED and now self-murderers are not to be deemed *felons* and their remains *are not to be stigmatised in this way*!

Let me come back to my pilgrimage. We retraced our steps back through North Cray and that gave me another look at Castlereagh's windows. As I came along, casting my eyes on the church and churchyard, I once more thought of the monstrous folly of his late coadjutors in not '*digging a hole*' there '*one day and filling it up the next*' with his carcase in it, instead of bringing that carcase with its cut throat up to Westminster Abbey, there to receive that *exulting huzza* from the honest and just mechanics and labourers of London, which must have stung those coadjutors to the soul and which, perhaps, must have done more to humble them than anything which has happened to them during their lives.

This little town, or rather village, of Foot's Cray crosses, along the London and Maidstone Road, the pretty little river Cray, which rises at the foot of the high land a few miles to the south of us and which takes its name from the word *craie* (chalk) between the hills on which subsoil it runs. From its source to its mouth it has a village and a church on one or the other of its sides in the space of almost every mile, and almost every village has its corn-mill or paper-mill, and, I believe, sometimes both.

This 'Seven Stars' where we are is a very pretty little inn, close by the Cray-side, a very neat paper-mill below it, seats under arbours by the water's edge, where I am now sitting writing on a table intended solely for bottles, glasses, pipes and tobacco, while two swans are eating bits of bread that Richard is tossing to the water to them.

FARNINGHAM
[29th July, 1825]
Last evening, at Foot's Cray, we got, after dinner, rather sleepy. We had not, since we left home, had fair play. We had got up at

four, our usual hour at Kensington, but we had not, as we do there, got to bed at *eight*. We had not had ALFRED's eight hours, and anything at all short of that satisfies neither of us. I laid myself down, or rather a part of myself, upon a *short* sofa. It was in the sun, and the flies teazed me. I roused up, and found my companion stretched on the floor, in a shady part of the room, with two chair cushions for a pillow. I followed his example, and we recovered what had been our due the previous night.

This morning, I despatched my scout to Captain Cater's at North Cray to find whether the Captain had returned home, while I prepared eggs, milk, gooseberries and currants for breakfast. The Captain was come back. We breakfasted, and set off for his house. He made out a *summons* for the gatekeeper to answer my complaint at the Bench at Bromley on Monday next, the 1st of August.

FARNINGHAM
[30th July, 1825]
The weather being famously hot, here being (at the Lion Inn) another little river, the Dart, which, just like the Cray and in a course almost parallel with it, is set with villages, churches, corn-mills and paper-mills and, like the Cray, abounding with trout: and Richard liking this place exceedingly, it being near to some farmers who keep hounds and talk about hunting; all this being thus, I have made up my mind to stay here until Monday morning, and then go thence to Bromley; and, in the meantime, to read a little of the works of Mr BROUGHAM's '*best public*

instructor', one 'broad sheet' of which, the *Morning Chronicle*, dated *this very morning*, has just come into my hands.

BROMLEY
[1st August, 1825, Monday]
I intended to go yesterday to the church at North Cray, in order to see that *table* at which (as the newspapers told us) CASTLEREAGH used to go constantly to *receive the Sacrament* along with the poor villagers, and which act the pious newspaper editors set down as being, of course, a complete proof of the great piety and humility and humanity of 'the *Noble* Lord'! But the day being very hot and the road dusty, and I being engaged to dinner with a farmer living in another direction, I took that other direction and spent a most pleasant day at a very delightful farm and with very sensible and agreeable people. This morning, at half-past five, we set off from Farningham, came through St Mary's Cray and Chiselhurst, and got to this place about eight o'clock and came to the Bell Inn, in which the GREAT UNPAID hold their BENCH. They meet at 12 o'clock.

I had just received the preceding, when I was called upstairs, before the GREAT UNPAID. After due hearing and deliberation they determined that the gate-keeper *was justified* in taking toll for a wagon going for manure and not returning it when the wagon returned the next day, *loaded with manure*. This determination having been declared to me, I got from this same bench, summonses for this same gate-keeper and for another gate-keeper to answer my complaint of their NOT having taken toll in other cases, on the same identical wagon and under the *precisely same circumstances* as to *time*. The summons will be answered at the same bench at Bromley, on the first Monday in *next month*.

FROM KENSINGTON, ACROSS SURREY,
AND ALONG THAT COUNTY
Reigate
[Wednesday evening, 19 October, 1825]
Having some business at Hartswood, near Reigate, I intended to come off this morning on horseback, along with my son

Richard, but it rained so furiously the last night that we gave up
the horse project for today. But we are under a farmhouse roof
and the wind may whistle and the rain fall as much as it like.
Reigate

[Thursday evening, 20 October]
Having done my business at Hartswood today about eleven
o'clock, I went to a sale at the farm which the farmer is quitting.
Here I had a view of what has been going on all over the
country.

Everything about this farm-house was formerly the scene of
plain manners and *plentiful living*. Oak clothes-chests, oak bed-
steads, oak chests and drawers, and oak tables to eat on, long,
strong and well supplied with joint stools. Some of the things
were many hundreds of years old. But all appeared to be in a
state of decay and nearly of disuse. There appeared to have been
hardly any *family* in that house, where formerly there were, in all
probability, from ten to fifteen men, boys and maids and, which
was worst of all, there was a *parlour*. Aye, and a *carpet* and a *bell-
pull* too. One end of the front of this once plain and substantial
house had been moulded into a '*parlour*', and there was a
mahogany table, and the fine chairs and the fine glass and all as
barefaced upstart as any stock-jobber in the kingdom can boast
of. And there were the decanters, the glasses, the 'dinner-set' of
crockery ware, and all just in the true stock-jobber style. And I
dare say it has been 'Squire Charington and the *Miss*
Charingtons', and not plain Master Charington and his son
Hodge, and his daughter Betty Charington, all of whom this
accursed system has, in all likelihood, transmuted into a species
of mock gentlefolks while it has ground the labourers down into
real slaves. Why do not farmers now *feed* and *lodge* their work-
people, as they did formerly? Because they cannot keep them
upon so little as they give them in wages. This is the real cause of
the change.

The land produces, on an average, what it always produces
but there is a new distribution of the produce. This 'Squire
Charington's father used, I dare say, to sit at the head of the oak-
table along with his men, say grace to them, and cut up the meat
and the pudding. He might take a cup of *strong beer* to himself,
when they had none, but that was pretty nearly all the difference

in their manner of living. So that *all* lived well. But the *'squire* had many *wine-decanters* and *wine-glasses* and a *'dinner set'* and a *'breakfast set'* and *'dessert knives'*, and these evidently imply carryings on and a consumption that must of necessity have greatly robbed the long oak table if it had remained fully tenanted. The long oak table could not share in the work of the decanters and the dinner set. Therefore it became almost untenanted: the labourers retreated to hovels called cottages, and, instead of board and lodging, they got money – so little of it as to enable the employer to drink wine. But then, that he might not reduce them to quite starvation, they were enabled to come to him, in the *king's name*, and demand food *as paupers*.

I could not quit this farmhouse without reflecting on the thousands of scores of bacon and thousands of bushels of bread that have been eaten from the long oak-table which, I said to myself, is not perhaps going at last to the bottom of a bridge that some stock-jobber will stick up over an artificial river in his cockney garden. *'By – it shan't,'* said I, almost in a real passion, and so I requested a friend to buy it for me. And if he do so, I will take it to Kensington or Fleet Street, and keep it for the good it has done in the world.

When the old farm-houses are down (and down they must come in time) what a miserable thing the country will be! Those that are now erected are mere painted shells, with a mistress within who is stuck up in a place she calls a *parlour* with, if she have children, the 'young ladies and gentlemen' about her; some show chairs and a sofa (a *sofa* by all means); half a dozen prints in gilt frames hanging up; some swinging book shelves with novels and tracts upon them; a dinner brought in by a girl that is perhaps better 'educated' than she; two or three nick nacks to eat instead of a piece of bacon and a pudding; the house too neat for a dirty-shoed carter to be allowed to come into; and everything proclaiming to every sensible beholder that there is here a constant anxiety to make a *show* not warranted by reality. The children (which is the worst part of it) are all too clever to *work*; they are all to be *gentlefolk*. Go to plough! Good God! What, 'young gentlemen go to plough'? They become *clerks*, or some skimmydish or other. They flee from the dirty work as cunning horses do from the bridle. What misery is all this!

I was going today, by the side of a plat of ground, where there was a very fine flock of *turkeys*. I stopped to admire them, and observed to the owner how fine they were, when he answered, 'We owe them entirely *to you*, sir, for we never raised one till we read your *Cottage Economy*.' I then told him that we had, this year, raised two broods at Kensington, one black and one white, one of nine and one of eight.

This town of Reigate had, in former times, a priory which had considerable estates in the neighbourhood. We all know how long it has been the fashion for us to take it for *granted* that the monasteries were *bad things*; but of late I have made some hundreds of thousands of very good Protestants begin to suspect that monasteries were better than *poor-rates*, and that monks and nuns, who *fed the poor*, were better than sinecure and pension men and women who *feed upon* the poor. But how came the monasteries? How came this that was at Reigate, for instance? Why, it was, if I recollect correctly, *founded by a Surrey gentleman* who gave this spot and other estates to it and who, as was usual, provided that masses were to be said in it for his soul and those of others, and that it should, as usual, give aid to the poor and needy.

FROM CHILWORTH, IN SURREY, TO WINCHESTER

THURSLEY, FOUR MILES FROM GODALMING, SURREY
[Sunday evening, 23 October, 1825]
We set out from Chilworth about noon. This is a little village, lying under the south side of St Martha's Hill, and on the other

side of that hill, a little to the north-west, is the town of Guildford which (taken with its environs) I, who have seen many, many towns, think the prettiest and, taken all together, the most agreeable and most happy-looking that ever I saw in my life. Here are hill and dell in endless variety. Here are the chalk and the sand, vieing with each other in making beautiful scenes. Here is a navigable river and fine meadows. Here are woods and downs. The vale, all the way down from Chilworth to Reigate, is very delightful.

Thursley
[Wednesday, 26 Oct.]

The weather has been very beautiful ever since last Thursday morning, but there has been a white frost every morning and the days have been coldish.

The great business of life, in the country, appertains in some way or other to the *game*, and especially at this time of year. If it were not for the game, a country life would be like an *everlasting honeymoon* which would, in about half a century, put an end to the human race. In towns, or large villages, people make a shift to find the means of rubbing the rust off each other by a vast variety of sources of contest. A couple of wives, meeting in the street and giving each other a wry look, or a look not quite civil enough, will, if the parties be hard pushed for a ground of contention, do pretty well. But in the country there is, alas! no such resource. Here are no walls for people to take of each other. Here they are so placed as to prevent the possibility of such local contact. Here, therefore, when all circumstances seem calcu-lated to cause never-ceasing concord with its accompanying dullness, there would be no relief at all, were it not for the *game*.

There is, however, an important distinction to be made between *hunters* (including coursers) and *shooters*. The latter are, as far as relates to their exploits, a disagreeable class compared with the former, and the reason is, their doings are almost wholly their own. I was once acquainted with a *famous shooter* called William Ewing. We spent scores of days together a shooting and were extremely well matched. In the course of a November day he had, just before dark, shot and sent to the farmhouse or kept in his bag, *ninety-nine* partridges. It was a grand achievement but, unfortunately, he wanted to make it a hundred. The sun was setting. I wanted to be off, as we had a very bad road to go and he, being under strict petticoat government, to which he most loyally and dutifully submitted, was compelled to get home that night, taking me with him. I therefore pressed him to come away. No; he would kill the *hundredth* bird. In vain did I talk of the bad road and its many dangers for want of a moon. The poor partridges, which we had scattered about, were *calling* all around us and, just at this moment, up got one under his feet. He shot and *missed*. 'That's it,' said he, running as if to *pick up* the bird. 'What!' said I, 'You don't think you *killed*, do you? Why, there is the bird now, not only alive but *calling* in that wood.' However, he began to *look about*, and I called the dog and affected to join him in his search. Pity for his weakness got the better of my dread of the bad road. After walking backwards and forwards many times with our eyes to the ground, looking for what both of us knew was not there, I had passed him (he going one way and I the other) and I happened to be turning round just after I had passed him when I saw him, putting his hand behind him, *take a partridge out of his bag and let it fall upon the ground*! I felt no temptation to detect him, but turned away my head. Presently he called out to me in a most triumphant tone, '*Here*! *Here*! Come here!' I went up to him and he, pointing with his finger down to the bird and looking hard in my face at the same time, said 'There, Cobbett! I hope that will be a *warning* to you never to be obstinate again!'

FARNHAM, Surrey
[Thursday, 27 Oct.]
We came hither by way of Waverley Abbey and Moore Park. On the commons, I showed Richard some of my old hunting scenes, when I was his age, or younger, reminding him that I was obliged to hunt on foot. We got leave to go and see the grounds at Waverley, where all the old monks' garden walls are totally gone, and where the spot is become a sort of lawn. I showed him a tree, close by the ruins of the Abbey, from a limb of which I once fell into the river in an attempt to take the nest of a *crow*, which had artfully placed it upon a branch so far from the

trunk as not to be able to bear the weight of a boy eight years old.
I showed him an old elm tree which was hollow even then, into
which I, when a very little boy, saw a cat go, that was as big as a
middle-sized spaniel dog, for relating which I got a scolding, for
standing to which I at last got a beating; but stand to which I
still did, and I would take my oath of it to this day. When in New
Brunswick I saw the great wild grey cat, which is there called a
Lucifer; and it seemed to me to be just such a cat I had seen at
Waverley.

From Waverley, we went to Moore Park, once the seat of Sir
William Temple. Here I showed Richard Mother Ludlum's
Hole, but, alas! it is not the enchanting place that I knew it, nor
that which Grose described in his antiquities. The semicircular
plain is gone: the basins, to catch the never-ceasing little
streams, are gone; the iron cups, fastened by chains for people to
drink out of, are gone: the stream that ran down a clean paved
channel now making a dirty gutter.

Near the mansion, I showed Richard the hill upon which
Dean Swift tells us he used to run for exercise, while he was
pursuing his studies here. And I would have showed him the
garden-seat, under which Sir William Temple's heart was
buried, agreeably to his will. But the seat was gone, also the wall
at the back of it, and the exquisitely beautiful little lawn in
which the seat stood was turned into a parcel of divers-shaped
cockney clumps, planted according to the strictest rules of
artificial and refined vulgarity.

FROM WINCHESTER TO BURGHCLERE

Burghclere [Monday morning, 31 October, 1825]
We had, or I had, resolved not to breakfast at Winchester, and
yet we were detained till nearly noon. But at last off we came,
fasting. After beginning to ascend the downs, we came to a
labourer's (*once a farm-house*) where I asked the man whether he
had any *bread and cheese*, and was not a little pleased to hear him
say '*Yes*'. Then I asked him to give us a bit, protesting that we
had not yet broken our fast. He answered in the affirmative at
once, though I did not talk of payment. His wife brought out the

cut loaf, and a piece of Wiltshire cheese, and I took them in hand, gave Richard a good hunch, and took one for myself. I verily believe that all the pleasure of eating enjoyed by all the feeders in London in a whole year does not equal that which we enjoyed in gnawing this bread and cheese, as we rode over this cold down, whip and bridle reins in one hand, and the hunch in the other. Richard, who was purse bearer, gave the woman, by my direction, about enough to buy two quartern loaves, for she told me that they had to buy their bread *at the mill*, not being able to bake themselves for *want of fuel*.

Before we got this supply of bread and cheese we, though in ordinary times a couple of singularly jovial companions and seldom going a hundred yards (except going very fast) without one or the other speaking, began to grow *dull* or rather *glum*. The way seemed long, and when I had to speak in answer to Richard, the speaking was as brief as might be. Unfortunately, just at this critical period one of the loops that held the straps of Richard's little portmanteau broke and it became necessary for me to fasten the portmanteau on before me, upon my saddle. This, which was not the work of five minutes, would, had I had *a breakfast*, have been nothing at all and, indeed, a matter of laughter. But *now*, it was *something*. It was his '*fault*' for capering and jerking about '*so*'. I jumped off, saying, '*Here*! I'll carry it *myself*.' And then I began to take off the remaining strap, pulling with great violence and great haste. Just at this time my eyes met his, in which I saw *great surprise*. And, feeling the just rebuke, feeling heartily ashamed of myself, I instantly changed my tone and manner.

Now, if such was the effect produced upon me by the want of food for only two or three hours; me, who had dined well the day before and eaten toast and butter the over-night: if the missing of only one breakfast made me what you may call '*cross*' to a child like this whom I must necessarily love so much and to whom I never spoke but in the very kindest manner: if this mere absence of a breakfast could thus put me *out of temper*, how great are the allowances that we ought to make for the poor creatures who, in this once happy and now miserable country, are doomed to lead a life of constant labour and of half-starvation.

FROM BURGHCLERE TO PETERSFIELD
Hurstbourn Tarrant (or Uphusband)
[Monday, 7 November, 1825]
We came off from Burghclere yesterday afternoon, going out of it on the west side of Beacon Hill and sloping away to our right over the downs towards Woodcote. The afternoon was singularly beautiful.

It is about six miles from Burghclere to this place. We came through a village called Woodcote, and another called Binley. I never saw any inhabited place more recluse than these. Yet into these the all-searching eye of the taxing THING reaches. Its excisemen can tell it what it is doing even in the little odd corner of Binley, for even there, I saw over the door of a place not half so good as the place in which my fowls roost, '*Licensed to deal in tea and tobacco*'. Poor, half-starved wretches of Binley. The hand of taxation, the collection for the sinecures and pensions, must fix its nails even in them.

EASTON, near Winchester
[Wednesday evening, 9 Nov.]
As we had to come to this place, which is three miles *up* the river Itchen, we crossed the Winchester and Basingstoke Road at King's Worthy. We saw, down by the waterside, a beautiful strawberry garden, capable of being watered by a branch of the Itchen which comes close by it, and which is, I suppose, brought there on purpose. Just by, on the greensward, is an alcove under the shade of very fine trees wherein to sit to eat the strawberries, coming from the little garden just mentioned, and met by bowls of cream coming from a little milk-house shaded by another clump a little lower down the stream. What delight! What a terrestrial paradise!

The water of the Itchen is, they say, famed for its clearness. As I was crossing the river the other day, at Avington, I told Richard to look at it, and I asked him if he did not think it very clear. I now find that this has been remarked by very ancient writers. I see, in a newspaper just received, an account of dreadful fires in New Brunswick. It is curious that, in my Register of the 29th October, I should have put a question relative to the white clover which starts up after the burning down of woods in America.

PETERSFIELD

[Friday Evening, 11 November]

We lost another day at Easton, the whole of yesterday it having rained the whole day. We started therefore this morning, coming through the Duke of Buckingham's park at Avington. This is certainly one of the very prettiest spots in the world. The wildfowl seem to take particular delight in this place. Now this is the advantage of going about on horseback. On foot, the fatigue is too great and you go too slowly. In any sort of carriage, you cannot get into the *real country places*. To travel in stage coaches is to be hurried along by force, in a box with an air-hole in it, the danger being much greater than that of ship-board, and the noise much more disagreeable, while the *company* is frequently not a great deal more to one's liking.

Before we got to Petersfield, we called at an old friend's and got some bread and cheese and small beer, which we preferred to strong. In approaching Petersfield, we began to descend from the high chalk country which, with the exception of the valleys of the Itchen and Test, had lasted us from Uphusband to this place. Here we quit flint and chalk and downs and take to sand, clay, hedges and coppices: and here, on the edge of Hampshire, we begin again to see those endless little bubble-formed hills that we before saw round the foot of Hindhead. We have got in in very good time, and got, at the Dolphin, good stabling for our horses. The waiters and people at inns *look so hard at us* to see us so liberal as to horse-feed, fire, candle, beds and room while we are so very, very sparing in the article of *drink*! They seem to pity our taste. I hear people complain of the 'exorbitant charges' at inns; but my wonder always is how the people can live with charging so little. Except in one single instance I have uniformly, since I have been away from home, thought the charges too low for people to live by.

FROM PETERSFIELD TO KENSINGTON
Petworth
[Saturday, 12 Nov. 1825]

I was at this town in the summer of 1823 when I crossed Sussex from Worth to Huntington. We came this morning from Petersfield, with an intention to cross to Horsham and then into Kent. But Richard's horse seemed not to be fit for so strong a bout and therefore we resolved to bend our course homewards.

At about four miles from Petersfield we passed through a village called Rogate. Just before we came to it, I asked a man who was hedging on the side of the road how much he got a day. He said *1s.6d.*; and he told me that the *allowed* wages was *7d.* a day for the man *and a gallon loaf a week for the rest of his family*: that is to say, one pound and two and a quarter ounces of bread for each of them, and nothing more! In the gaol, the convicted felons have a pound and a half each of bread a day to begin with: they have some meat generally, and it has been found absolutely necessary to allow them meat when they work at the treadmill. I asked this man how much a day they gave to a young, able man who had no family, and was compelled to come to the parish officers for work. About the borders of north Hampshire they give to these single men two gallon loaves a week or, in money, two shillings and eightpence and nothing more. Here, in this part of Sussex, they give the single man sevenpence a day, that is

to say, enough to buy two pounds and a quarter of bread for six days in the week, and as he does not work on Sunday there is no sevenpence allowed for the Sunday and, of course, nothing to eat.

When we came into the village of Rogate I saw a little group of persons standing before a blacksmith's shop. The churchyard was on the other side of the road, surrounded by a low wall. The earth of the churchyard was about four and a half feet higher than the common level of the ground about, and you may see, by the nearness of the church windows to the ground, that this bed of earth has been made by the innumerable burials that have taken place in it. The group, consisting of the blacksmith, the wheelwright perhaps, and three or four others, appeared to me to be in a deliberative mood. So I said, looking significantly at the churchyard, 'It has taken a pretty many thousands of your forefathers to raise the ground up so high.' 'Yes, sir,' said one of them. 'And,' said I, 'for about nine hundred years those that built that church thought about religion very differently from what we do.' 'Yes,' said another. 'And,' said I, 'do you think that all those who made that heap there are gone to the devil?' I got no answer to this. 'At any rate,' added I, 'they never worked for a pound and a half of bread a day.' They looked hard at me, and then looked hard at one another, and I, having trotted off, looked round at the first turning and saw them looking after us still.

From Rogate we came on to Trotten, where a Mr Twyford is squire. I saw the squire looking at some poor devils who were making 'wauste improvements, m'am,' on the road which passes the squire's door. He looked uncommonly hard at me. It was a scrutinising sort of look, mixed, as I thought, with a little surprise, if not of jealousy, as much as to say 'I wonder who the devil you can be?' My look at the squire was with the head a little on one side and with the cheek drawn up from the left corner of the mouth, expressive of anything rather than a sense of inferiority to the squire, of whom, however, I had never heard speak before.

From Trotten we came to Midhurst, and, having baited our horses, went into Cowdry Park to see the ruins of that once noble mansion from which the Countess of Salisbury (the last of the

Plantagenets) was brought by the tyrant Henry VIII to be cruelly murdered in revenge for the integrity and other great virtues of her son, Cardinal Pole. This noble estate, one of the finest in the whole kingdom, was seized on by the king after the possessor had been murdered on his scaffold. The estate was then granted to a Sir Anthony Brown, who was physician to the king. By the descendants of this Brown the estate has been held to this day, and Mr Poyntz, who married the sole remaining heiress, a Miss Brown, is now the proprietor of the estate, comprising, I believe, *forty or fifty manors*. I asked the people at Midhurst where Mr Poyntz himself lived, and they told me at the *lodge* in the park, which lodge was formerly the residence of the head keeper.

We got to Petworth pretty early in the day. On entering it you see the house of Lord Egremont, which is close up against the park wall. There is a sort of town hall here, and on one side of it is the bust of Charles II, I should have thought, but they tell me that it is of Sir William Wyndham, from whom Lord Egremont is descended. But there is *another building* much more capacious and magnificent than the town hall, namely, the Bridewell. This structure vies, in magnitude, with the house of Lord Egremont itself. This place was not wanted when the labourer got twice as much, instead of half as much, as the common standing soldier.

THURSLEY
[Sunday, 13 November]
To our great delight we found Richard's horse quite well this morning, and off we set for this place.

North Chapel is a little town in the Weald of Sussex where there were formerly post-chaises kept, but where there are none now. And here is another complete revolution. In almost every country town the post-chaise houses have been lessened in number, and those that remain have become comparatively solitary and mean. The guests at inns are not now gentlemen, but *bumpers* who, from being called (at the inns) 'riders', became 'travellers' and are now 'commercial gentlemen' who go about in *gigs*, instead of on horseback, and who are in such numbers as to occupy a great part of the rooms in all inns in every part of the

country. There are probably twenty thousand of them always
out who may perhaps have, on average, throughout the year,
three or four thousand 'ladies' travelling with them. The
expense of this can be little short of fifteen millions a year, all to be
paid by the country people who consume the goods, and a large
part of it to be drawn up to the Wen.

We came through Chiddingfold, a very pretty place. There is
a very pretty and extensive green opposite the church, and we
were at the proper time of day to perceive that the modern
system of education had by no means overlooked this little
village. We saw the *schools* marching towards the church in
military order. Two of them passed us on our road. The boys
looked very hard at us, and I saluted them with 'There's brave
boys, you'll all be parsons or lawyers or doctors.' Another school
seemed to be in a less happy state. The scholars were too much in
uniform to have had their clothes purchased by their parents,
and they looked, besides, as if a little more victuals and a little
less education would have done as well. There were about
twenty of them, without one single tinge of red in their whole
twenty faces. Can it be of any use to expend money in this way
upon poor creatures that have not half a belly of food?

We got to Thursley and, the weather being pretty cold, we
found ourselves most happily situated here by the side of an
American fireplace, making extremely comfortable a room which
was formerly amongst the most uncomfortable in the world.
This is another of what the malignant parsons call Cobbett's
Quackeries. But my real opinion is that the whole body of them,
all put together, have never, since they were born, conferred so
much benefit upon the country as I have conferred upon it by
introducing this fireplace.

KENSINGTON
[Sunday, 20 Nov.]
Coming to Godalming on Friday, where business kept us that
night, we had to experience at the inn the want of our American
fireplace. A large and long room to sit in, with a miserable thing
called a screen to keep the wind from our backs, with a smoke in
the room half an hour after the fire was lighted, we, consuming a

bushel of coals in order to keep us warm, were not half so well off as we should have been in the same room, and without any screen, and with two gallons of coals, if we had had our American fireplace. I gave the landlord my advice upon the subject, and he said he would go and look at the fireplace at Mr Knowle's.

It looked like rain on Sunday morning, we therefore sent our horses on from Godalming to Ripley, and took a post-chaise to convey us after them. Being shut up in the post-chaise did not prevent me taking a look at a snug little house stuck under the hill on the road side, just opposite the old chapel on St Catherine's Hill, which house was not there when I was a boy. I found that this house is now occupied by the family of Molyneux, for ages the owners of Losely Park, on the outskirts of which estate this house stands. The house at Losely is of great antiquity and had, or perhaps has, attached to it the great manors of Godalming and Chiddingfold. I believe that Sir Thomas More lived at Losely, or, at any rate, that the Molyneux's are, in some degree, descended from him.

When we got to Ripley we found the day very fine, and we got upon our horses and rode home to dinner, after an absence of just one month.

But Richard and I have done something else beside ride and hunt, and course, and stare about us during this month. He was eleven years old last March and it was not time for him to begin to know something about letters and figures. He has learned to work in the garden and, having been a good deal in the country, knows a great deal about farming affairs. He can ride anything of a horse, and over anything that a horse can go over. When he and I went from home, he began to talk in anticipation of the sport he was going to have, which gave me occasion to address him thus: 'Fox hunting is a very fine thing, and very proper for people to be engaged in, and it is very desirable to be able to ride well and to be in at the death. But that is not ALL. Any fool can ride a horse and draw a cover: any groom or stable fellow can do these things. But all gentlemen that go a-foxhunting (I hope God will forgive me the lie) are scholars, Richard. You must now begin to learn something, and you must begin with arithmetic.'

I began with a pretty long lecture on the utility of arithmetic, and proceeded to explain to him the power of figures, according to the place they occupied. I then, for it was still dark, taught him to add a few figures together, I naming the figures one after the other. Thus we went on, mixing our riding and hunting with our arithmetic. Now when there is so much talk about education, let me ask how many pounds it generally costs parents to have a boy taught this of arithmetic; how much mortification and very often how much loss of health it costs the poor, scolded, broken-hearted child. I never once desired him to stay a moment from any other things he had a mind to go at. I just wrote down the sums upon paper, laid them upon the table and left him to tackle them when he pleased.

I think I shall be tempted to mould into a little book these lessons of arithmetic given to Richard. Some people will say, here is a monstrous deal of vanity and egotism, and if they will tell me how such a story is to be told without exposing a man to this imputation, I will adopt their mode another time. I get nothing by telling the story. I should get full as much by keeping it to myself. But it may be useful to others and therefore I tell it.

As to the *age* at which children ought to begin to be taught, it is very curious that, while I was at a friend's house during my ride, I looked into, by mere accident, a little child's abridgement of the History of England; a little thing about twice as big as a crown piece. Even into this abridgement the historian had introduced the circumstances of Alfred's father who, 'through a *mistaken notion* of kindness to his son, had suffered him to live to the age of 12 years without any attempt being made to give him education.' How came the writer to know that it was '*a mistaken notion*'? It appears from the result that the notions of the father were perfectly correct: and I am satisfied that if they had begun to thump the head of Alfred when he was a child, we should not have this day heard talk of Alfred the Great.

KENSINGTON TO EAST EVERLEY
[Sunday, 27 August, Evening]
I set off from Kensington on Friday morning on my way to the West. I got, at one time, a little out of my road in, or near, a

place called Tangley. I rode up to the garden-wicket of a cottage and asked the woman which was the way to LUDGERSHALL, which I knew could not be more than about *four miles* off. She did *not know*! A very neat, smart and pretty woman, but she did not know the way to this rotten borough which was, I was sure, only about four miles off! 'Well, my dear good woman,' said I, 'but you *have been* at LUDGERSHALL?' – 'No.' – 'Nor at Andover?' (six miles another way). 'No' – 'Nor at Marlborough?' (nine miles another way). 'No' – 'Pray, were you born in this house?' – 'Yes.' – 'And how far have you ever been from this house?' 'Oh! I have been *up in the parish* and over *to Chute*.' That is to say, the utmost extent of her voyages had been about *two and a half miles*. Let no one laugh at her and, above all others, let not me, who am convinced that the *facilities*, which now exist, of *moving human bodies from place to place* are amongst the *curses* of the country, the destroyers of *industry*, of morals and, of course, of happiness.

Everley is but about three miles from LUDGERSHALL, so that we got here in the afternoon of Friday. I was here, in this very inn, with a party eighteen years ago, and the landlord, who is still the same, recognised me as soon as he saw me. This inn is one of the nicest and, in summer, one of the pleasantest in England. The house is large, the yard and the stables good, the landlord *a farmer* also, and therefore no cribbing your horses in hay or straw and yourself in eggs and cream. I am sitting at one of the southern windows of this inn, looking across the garden towards the rookery. It is nearly sun-setting: the rooks are skimming and curving over the tops of the trees, while under the beeches I see a flock of several hundred sheep come nibbling their way in from the down, going to the fold.

My sons set off about three o'clock on their way to Herefordshire, where I intended to join them when I have had a pretty good ride in this country.

EAST EVERLEY
[Monday morning, 5 o'clock, 28 August, 1826]
A very fine morning. A man *eighty-two years* of age, just beginning to mow the short-grass in the garden. I thought it, even when I was young, the hardest work that man can do. To *look on*, this

work seems nothing, but it tries every sinew in your frame if you go upright and do your work well.

DOWN THE VALLEY OF THE AVON IN WILTSHIRE
Milton
[Monday, 28 August]

I came off this morning on the Marlborough road and then turned off, over the downs, in search of the source of the Avon river which goes down to Salisbury. But before I begin to ride down this beautiful vale let me give, as well as my means will enable me, a plan or map of it. A friend of mine has lent me a very old map of Wiltshire describing the spots where all the churches stood, and also the spots where manor-houses or mansion houses stood. I laid a piece of very thin paper upon the map, and thus traced the river upon the map, putting *figures* to represent the spots where churches stood and putting *stars* to represent the spots where manor houses or mansions formerly stood.

I proceeded on to the village of Milton. I left Easton away at my right, and I did not go up to Watton Rivers where the river Avon rises. Lower down the river, as I thought, there was a friend who was a great farmer and whom I intended to call on.

When I set out this morning, I intended to go all the way down to the city of Salisbury *today*; but I soon found that to refuse to sleep at Fifield would cost me a great deal more trouble than a day was worth. So that I made my mind up to stay in this farm-house, which has one of the nicest gardens that I ever saw.

Here I am, then, just going to bed after having spent as pleasant a day as ever I spent in my life.

AMESBURY
[Tuesday, 29 August]
I set out from Fifield this morning and got here about one o'clock, with my clothes wet. While they are drying, and while a mutton chop is getting ready I sit down to make some notes of what I had seen since I left Enford . . . but here comes my dinner; and I must put off my notes until I have dined.

SALISBURY
[Wednesday, 30 August]
My ride yesterday, from Milton to this city of Salisbury was, without any exception, the most pleasant that I ever had in my life as far as my recollection serves me. I arrived here in very good time, though I went over the Accursed Hill (Old Sarum) and went across to Laverstoke, before I came to Salisbury.

It is manifest enough that the *population* of this valley was, at one time, many times over what it is now: for, in the first place, what were the twenty-nine churches built for? The *stars*, in my map, mark the spots where manor houses or gentlemen's mansions formerly stood, and stood, too, only about sixty years ago. In this distance of about thirty miles there stood fifty mansion houses. Where are they *now*? I believe there are but eight that are at all worthy of the name of mansion houses, and even these are but poorly kept up. The state of this valley seems to illustrate the infamous and really diabolical assertion of Malthus, which is, that the human kind have a natural tendency *to increase beyond the means of sustenance for them*.

In taking my leave of this beautiful vale, I have to express my deep shame as an Englishman, at beholding the general *extreme poverty* of those who cause this vale to produce such quantities of food and raiment. This is, I verily believe it, the *worst used labouring people upon the face of the earth*. This state of things never can continue many years! By *some* means or other there must be an end to it; and my firm belief is that that end will be dreadful.

When I came down to Stratford Dean I wanted to go across to Laverstoke, but just on the other side of the road here rises the *Accursed Hill*. The hill is very steep and I dismounted and led my horse up. Being as near to the top as I could conveniently get, I stood a little while reflecting not so much on the changes which that hill had seen, as on the changes, the terrible changes, which in all human probability it had *yet to see*, and which it would have greatly *helped to produce*.

FROM SALISBURY TO WARMINSTER . . . TO HIGHWORTH
Heytesbury (Wilts)
[Thursday, 31 August, 1826]
This place, which is one of the rotten boroughs of Wiltshire and which was formerly a very considerable town, is now but a very miserable affair. Yesterday morning I went into the cathedral at Salisbury about 7 o'clock. When I got into the nave of the church and was looking about and admiring the columns and the roof, I heard a sort of *humming*, in some place which appeared to be the transept of the building. I wondered what it was, and made my way towards the place where the noise appeared to issue. Still following the sound, I at last turned in at a doorway at my left, where I found a priest and his congregation assembled. It was a parson of some sort, with a white covering on him, and five women and four men; when I arrived, there were five couple of us. I joined the congregation until they came to the *litany*; and then, being monstrously hungry, I did not think myself bound to stay any longer. I wonder what the founders would say if they could rise from the grave and see such a congregation as this in this most magnificent and beautiful cathedral.

Today has been exceedingly hot. Hotter, I think, for a short time, that I ever felt it in England before. In coming through a village called Wishford, I thought the heat on my back was as great as I had ever felt it in my life.

My next village was one that I had lived in for a short time when I was only about ten or eleven years of age. I had been sent down with a horse from Farnham, and I remember that I went by *Stonehenge* and rode up and looked at the stones. From Stonehenge I went to the village of Steeple Langford, where I

remained from the month of June to the fall of the year. I
remembered the beautiful villages up and down this valley. I
also remembered, very well, that the women of Steeple Langford used to card and spin dyed wool. I was therefore filled with
curiosity to see this Steeple Langford again. I was impatient to
get to it, hoping to find a public house, and a stable to put my
horse in, to protect him, for a while, against the flies which
tormented him to such a degree that to ride him was work as
hard as threshing. When I got to Steeple Langford, I found no
public house, and I found it a much more miserable place than I
had ever remembered it. The *Steeple*, to which it owed its
distinctive appellation, was gone; and the place seemed to me to
be very much altered for the worse. A little further on, however,
I came to a very famous inn, called Deptford Inn, which is in the
parish of Wyly. I stayed at this inn until about four o'clock in the
afternoon. I remembered Wyly very well and thought it a gay
place when I was a boy. I remembered a very beautiful garden
belonging to a rich farmer and miller and I went to see it; but
alas! though the statues in the water and on the grass-plat were
still remaining, everything seemed to be in a state of perfect
carelessness and neglect.

This Deptford Inn was a famous place of meeting for the
yeoman cavalry in glorious anti-jacobin times, when wheat was
twenty shillings a bushel, and when a man could be crammed
into gaol for only *looking* awry. The shape of the garden shows
you what revelry used to be carried on here.

WARMINSTER (Wilts)
[Friday, 1 Sept.]
I set out from Heytesbury this morning about six o'clock. Last
night, before I went to bed, I found that there were some men
and boys in the house who had come all the way from Bradford,
about twelve miles, in order to get *nuts*. These people were men
and boys that had been employed in the *cloth* factories at
Bradford and about Bradford. I had some talk with some of
these nutters, and I am quite convinced, not that the cloth
making is at *an end*, but that it will never again be what it has
been.

These poor nutters were extremely ragged. I saved my supper, and I fasted instead of breakfasting. That was three shilling which I had saved, and I added five to them with a resolution to save them afterwards, in order to give these chaps a breakfast for once in their lives. There was eight of them, six men and two boys; and I gave them two quartern loaves, two pounds of cheese and eight pints of strong beer. The fellows were very pleased, but the conduct of the landlord and landlady pleased me exceedingly. When I came to pay my bill, they had said nothing about my bed; and when I asked why they had not put the bed in the bill, they said they would not charge me anything for the bed since I had been so good to the poor men. Yes, said I, but I must not throw the expense on you. I had no supper and I have had no breakfast and, therefore, I am not called upon to pay for them. But *I have had* the bed. It ended by my paying for the bed, and coming off, leaving the nutters at their breakfast, and very much delighted with the landlord and his wife. And here I must observe, that I have pretty generally found a good deal of compassion for the poor people to prevail amongst publicans and their wives.

[Saturday, 2 September]
After I got to Warminster yesterday it began to rain, which stopped me in my way to Frome in Somersetshire. But as I meant to be quite in the northern part of the county by tomorrow noon, or thereabouts, I took a post-chaise in the afternoon of yesterday and went to Frome where I saw, upon my entrance into the town, between two and three hundred weavers, men and boys, cracking stones, moving earth, and doing other sorts of work towards making a fine principal road into the town. The parish pay, which they get upon the roads, is 2s. 6d. for a man, 2s. for his wife, 1s. 3d. for each child under eight years of age, 3d. a week in addition for each child above eight years old, who can go to work: and if the children above eight years old, whether boy or girl, do not go to work upon the roads they have *nothing*! These poor creatures of Frome have pawned all their things, or nearly all. All their best clothes, their blankets and sheets; their looms; any little piece of furniture that they had, and that was good for anything.

Devizes (Wilts)
[Sunday morning, 3 Sept.]
I left Warminster yesterday about one o'clock. It is contrary to
my practice to set out at all unless I can do it early in the
morning, but at Warminster I was at the south-west corner of
this county, and I had made a sort of promise to be today at
Highworth, which is at the north-east corner. The distance,
including my little intended deviations, was more than fifty
miles, and not liking to attempt it in one day I set off in the
middle of the day and got here in the evening, just before a
pretty heavy rain came on.

I must once more observe that Warminster is a very nice
town: everything belonging to it is *solid* and *good*. There are no
villainous gingerbread houses running up, and no nasty shabby-
genteel people; no women trapesing around with showy gowns
and dirty necks; no Jew-looking fellows with dandy coats, dirty
shirts and half-heels to their shoes. A really nice and good town.
It is a corn market, one of the greatest in this part of England,
and here things are conducted in the good old honest way. The
corn is brought and pitched in the market before it is sold; and
when sold, it is paid for on the nail; and all is over and the
farmers and millers gone home by daylight. Almost everywhere
else the corn is sold by sample; it is sold by juggling in a corner;
the parties meet and drink first; it is night work; there is no fair
and open market; the mass of the people do not know what the
prices are; and all this favours that monopoly which makes the
corn change hands many times, perhaps, before it reaches the
mouth, leaving a profit in each pair of hands.

HIGHWORTH (Wilts)
[Monday, 4 Sept.]
I got here yesterday after a ride, including my deviations, of
about thirty-four miles, and that, too, *without breaking my fast*.
Before I got to the rotten borough of Calne I had two *tributes* to
pay to the aristocracy, namely two *Sunday* tolls, and I resolved
that the country in which these tolls were extorted should not
have a farthing of my money that I could, by any means, keep
from it. Therefore I fasted until I got into the free quarters in

which I now am. I would have made my horse fast too if I could
have done it without the risk of making him unable to carry me.

FROM HIGHWORTH TO CRICKLADE
AND THENCE TO MALMESBURY
Highworth (Wilts)
[Monday, 4 Sept., 1826]
When I got to Devizes on Saturday evening, and came to look out
of the inn window into the street, I perceived that I had seen that
place before, and always having thought that I should like to *see*
Devizes, of which I had heard so much talk as a famous corn-
market, I was very much surprised to see that it was not new to
me. Presently a stage coach came up to the door with 'Bath and
London' upon its panels; and then I recollected that I had been at
this place on my way to Bristol last year.

In quitting Devizes yesterday morning, I saw just on the
outside of the town a monstrous building, which I took for a
barrack; but upon asking what it was I found it was one of those
marks of the JUBILEE REIGN; namely, *a most magnificent gaol.*
It seemed to me sufficient to hold one-half of the able-bodied
men in the county! As I came on the road, for the first three or
four miles, I saw great numbers of labourers either digging

potatoes for their Sunday's dinner, or coming home with them, or going out to dig them. The land-owners or occupiers let small pieces of land to the labourers, and these they cultivate with the spade for their own use. They pay, in all cases, a high rent, and in most cases an enormous one. The practice prevails all the way from Warminster to Devizes, and from Devizes to nearly this place. The rent is, in some places, a shilling a rod which is, mind you, 160s. or £8 an acre!

HIGHWORTH
[Wednesday, 6 Sept.]

The great object of my visit to the northern border of Wiltshire will be mentioned when I get to Malmesbury, whither I intend to go tomorrow, or next day, and thence through Gloucestershire, in my way to Herefordshire.

MALMESBURY (Wilts)
[*Monday, 11 Sept.*]

I was detained at Highworth partly by rain and partly by company that I liked very much. I left at 6 o'clock yesterday morning and got to this town about three or four o'clock in the afternoon after a ride, including my deviations, of 34 miles and as pleasant a ride as ever man had. I got to a farmhouse in the neighbourhood of Cricklade to breakfast, at which house I was very near to the source of the river Isis, which is, they say, the first branch of the Thames. They call it the 'Old Thames', and I rode through it here, it not being above four or five yards wide and not deeper than the knees of my horse.

I observed that, when I got to Malmesbury, I would have to explain my main object in coming to the north of Wiltshire. In the year 1818, by *an Act*, parliament ordered the bishops to cause the beneficed clergy to give in an account of their livings, which account was to contain the following particulars relating to each parish:

1 Whether a rectory, vicarage or what.
2 In what rural deanery.
3 Population.

4 Number of churches and chapels.

5 *Number of persons they* (the churches and chapels) *can contain.*

In looking into this account, as it was finally made up and printed by the parliamentary officers, I saw that it was impossible for it to be true. I have always asserted, and indeed I have clearly proved, that one of the last two population returns is false, bare-facedly false, and I am sure that the account of which I am now speaking was equally false.

The falsehood consisted, I saw principally, in the account of the capacity of the church to contain people. I saw that, in almost every instance, this account must of necessity be false, though coming from under the pen of a beneficed clergyman. I saw that there was a constant desire to make it appear that the church was now become too small! And thus to help along the opinion of a great recent increase of population, an opinion so sedulously inculcated by all the tax-eaters of every sort.

There was one instance in which the parson had been singularly impudent, for he had stated the population at eight persons, and had stated that the church could hold eight persons. This was the account of the parish of Sharncut. To this Sharncut, therefore, I was resolved to go and to try the fact with my own eyes.

I got to Sharncut, which I found to consist of a church, two farm houses and a parsonage house. I found in the church eleven pews that would contain eighty-two people, and these do not occupy a third area of the church; and thus more than two hundred persons can be accommodated, with perfect convenience, in this church which the parson says *can* contain *eight*! The *motive* for making out the returns in this way is clear enough. The parsons see that they are getting what they get in a declining and mouldering country. They feel the facts, but they wish to disguise them because they know they have been the one great cause of that country being in its present impoverished and dilapidated state.

From Sharncut I came through a very long and straggling village, called Somerford, another called Ocksey and another called Crudwell. Between Somerford and Ocksey I saw, on the side of the road, more *goldfinches* than I had ever seen together; I think fifty times as many as I had ever seen at one time in my life.

The favourite food of the goldfinch is the seed of the *thistle*. The seed is just now dead ripe. The thistles are all cut and carried away from the fields by the harvest; but they grow alongside the roads and, in this place, in great quantities. So that the goldfinches were got here in flocks and, as they continued to fly along before me, for nearly half a mile, and still sticking to the road and the banks, I do believe I had, at last, a flock of ten thousand flying before me. *Birds* of every kind, including partridges and pheasants and all sorts of poultry, are most abundant this year. The fine, long summer has been singularly favourable to them, and you see the effect of it in the great broods of chickens and geese and turkeys in and about every farmyard.

When I got here yesterday, I went first to an inn, but I very soon changed my quarters for the house of a friend and whose family, though I had never seen them before, and had never heard of them until I was at Highworth, gave me a hearty reception. This town, though it has nothing particularly engaging in itself, stands upon one of the prettiest spots that can be imagined. There remains more of the abbey than, I believe, of any of our monastic remains, except that of Westminster, and those that have become cathedrals. The church service is performed in the part of the abbey that is left standing. It was once a most magnificent building and there is now a *doorway* which is one of the most beautiful things I ever saw and which was nevertheless built in Saxon times, in 'the *dark* ages', and was built by men who were not begotten by Pitt nor by Jubilee George.

There is a *market-cross* in this town, the sight of which is worth a journey of hundreds of miles. Time, with his scythe, and 'enlightened Protestant piety' with its pick-axe and crow-bars; these united have done much to efface the beauties of this monument of ancient skill and taste, and proof of ancient wealth; but in spite of all their destructive efforts this cross still remains a most beautiful thing, though possibly, and even probably, nearly or quite a thousand years old. There is a *market-cross* lately erected at Devizes and intended to imitate the ancient ones. Compare that with this, and then you have, pretty fairly, a view of the difference between us and our forefathers of the 'dark ages'.

Tomorrow I start for Bollitree, near Ross, Herefordshire, my road being across the county and through the city of Gloucester.

FROM MALMESBURY, THROUGH GLOUCESTERSHIRE,
HEREFORDSHIRE, AND WORECESTERSHIRE
Stroud, Gloucestershire
[Tuesday forenoon, 12 Sept., 1826]
I set off from Malmesbury this morning at 6 o'clock in as sweet and bright a morning as ever came out of the heavens, and leaving behind me as pleasant a house and as kind hosts as I ever met with in the whole course of my life, either in England or America. And now, before I take my leave of Wiltshire, I must observe that, in the whole course of my life (days of *courtship* being excepted, of course) I never passed seventeen pleasanter days.

I saw again this morning large flocks of goldfinches feeding on the thistle-seed on the roadside. The French call this bird by a name derived from the thistle, so notorious has it always been that they live upon this seed. *Thistle* is, in French, *chardon*; and the French call this beautiful little bird *chardonneret*. I never could have supposed that such flocks of these birds would ever be seen in England.

Just before I got into Tutbury I was met by a good many people, in twos, threes, or fives, some running and some walking fast, one of the first of whom asked me if I had met an 'old man' some distance back. I asked what *sort* of a man. 'A *poor* man.' 'I don't recollect, indeed; but what are you all pursuing him for?' 'He has been *stealing*.' 'What has he been stealing?' 'Cabbages.' 'Where?' 'Out of Mr Glover, the hatter's, garden.' 'What? Do you call that *stealing*? And would you punish a poor man, and therefore in all likelihood a hungry man, and moreover an old man; do you set up a hue and cry after, and would you punish, such a man for taking a few cabbages, when that Holy Bible which, I dare say, you profess to believe in and perhaps assist to circulate, teaches you that the hungry man may, without committing any offence at all, go into his neighbour's vineyard and eat his fill of grapes, one bunch of which is worth a sackfull of cabbages?' 'Yes; but he is a very bad character.'

Another group or two of the pursuers had come up by this

time and I, bearing in mind the fate of Don Quixote when he interfered in somewhat similar cases, gave my horse the hint and soon got away. But though doubtless I made no converts, I, upon looking back, perceived that I had slackened the pursuit. It is impossible for me to behold such a scene, without calling in mind the practice in the United States of America where, if a man were even to talk of prosecuting another (especially if that other were poor or old) for taking from the land, or from the trees, any part of a growing crop for his own personal and immediate use, such talker would be held in universal abhorrence.

Tutbury is a very pretty town, and has a beautiful ancient church. The country is high along here for a mile or two towards Avening. I was upon the edge of the high land, looking right down upon the village of Avening and seeing, just close to it, a large and fine mansion house, a beautiful park and, making part of the park, one of the finest, most magnificent woods (of 200 acres, I dare say) lying facing me. While I was sitting on my horse, admiring this spot, a man came along with some tools in his hand, as if going somewhere to work as a plumber. 'Whose beautiful place is that?' said I. 'One 'Squire Ricardo, I think they call him, but . . .' – You might have knocked me down with a feather, as the old woman said . . . 'but' (continued the plumber), 'the Old Gentleman's dead,' 'God – the Old Gentleman and the young gentleman too,' I said, and giving my horse a blow, instead of a word, on I went down the hill.

One of the first objects that struck my eye in the village was the sign of the Cross, and of the Red, or Bloody Cross too. I asked the landlord some questions, which began a series of joking and bantering that I had with the people, from one end of the village to the other. I set them all a laughing, and though they could not know my name, they will remember me for a long while.

HUNTLEY (between Gloucester and Ross)
From Stroud I came up to Pitchcomb, leaving Painswick on my right. From the lofty hill at Pitchcomb I looked down into the great flat and almost circular vale, of which the city of Gloucester is in the centre. When I came to Gloucester, I found I

should run a risk of having no bed if I did not bow very low and pay very high; for what should there be here, but one of those scandalous and beastly fruits of the system, called a 'music-meeting'. Those who founded the cathedrals never dreamed, I dare say, that they would have been put to such uses as this! They are, upon these occasions, made use of as *Opera-houses*, and I am told that the money which is collected goes, in some shape or other, to the clergy of the church, or their widows or children, or something.

From this scene of prostitution and of pocket-picking I moved off with all convenient speed, but not before the ostler made me pay 9*d.* for merely letting my horse *stand* about ten minutes, and not before he had begun to *abuse* me for declining, though in a very polite manner, to make him a present in addition to the 9*d.* How he ended I do not know, for I soon set the noise of the shoes of my horse to answer him. I got to this village, about eight miles from Gloucester, about five o'clock; it is now half past seven and I am going to bed with an intention of getting to Bollitree (six miles only) early enough in the morning to catch my sons in bed if they play the sluggard.

BOLLITREE
[Wednesday, 13 Sept.]
This morning was most beautiful. There has been rain here now, and the grass begins (but only begins) to grow. When I got to within two hundred yards of Mr Palmer's, I had the happiness to meet my son Richard, who said that he had been up an hour. As I came along, I saw one of the prettiest sights in the *flower* way that I ever saw in my life. It was a little orchard; the grass in it had just taken a start, and was beautifully fresh, and very thickly growing among the grass was the purple flowered *Colchicum* in full bloom. They say that the leaves of this plant, which come out in the spring and die away in the summer, are poisonous to cattle if they eat much of them in the spring. The flower, if standing by itself, would be no great beauty; but contrasted thus with the fresh grass, which was a little shorter than itself, it was very beautiful.

RYALL, near Upton upon Severn (Worcestershire)
[Monday, 25 Sept.]
I set off from Mr Palmer's yesterday, after breakfast, having his
son (about 13 years old) as my travelling companion. We came
across the country, a distance of about 22 miles, and having
crossed the Severn at Upton, arrived here, at Mr John Price's,
about two o'clock. On the road we passed by the estate of *another
Ricardo!* This is Osmond, the other is David. This one has ousted
two families of Normans, the Honeywood Yateses and the
Scudamores. They suppose him to have ten thousand pounds a
year in rent here! Famous 'watching the turn of the market'!

Mr Hanford, of this county, and Mr Canning of Gloucestershire having dined at Mr Price's yesterday, I went today with
Mr Price to see Mr Hanford at his house and estate at Bredon
Hill, which is, I believe, one of the highest in England. At the
very highest part of it there are remains of an encampment, or
rather, I should think, a citadel. In many instances in Wiltshire
these marks of fortifications are called castles still, and doubtless
there were once castles on this site. From Bredon Hill you see
into nine or ten counties, and those curious bubblings up, the
Malvern Hills, are right before you and only at about ten miles
distance, in a straight line.

Mr Hanford's house is on the side of Bredon Hill, about a
third part up it, and is a very delightful place. The house is of
ancient date and it appears to have been always inhabited by,
and the property of, Roman Catholics, for there is, in one corner
of the very top of the building, up in the very roof of it, a Catholic
chapel, ancient as the roof itself. At the back of the altar there is a
little room, which you enter through a door going out of the
chapel, and adjoining this little room there is a closet, in which is
a trap door made to let the priest down into one of those
hiding places which were contrived for the purpose of evading
the grasp of those greedy Scotch minions to whom that pious
and tolerant Protestant, James I, delivered over these English
gentlemen who remained faithful to the religion of their fathers.

WORCESTER
[Tuesday, 26 Sept.]
Mr Price rode with us to this city, which is one of the cleanest,

neatest, and handsomest towns I ever saw; indeed, I do not recollect to have seen any one equal it. The *cathedral* is indeed a poor thing compared with any of the others, except that of Hereford; and I have seen them all but those of Carlisle, Durham, York, Lincoln, Chester, and Peterborough. But the *town* is, I think, the very best I ever say: the *people* are, upon the whole, the most suitably dressed and most decent looking people.

At Worcester, as everywhere else, I find a group of cordial and sensible friends, at the house of one of whom, Mr George Brooke, I have just spent a most pleasant evening. I here learned a fact which I must put on record before it escapes my memory. Some few years ago (about seven, perhaps), at the public sale by auction of the goods of a then recently deceased attorney, there were amongst the goods to be sold, the portraits of *Pitt*, *Burdett*, and *Paine*. Pitt, with hard driving and very lofty praises, fetched fifteen shillings: Burdett fetched twenty-seven shillings. Paine was, in great haste, knocked down at five pounds.

STANFORD PARK
[Wednesday morning, 27 Sept.]
In a letter which I received from Sir Thomas Winnington (one of the members for this county) last year, he was good enough to request that I would call upon him if ever I came into Worcestershire, which I told him I would do: and accordingly we are here in his house, situated certainly in one of the finest spots in all England.

We left Worcester yesterday about ten, crossed the Severn which runs close by the town and came on to this place. About four miles back, we passed through the park and estate of Lord Foley, to whom is due the praise of being a most indefatigable and successful *planter of trees*; and he has the merit of dis-interestedness, the trees being chiefly oak, which he is *sure* he can never see grow to timber.

Sir Thomas was out shooting, but he soon came home and gave us a very polite reception. I wished to get away early this morning, but being prevailed on to stay to breakfast, here I am, at six o'clock in the morning, in one of the best, and best-stocked private libraries that I ever saw.

The house and stables are such as they ought to be for the great estate that surrounds them and the park is everything that is beautiful. 'Well, then,' says the devil of laziness, 'and could you not be contented to live here all the rest of your life? and never again pester yourself with the cursed politics?' 'Why, I think I have laboured enough. Let others work now. And such a pretty place for coursing and for hare-hunting and woodcock shooting, I dare say. And then those pretty wild ducks in the water and the flowers and the grass and the trees and the fresh air, and never, never again to be stifled with the smoke that from the infernal Wen ascendeth for ever more and that every easterly wind brings to choke me at Kensington!'

The last *word* of this soliloquy carried me back, slap to my own study (very much unlike that in which I am in) and bade me think of the complete triumph that I have yet to enjoy; promised me the pleasure of seeing a million trees of my own, and sown by my own hands, this very year.

RYALL
[Wednesday night, 27 Sept.]
After breakfast we took our leave of Sir Thomas Winnington and of Stanford, very much pleased with our visit. We wished to reach Ryall as early as possible in the day and we did not, therefore, stop at Worcester. We got here about three o'clock.

FROM RYALL IN WORCESTERSHIRE
TO BURGHCLERE IN HAMPSHIRE
Ryall
[Friday morning, 29 September, 1826]
I have observed in this country, and especially near Worcester, that the working people seem to be better off than in many other parts, one cause of which is, I dare say, that *glove manufacturing*, which cannot be carried on by fire or wind or water and which is, therefore, carried on by the *hands* of human beings. It gives work to women and children, as well as to men, and that work is, by a great part of the women and children, done in their cottages, and amidst the fields and hop-gardens. This is a great

thing for the land. If this glove-making were to cease, many of these women and children, now not upon the parish, must instantly be upon the parish. The glove trade is, like all others, slack from this last change in the value of money; but there is no horrible misery here, as at Manchester, Leeds, Glasgow, Paisley and other Hell-Holes of 84 degrees of heat.

I cannot take leave of this county without observing that I do not recollect to have seen one miserable object in it. The working people all seem to have good large gardens, and pigs in their styes; and this last, say the *feelosofers* what they will about 'antallectual enjoyments', is the *only* security for happiness in a labourer's family.

On my return from Worcester to this place, yesterday, I noticed, at a village called Severn Stoke, a very curiously constructed grape house; that is to say, a hot-house for the raising of grapes. Upon enquiry, I found that it belonged to a parson of the name of St John, whose parsonage house is very near to it and who, being *sure* of having the benefice when the then rector should die, bought a piece of land and erected his grapery on it, just facing and only about 50 yards from the windows out of which the *old parson* had to look until the day of his death, with a view, doubtless, of piously furnishing his aged brother with a *momento mori* (remember death), quite as significant as a death's head and cross bones, and yet done in a manner expressive of that fellow feeling, that delicacy, that abstinence from self-gratification, which are well known to be characteristics almost peculiar to 'the cloth'.

HAYDEN
[Saturday night, 30 Sept.]
From Ryall, in Worcestershire, we came yesterday (Friday) morning first to Tewkesbury in Gloucestershire. This is a good, substantial town which for many years sent to parliament that sensible, honest and constant hater of Pitt and his infernal politics, James Martin, and which now sends to the same place Mr John Martin, his son.

The Warwickshire Avon falls into the Severn here, and on the sides of both, for many miles back, there are the finest meadows that ever were seen. In looking over them, and beholding the endless flocks and herds, one wonders what can become of all the meat! By riding on about eight or nine miles farther, however, this wonder is a little diminished; for here we come to one of the devouring Wens; namely Cheltenham, which is what they call a 'watering place'; that is to say, the place to which East India plunderers, West India floggers, English tax-gropers, together with gluttons, drunkards and debauchees of all descriptions, female as well as male, resort at the suggestion of silently laughing quacks in the hope of getting rid of the bodily consequences of their manifold sins and iniquities. When I enter a place like this, I always feel disposed to squeeze up my nose with my fingers. It is nonsense, to be sure, but a conceit that every two-legged creature that I see coming near me is about to cover me with the poisonous proceeds of its impurities. To places like this come all that is knavish and all that is foolish and base; gamesters, pickpockets and harlots; young wife-hunters in search of rich and wrinkled and half-rotten women, the former resolutely bent, be the means what they may, to give the latter heirs to their lands and tenements.

We rode up the main street of the town for some distance. The whole town (and it was now ten o'clock) looked delightfully dull. I did not see more than four or five carriages and perhaps twenty people on horseback; and these seemed by their hook-noses and round eyes, and by the long and sooty necks of the women, to be, for the greater part, *Jews and Jewesses*. The place really seems to be sinking very fast, and I have been told, and believe the fact, that houses in Cheltenham will now sell for only just about one-third as much as the same would have sold in last October.

It is curious to see the names which the vermin owners have put upon the houses here. There is a neat row of most gaudy and fantastical dwelling places called 'Colombia Place', given it, doubtless, by some dealer in *bonds*. There is what a boy told us was the '*New Spa*': there is '*Waterloo House*'! Oh! How I rejoice at the ruin of the base creatures! There is '*Liverpool Cottage*,' '*Canning Cottage*', '*Peel Cottage*'; and the good of it is that the ridiculous beasts have put this word *cottage* upon scores of houses, and some very mean and shabby houses, standing along and making part of an unbroken street. What a figure this place will cut in another year or two! I should not wonder to see it wholly deserted.

After Cheltenham we had to reach this pretty little town of Fairford, the regular turnpike to which lay through Cirencester; but I had from a fine map, at Sir Thomas Winnington's, traced out a line for us along through a chain of villages, leaving Cirencester away to our right and never coming nearer than seven or eight miles to it.

A *route*, when it lies through *villages*, is one thing on a *map* and quite another on the ground. Our line of villages from Cheltenham to Fairford was very nearly straight on the map, but upon the ground it took us round about a great many miles, and, which was a great inconvenience, not a public house was there on the road until we got within eight miles of Fairford. Resolved that not a single farthing of my money should be spent in the Wen of Cheltenham, we came through that place, expecting to find a public house in the first or second of the villages: but not one was there over the whole of the wold. And though I, by pocketing some slices of meat and bread at Ryall, provided against this contingency, as far as related to ourselves, I could make no such provision for our horses, and they went a great deal too far without baiting. Plenty of farmhouses, and, if they had been in America, we need have looked for no other. Very likely (I hope it at any rate) almost any farm on the Cotswold would have given us what we wanted, and we asked for it. But the fashion, the good old fashion was, by the hellish system of funding and taxing and monopolising, driven across the Atlantic. And is England *never* to see it return! Is the hellish system to last *for ever*!

Doctor Black, in remarking upon my Ride down the Vale of the Salisbury Avon, says that there has doubtless been a falling off of population of the villages 'lying amongst the chalk hills': aye, and lying everywhere else, too, or how comes it that four-fifths of the parishes of Herefordshire, abounding in rich land, in meadows, orchards and pastures, have either no parsonage house at all, or have none that a parson thinks fit for him to live in? I vouch for the fact.

BURGHCLERE (Hampshire)
[Monday, 2 October]

Yesterday was a really *unfortunate day*. The morning promised fair, but its promises were like those of Burdett! There was a little, snivelling, wet frost.

Just before we got to Swindon, we crossed a canal at a place where there is a wharf and a coal-yard, and close by these a gentleman's house, with coach-house, stables, walled-in garden, a paddock *orne'* and the rest of those things which, all together, make up a *villa*. Seeing a man in the coal-yard, I asked him to what gentleman the house belonged. 'To the *head 'un* of the canal,' said he. And when, upon further enquiry of him, I found that it was the villa of the chief manager, I could not help congratulating the proprietors of this aquatic concern, for though I did not ask the name of the canal, I could readily suppose that the profits must be prodigious when the residence of the manager would imply no disparagement of dignity if occupied by a Secretary of State for the Home or even the Foreign Department.

A little after we came through Auborne, we turned off to our right to go through Ramsbury to Shallburn, where Tull, the father of the drill-husbandry, began and practised that husbandry at a farm called 'Prosperous'. We pushed through coppices and across fields to a little village called Froxfield, which we found to be on the great Bath road. I had been at Prosperous before, so that I knew Mr Blandy, the owner, and his family, who received us with great hospitality. About three

quarters of an hour before sunset we set off. Including the numerous angles and windings we had nine or ten miles yet to go, but I was so anxious to get to Burghclere that, contrary to my practice as well as my principle, I determined to encounter the darkness for once, though in cross-country roads presenting us, at every mile, with ways crossing each other, or forming a Y; or kindly giving us the choice of three, forming the upper part of a Y and a half. Add to this that we were in enclosed country, the lanes very narrow, deep-worn, and banks and hedges high. There was no moon; but it was starlight, and as I could see the Hampshire hills all along to my right, and knew that I must not get above a mile or so from them, I had a guide that could not deceive me: for as to *asking* the road in a case like this it is of little use, unless you meet someone at every half mile: for the answer is *keep right on*: aye, but in ten minutes, perhaps, you come to a Y or to a T, or a +.

A fellow told me once, in my way from Chertsey to Guildford, 'keep *right on*, you can't miss your way.' I was in the perpendicular part of the T, and the top part was only a few yards from me. '*Right on*,' said I; 'what, over *that bank* into the wheat?' 'No, no,' said he, 'I mean *that road*, to be sure,' pointing to the road that went off to the left. In *down countries* the direction of shepherds and pig and bird boys is always in precisely the same words; namely, '*right* over the down', laying great stress upon the word *right*. 'But,' said I to a boy at the edge of the down at King's Worthy (near Winchester), 'But what do you mean by *right* over the down?' 'Why,' said he, '*right* on to Stoke, to be sure, zur.' 'Aye,' said I, 'but how am I, who was never here before, to know *what is* right, my boy?' That posed him. It set him to thinking, and after a bit he proceeded to tell me that when I got up the hill I should see '*some trees*'; that I should go along by them; that I should then see a *barn* right before me; that I should go down to the barn; and that I should then see a wagon track that would lead me all the way down to Stoke. 'Aye,' said I. 'Now, indeed, you are a real clever fellow.' And I gave him a shilling, being part of my savings of the morning.

Whoever tries it will find that the *less they eat and drink* while travelling, the better they will be. I act accordingly. Many days I have no breakfast and no dinner. I went from Devizes to Highworth without breaking my fast, a distance, including deviations, of more than *thirty miles*. I sometimes take, from a friend's house, a little bit of meat between two bits of bread which I eat as I ride along; but whatever I save from this fasting work, I think I have a clear right to give away. And, accordingly, I generally put the amount, in copper, into my waistcoat pocket and dispose of it during the day. I know well that *I am the better* for not stuffing and blowing myself out, and with the savings I make many and many a happy boy. And now and then I give a whole family a good meal with the cost of a breakfast or dinner, that would have done me mischief. I do not do this because I grudge inn-keepers what they charge: for my surprise is how they can live without charging *more* than they do in general.

It was dark by the time we got to a village called East Woodhay. Sunday evening is the time *for courting* in the country. It is not convenient to carry this on before faces, and at farm-houses and cottages there are no spare apartments; so that the pairs turn out and pitch up, carry on their negotiations by the side of stile or gate. The evening was auspicious; it was *pretty dark*, the weather mild, and Old Michaelmass (when yearly services end) was fast approaching; and accordingly I do not recollect ever having before seen so many negotiations going on within so short a distance. At West Woodhay my horse *cast a shoe*, and as the road was abominably flinty, we were compelled to go at a snail's pace; and I should have gone crazy with impatience had it not been for these ambassadors and ambassadresses of Cupid, to every pair of whom I said something or the other. I began asking the fellow *my road*, and from the tone and manner of his answer I could tell pretty well what prospect he had of success, and knew what to say to draw something from him. I had some famous sport with them, saying more to them than I should have said by daylight, and a great deal less than I should have said if my horse had been in a condition to carry me away as swiftly as he did from Osmond Ricardo's terrific cross!

HURSTBOURNE TARRANT (commonly called Uphusband)
[Wednesday, 11 October, 1826]
When quarters are good you are apt to *lurk* in them, but really it

was so wet that we could not get away from Burghclere till Monday evening. Being here, there were many reasons for our going to the great fair at Weyhill which began yesterday.

From Weyhill I was shown the wood in which took place the battle in which was concerned poor Turner, one of the young men who was hanged at Winchester in the year 1822. There was a young man, named Smith, who was on account of another game-battle hanged on the same gallows! And this for the preservation of the *game*, you will observe. James Turner, aged 28 years, was accused of assisting to kill Robert Baker, gamekeeper to Thomas Asheton Smith, Esq., in the parish of South Tidworth; and Charles Smith, aged 27 years, was accused of shooting at (not killing) Robert Snelgrove, assistant game-keeper to Lord Palmerston at Broadlands in the parish of Romsey. Poor Charles Smith had been better hunting after *shares*, than *hares*. *Mines*, however *deep*, he would have found less perilous than the pleasure grounds of Lord Palmerston! I deem this hanging worthy of general attention: it shall make me repeat here that which I published in the *Register* of the 6th April 1822.*

Such was what I *then* addressed to the landlords. How well it fits the *present* time! They are just in the same sort of *mess* now that they were in 1822.

ANDOVER
[Sunday, 15 October]
After the Weyhill Fair was over yesterday, I came down from the hill to this town of Andover. Having made my plans to sleep at Andover last night, I went with two Farnham friends to dine at the ordinary at the George Inn, which is kept by one Sutton, a rich old fellow, who wore a round-skirted, sleeved fustian waistcoat, with a dirty white apron tied round his middle and with no coat on; having a look the *eagerest* and the *sharpest* that I ever saw in any set of features in my life, having an air of authority and mastership which, to a stranger as I was, seemed

---

* Cobbett here inserts the lengthy Letter on the Agricultural Report describing the background to the trial of Turner and Smith.

quite incompatible with the meaness of his dress and the vulgarity of his manners.

A great part of the farmers and other fair-people having gone off home, we found preparations made for dining only about ten people. But after we sat down, and it was seen that we designed to dine, guests came in apace. After the dinner was over, the room became fuller and fuller. Our chairman gave *my health*, which of course was followed by a speech; and, as the reader may readily suppose, to have an opportunity of making a speech was the main motive for my going to dine at an *inn*, at any hour, and especially at seven o'clock at night. Just at this time, a noise was heard, and a sort of row was taking place in the passage, the cause of which was, upon inquiry, found to be no less a person than our landlord, our host Sutton, who, it appeared, finding that my speech-making had cut off or at least suspended all intercourse between the dining, now a drinking, room and the bar; finding, or rather supposing, that, if my tongue were not stopped from running his taps would be, had, though an old man, fought, or at least forced his way up through the thronged stairs and through the passage and door-way into the room and was (with what breath the struggle had left him) beginning to bawl out to me, when someone called to him, and told him that he was causing an interruption, to which he answered that that was what he had come to do. And then he went on to say, in so many words, that my speech injured his sale of liquor!

The old fellow, finding himself *tackled*, saved the labour of shoving or kicking him out of the room by retreating out of the doorway. After this, I proceeded with my speech-making, and this being ended, the great business of the evening began; namely, drinking, smoking and singing was about to be proceeded in by a company who had just closed an arduous and anxious week, who had before them a Sunday morning to sleep in, and whose wives were, for the greater part, at a convenient distance.

But now behold, the old fustian-jacketed fellow, whose head was, I think, *powdered*, took it into that head not only to lay 'restrictions' upon trade, but to impose an absolute embargo; cut off entirely all supplies whatever from his bar to this room, *as long as I remained in that room*. A message to this effect from the old fustian man having been, through the waiter, communicated to the chairman, and he having communicated it to the company, I addressed the company in nearly these words: 'I like your company too well to quit it. I have paid this fellow *six* shillings for the wing of a fowl, a bit of bread and a pint of small beer. I have a right to sit here. I want no drink, and those who do, being refused it, have a right to send to other houses for it, and drink it here.'

However, Mammon soon got the upper hand downstairs, all the fondness for 'free trade' returned, and up came the old fustian-jacketed fellow, bringing pipes, tobacco, wine, grog, sling, and seeming to be as pleased as he had just sprung a mine of gold! Nay, he soon after this came into the room with two gentlemen, who had come to ask him where I was. He actually came up to me, making his bow, and, telling me that those gentlemen wished to be introduced to me, he, with a fawning look, laid his hand on my knee! It was not politics; it was not *personal* dislike to me. It was, as I told the company, just this; he looked upon their bodies as so many gutters to drain off the contents of his taps, and upon their purses as so many small heaps from which to take the means of augmenting his great one; and, finding that I had been the cause of suspending this work of 'reciprocity', he wanted, and no matter how, to restore the reciprocal system to motion.

Tomorrow morning we set off for the New Forest; and, indeed, we have lounged about here long enough.

WESTON GROVE
[Wednesday, 18 Oct., 1826]
Yesterday, from Lyndhurst to this place was a ride, including our roundabout, of more than forty miles, but the roads the best in the world, one half of the way green turf, and the day as fine a one as ever came out of the heavens.

We had slept in a room, the access to which was only through another sleeping room, which was also occupied, and as I had got to bed about two o'clock at Andover, we went to bed, at Lyndhurst, about *half-past seven* o'clock. I was, of course, awake by three or four. I had eaten little over night so that here I lay,

not liking (even after daylight began to glimmer) to go through
a chamber where, by possibility, there might be 'a lady' actually
in bed. Here lay I, my bones aching with lying in bed, my
stomach growling for victuals, imprisoned by my *modesty*. But at
last I grew impatient; for modesty here, or modesty there, I was
not to be penned up and starved. So after having shaved and
dressed and got ready to go down I thrusted George out a little
before me into the other room and through we pushed,
previously resolving, of course, not to look towards *the bed* that
was there. But the devil would have it just as I was about the
middle of the room I, like Lot's wife, turned my head! All that I
shall say is, first, that the consequences that befell her did not
befall me and, second, that I advise those who are likely to be
hungry in the morning not to sleep in *inner rooms*.

Having got safe downstairs, I lost no time in inquiry after the
means of obtaining a breakfast to make up the bad fare of the
previous day. And finding my landlord rather tardy in the work,
I went myself and, having found a butcher's shop, bought a loin
of small, fat wether mutton which I saw cut out of the sheep and
cut into chops. These were brought to the inn. George and I ate
about 2lb out of the 5lb, and while I was writing a letter, and
making up my packet to send from Southampton, George went
out and found a poor woman to come and take away the rest of
the loin of mutton.

Having made all preparations for a day's ride we set off, as our
first point, for a station in the New Forest called New Park. We
got to this place about 9 o'clock. There is a good and large
mansion house here, in which the 'commissioners of woods and
forests' reside when they come in the forest. The place looks a
considerable gentleman's seat; the house stands in a sort of *park*,
and you can see that a great deal of expense has been incurred in
levelling the ground and making it pleasing to the eye of my
lords 'the commissioners'.

My business here was to see whether anything had been done
towards the making of *locust* plantations*. I found that last fall
some few locusts had been put out into plantations of other trees
already made, but that they had *not* thrived, and had been *barked*

---

* Acacia trees

by the hares. And what are these *hares* kept *for* here? *Who* eats them? What *right* have these commissioners to keep hares here to eat up the trees? And what are these *deer* for? *Who* is all this game and venison *for*? There is more game even in Kew Gardens than the royal family can want. And do they ever taste, or even hear of, any game or any venison in the New Forest?

What a pretty thing here is, then. Here is another deep bite into us by the long and sharp-fanged aristocracy. This New Forest is a piece of property as much belonging to *the public* as the Custom House at London is. There is no man, however poor, who has not a right in it. Every man is owner of part of a deer, the game, and of the money that goes to the keepers. And yet any man may be *transported* if he go out by night to catch any part of this game!

From New Park I was bound for Beaulieu Abbey. The name, meaning *fine place*, the place is one of the finest that was ever seen in this world. The ruins consist of the walls of a building about 200 feet long and about 40 feet wide. It has been turned into a barn, in part. But there is another ruin which was a church or chapel and which stands now very near to the farmhouse of Mr John Biel, who now rents the farm of the Duchess of Buccleugh, who is now the owner of the abbey lands. The little church, or chapel, of which I have been speaking, appears to have been a very beautiful building. Part of the outside is now surrounded by the farmer's garden: the interior is partly a pig-stye and partly a goose-pen. Under that arch which had once seen so many rich men bow their heads, we entered into the goose-pen, which is by no means one of the *nicest* concerns in the world. Beyond the goose-pen was the pig-stye, and in it a hog which, when fat, will

weigh about 30 score, actually rubbing his shoulders against a little sort of column which had supported the font and its holy water. The farmer told us that there was a hole, which indeed we saw, going down into the wall or rather into the column where the font had stood. And he told us that many attempts had been made to bring water to fill that hole, but that it had never been done.

Mr Biel was very civil to us. He asked us to dine with him, which we declined for want of time. But being exceedingly hungry we had some bread and cheese and very good beer. The farmer told me that a great number of gentlemen had come there to look at that place, but that he could never find out what that place had been. I told him that I would, when I got to London, give him an account of it. He seemed surprised that I should make such a promise, and expressed his wish not to give me so much trouble. I told him not to say a word about the matter, for that his bread and cheese and beer were so good that they deserved a full history to be written of the place where they had been eaten and drunk. 'God bless me, sir! No! No!' I said I will, upon my soul, farmer. I now left him, very grateful on our part for his hospitable reception and he, I dare say, hardly able to believe his own ears at the generous promise I had made him, which promise, however, I am now about to fulfill.

The Abbey of Beaulieu was founded in the year 1204, by King John, for 30 monks of the reformed Benedictine Order. It flourished until the year 1540, when it was suppressed and the lands confiscated in the reign of Henry VIII. The lands and abbey and all belonging to it were granted by the king to one Thomas Wriothsley, who was a court-pander of that day. From him, it passed by sale, by will, by marriage or by something or the other, till at last it has got into the hands of the Duchess of Buccleugh. So much for the ruins of the abbey: and now as for the ruins on the farm of Mr John Biel: they were the dwelling places of the Knights Templar, or Knights of St John of Jerusalem. The building they inhabited was called a hospital, and their business was to relieve strangers, and persons in distress.

Now farmer John Biel, I dare say you are a very good Protestant: and I am a monstrous good Protestant too. We cannot bear the pope, nor 'they there priests that makes men confess their sins and go down upon their marrow bones before them.' But, master Biel, let us give the devil his due. Here were a set of monks, and also a set of Knights Templars. Neither of them could marry, of course. They could possess no private property: they could hoard no money: they could save nothing. Whatever they received as rent for their lands, they must necessarily spend upon the spot, for they never could quit that spot. They did spend it all upon the poor: Beuley, and all around Beuley, saw no misery, and had never heard the damned name of pauper pronounced as long as these monks and Templars continued. You and I are excellent Protestants, farmer John Biel: you and I have often assisted on the 5th of November to burn Guy Fawkes, the pope and the devil. But you and I, farmer John Biel, would much rather be life-holders under monks and Templars, than rack-renters under duchesses.

FROM WESTON TO KENSINGTON
Weston Grove
[18 October, 1826]
It was nightfall when we arrived at Eling, that is to say, at the head of the Southampton Water. Our horses were very hungry. We stopped to bait them and set off just about dusk to come to this place (Weston Grove), stopping at Southampton on our way, and leaving a letter to come to London.

The moon shone very bright by the time we mounted the hill. It was eight o'clock before we arrived at Mr Chamberlayne's, whom I had not seen since, I think, the year 1816; for in the fall of that year I came to London, and I never returned to Botley (which is only about three and a half miles from Weston) to stay there for any length of time.

To those who like water-scenes (as nineteen-twentieths of people do) it is the prettiest spot in all England. Let me describe, as well as I can, what this land and its situation are. The Southampton Water begins at Portsmouth, and goes up to Redbridge, being, on average, about two miles wide, having on one side the New Forest and on the other, for a great part of the way, this fine and beautiful estate of Mr Chamberlayne. The views from this place are the most beautiful that can be imagined. You see up the water, and down the water, to Redbridge one way and Spithead the other. Through the trees, to the right, you see the spires of Southampton, and you only have to walk a mile, over a beautiful lawn and through a not less beautiful wood, to find, in a little dell surrounded with lofty woods, the venerable ruins of Netley Abbey which make part of Mr Chamberlayne's estate.

Everything that nature can do has been done here: and money most judiciously employed to come to her assistance. Here are a thousand things to give pleasure to any rational mind; but there is one thing which, in my estimation, surpasses, in pleasure to contemplate, all the lawns and all the groves and all the gardens and that is the real, unaffected goodness of the owner of the estate. When he came to this place the common wages of day-labouring men were *thirteen shillings a week*. Those wages he has *given, from that time to this*, without any abatement whatever. He has got less money in his bags than he would have if he had ground men down in their wages; but if his sleep be not sounder than that of the hard-faced wretch that can walk over grass and gravel, kept in order by a poor creature that is half-starved, then all we have been taught is false and there is no difference between the man who feeds, and the man who starves the poor.

HAMBLEDON
[Sunday, 22 Oct., 1826]
We left Weston Grove on Friday morning, and came across to Botley where we remained during the rest of the day, and until after breakfast yesterday.

We are now at about a mile from the village of Hambledon. A village it *now* is; but it was formerly a considerable market town, and it had three fairs in the year. There is now not even the name of market left, I believe, and the fairs amount to little more than a couple or three gingerbread stalls, with dolls and whistles for children. *Wens* have devoured market towns and *shops* have devoured markets and fairs. Shop-keeping, merely as shop-keeping, is injurious to any community. What are the shop and shop-keeper for? To receive and distribute the produce of the land. The shop must be paid for: the shop-keeper kept, and the one must be paid for and the other kept by the consumer of the produce. When fairs were very frequent, shops were not needed. A manufacturer of shoes, of stockings, of hats, of almost anything that man wants could manufacture at home, in an obscure hamlet with cheap house-rent, good air, and plenty of room. He need pay no heavy rent for a shop, and, by attending three or four or six fairs a year, he sold the work of his hands, unloaded with a heavy expense attending the keeping of a shop. He would get more for ten shillings in a booth at a fair or market than he would get in a shop for ten or twenty pounds.

THURSLEY
[Friday evening, 23 October]
Our way this morning was over Butser Hill to Petersfield; then to Lyphook, then to this place, in all about twenty-four miles. Butser Hill belongs to the back chain of the South Downs; and indeed it terminates that chain to the westward. Some think that Hindhead, which is the famous sand-hill over which the Portsmouth road goes at sixteen miles to the north of this great chalk-hill; some think that Hindhead is the highest hill of the two. Be this as it may, this Butser Hill is quite high enough, for it took us up among the clouds which wet us very nearly to the skin. The hill appears, at a distance, to be a sharp ridge on its top. It is, however, not so. It is, in some parts, half a mile wide or more.

We came through Petersfield without stopping and baited our horses at Lyphook, where we stayed about half an hour. In coming from Lyphook to this place we overtook a man who asked for relief. He told me he was a weaver, and as his accent was northern, I was about to give him a balance I had in hand arising from our savings in the fasting way, amounting to about three shillings and sixpence. But unfortunately for him, I asked him what place he had lived at as a weaver, and he told me he was a Spitalfields weaver. I instantly put on my glove and returned my purse into my pocket, saying, 'Go then to Sidmouth and Peel and the rest of them and get relief, for I have this minute, while I was stopping in Lyphook, read in the *Evening Mail* newspaper, an address to the king from the Spitalfield weavers for which they ought to suffer death from starvation. In that address those base wretches tell the king that they were loyal men; that they detested the designing men who were guilty of seditious practices in 1817; they, in short, express their approbation of the Power-of-Imprisonment Bill, of all the deeds committed against the reformers in 1817 and 1819. You are one of them, my name is William Cobbett and I would sooner relieve a dog than relieve you.' The weaver attempted explanations. He said that they only said it in order to get relief, but that they did not mean it in their hearts. 'Oh, base dogs,' said I, 'it is precisely by such men that ruin is brought upon nations; it is precisely by such baseness and insincerity, such scandalous cowardice, that ruin has been brought upon them.'

Before we got to Thursley, I saw three poor fellows getting in turf for their winter fuel and I gave them a shilling apiece. To a boy at the bottom of Hindhead I gave the other sixpence towards buying him a pair of gloves, and thus I disposed of the money which was, at one time, actually out of my purse and going into the hand of the 'loyal Spitalfield weaver'.

KENSINGTON
[Thursday, 26 Oct.]
We left Mr Knowles on Thursday morning, came through Godalming, stopped at Mr Rowland's at Chilworth and then came on through Dorking. I have put an end to my ride of August, September and October 1826, during which I have travelled five hundred and sixty-eight miles, and have slept in thirty different beds, having written three monthly pamphlets, called the *Poor Man's Friend*, and I have also written (including the present one) eleven *Registers*. I have been in three cities, in about twenty market towns, in perhaps five hundred villages. During the whole of this ride, I have very rarely been a-bed after daylight; I have drunk neither wine nor spirits. I have eaten no vegetables; and only a very moderate quantity of meat. And it may be useful to my readers to know that the riding of twenty miles was not so fatiguing to me at the end of my tour as the riding of ten miles was at the beginning of it.

ST SWITHIN AND THE BOROUGHMONGERS
Uphusband (Hants)
[11th August, 1827]
This famous old Saint seems likely to give the Boroughmongers a
stiffer tackling than they have had for some time: whatever *prices*
may be, there must, on a general scale, be injury to *them* in the
destruction of the crop; they cannot suck blood out of nothing.

From KENSINGTON all along to ANDOVER, where I
slept, the wheat is a very *poor* crop. Of that which is not cut, a
third part lies on the ground: and of that which is standing up
the high wind of yesterday and the day before has shaken out a
considerable part. So that we are not to be surprised when we see
reapers at work in the rain; the grain *may* be spoiled by lying on
the ground, or by being in wet bundles, but if you suffer the
straw to stand, the grain *must* tumble out. The wet *swells* the
grain and therefore *loosens* it from the hold which the chaff has on
it. The price, however, does not seem disposed to mount in
proportion to the diminished supply and the dismal prospects.

Andover (Hants)
[12th August, 1828]
Yesterday morning we had weather fair, with some sun. This set
the farmers to *carting wheat* and several ricks were begun in the
parish of Uphusband. The rain, however, came on at half-past
two and continued until night. Some of the ricks were half built,
others less; the rain must have descended several feet down into
them. But such is the fear of the farmers of *losing all*, that some of
them actually carried the wheat under the falling rain. These
ricks will be little better than muck-heaps.

Andover
[13th August, 1828]
Yesterday afternoon the rain came on again in torrents,
accompanied with heavy thunder. This will nearly complete the
destruction of more than half the wheat in this neighbourhood. I
give it as my well-considered opinion, that from London to
NEWBURY, and then across the country to this place, *more than
half* the wheat is destroyed. There is little ground for belief that
the destruction is not general and, if this be the case, ought the
Corn-bill to remain in force a day? The weather has given the
Government abundant warning.

KENSINGTON
[14th August, 1828]
Yesterday morning, when I wrote the above article from
Andover, there was, at five o'clock, a very thick fog. From
thence I set off to Newbury, and found the fog collecting on the
tops of the highest hills, sure sign of rain. I left Newbury about
twelve, and it began to rain about one. After stopping to dine at
Reading, I came on and got to Kensington about nine. As I
came in this whole distance in a post chaise, I had time to look
about me, to make inquiries of intelligent persons, and to
examine the state of the wheat with my own hands. Again I say,
a dreadful responsibility must rest somewhere, if great suffering
from a want of food should come upon us. I say that the Corn Bill
should have been suspended for twenty days past or, at least, the
parliament called together.

BARN-ELM INTO THE EAST OF SUSSEX
Barn-Elm Farm
[24th June, 1829]
On Friday last, the 19th instant, I set off for the neighbourhood
of BATTLE in Sussex. The object of this journey was to obtain
some authentic information upon a subject which is at this time
of great interest to many of my readers: namely, on the *subject of
emigration to the United States.*

I heard several years ago, that some of the parishes in the
eastern part of Sussex were actually shipping off families of
labouring people to the United States, in order to protect
themselves against the consequences of men with large families

becoming paupers. The labourers thus sent away wrote, as they naturally would, *letters home to their fathers and mothers and brethren.* A gentleman living in the neighbourhood of ROB-ERTSBRIDGE, about five or six miles from BATTLE, made a collection of these letters and published them.

This publication, which is by far the most interesting publication I ever read in my life, confirms in the fullest extent, under the hands of these simple people writing from the spot, everything that I have ever published relative to the happy state of farmers and labourers in America. But in a case so interesting I was not willing to stop short of being able to answer on my own word as to the *authenticity* of these letters and, therefore, I resolved *to go and see the parties* who had received these, as well as those who had received other letters. Therefore this RURAL RIDE was undertaken and on Friday morning last, I, accompanied by my Secretary (not knowing but there might be some copying of the letters to be performed) set off for the country inhabited by the relations of these happy emigrants.

In a light phaeton, drawn by one stout horse, I got to TONBRIDGE early in the afternoon, with the intention of getting to ROBERTSBRIDGE or to BATTLE by nine o'clock or thereabouts. But here a singular and, I hope, never to be repeated instance of *backsliding* fell upon me. I did not go to bed *till past twelve o'clock at night,* instead of going to bed at eight, as I ought to have done. The case is this, I had not long been in the town before somebody that knew me, saw me. The consequence was, that I soon had a *little group of disciples* to visit me at the inn. We talked and laughed and then talked and laughed again, till I was pretty nearly hoarse and until midnight compelled us to break off. I shall always remember that these seducing disciples of TONBRIDGE kept me out of my bed till past twelve o'clock at night, though I had been up at four o'clock in the morning.

Nevertheless, we were off on the Saturday morning by *six o'clock* and, after stopping about an hour at Lamberhurst, we arrived at the very pleasant hamlet of ROBERTSBRIDGE about eleven o'clock. I intended to go on the *Sunday to Church* at SEDLESCOMB. Besides mere religion there was another motive for going to church at the village. A young woman, who went out with her parent to AMERICA in the year 1823, in writing home to a grandfather and grandmother, has the following passage in one of her letters. 'I have now got *good clothes, and I can dress as well as any lady in* SEDLESCOMB. I can enjoy a silk frock, or a white frock, and my crape frock and crape veil and morocco shoes, *without the parish grumbling about it.*'

This passage in the letter of MARY JANE WATSON, who has been enabled to write by the goodness of a master and mistress in America, who put her to school *while she was in their service*, made me wish to see the ladies of SEDLESCOMB *with my own eyes*. I wished to see whether they had 'crape frocks and crape veils'. I wished to see whether the young woman which they had sent out as a *pauper* did not now surpass them in point of dress. I intended to write an account of what I saw, and send it to a friend in NEW YORK, signed with my own name, to be put in the newspapers. But when I reflected that these were very religious people, and that they might not wish to be withdrawn from their devotions on the Sunday, I determined to abandon my church-going project and to see the parties on Saturday in the afternoon.

With this intention, we set off about one o'clock and in the first place went to the village of SEDLESCOMB, which ought to be immortalised by the letters written to that place by divers persons belonging to this family and others. The village is a straggling, wide street, bending round in a sort of semi-circular form. The spot is very beautiful, the church ancient, the houses and little gardens generally very neat.

Our first point was the *public-house*, to feed the horses, refresh ourselves and make inquiry. The landlord did not know anything about the parties, not having lived long in the village. But there was a labouring man in the house, who had in his arms one of his *eleven* children, who knew everything about the whole of them, and who undertook to be our guide. We went to them, talked to them, and with the exception of four, found them all and they gave us the *original letters*.

STEPHEN WATSON, after having lived in the service of one master and on one spot, for *seven and twenty years*, had quitted that master. We found him at home. This man and wife, let it be remembered, were the grandfather and grandmother of MARY JANE WATSON. And I thought it due to that little lady (who from a state of pauperism in England was got to wear crape frocks and prunello shoes in America) to join her grandfather and grandmother in *drinking her health* in something a little better than water, for which purpose we took with us a couple of bottles of most excellent bottled ale. To describe the satisfaction with which these good people evinced at seeing a man, who *had been in the country* where their children and grandchildren were, and who was able to assure them, that those beloved children *would never know want*, is wholly out of my power.

It was Saturday, drawing towards evening. Watson, a man *still one year younger than I am*, though with eight or ten children and thirty or forty grandchildren, had come home from his work. And there he was, a man who had worked seven and twenty years for one master, and who had been for a great part of the time, the *principal seedsman* on the farm, finding no fault with that master, other than that it was become *too hard*, and that he could get too little victuals!

I was particularly desirous to see THOMAS COOKE of Crispe Corner, who had got a letter from his daughter and son-in-law dated at the CITY OF HUDSON: of this letter I will insert a small part, *letter for letter*: 'I must tell you how we are getting on in this world we are in the same place where we was (Hudson) and we are getting on very comfortly we have plenty to eat we never have to look far for food and we have got plenty for our use we have layd out about 100 dollars (£22.10s. sterling) for housel (household goods) we have not got much stock but we have got a sow will soon farow (have young ones) and we think of buying a cow or too'.

Now, my readers, pray look at this. This man (with a *wife and six children*) gets to New York a pauper, without a farthing in the world, on the 19th of May 1828, and in *March* 1829, he has laid out £22 10s. English money in 'housel', he has a *sow* ready to farrow, and he is about to purchase *a cow or two*!

I cannot quit this subject, even for the present, without observing upon the conduct of those who ought to be the friends and protectors of the labouring poor. They seem to look on them not as *men* and *women*, but merely as animals made for their service or sport. Our ears are everlastingly dinned with the charges of *immoralities* committed by the poor. I have known of twenty different projects for correcting the '*evil of pauperism*', but never of one project for making the lot of the labourer better than it is.

It will be an act of kindness, and, indeed, of nothing more than bare justice, to let the emigrants see this Register. And with this view of the matter, I beg Mr GEORGE WOODWARD of New York to take care that one copy of this Register reach Mr Stephen Watson, No. 535 South Market Street, Albany. He may have changed his address, but it will not be difficult to find him, or some one of so numerous a family.

TO TRING IN HERTFORDSHIRE
Barn-Elm Farm
[23rd September, 1829]

Mr Elliman, of Tring, had from me last March 25,000 *locust trees* wherewith to make a plantation near that town; and I, having a great desire to see this plantation, went thither for the purpose on Wednesday, the 16th instant. The morning was very wet and the whole day gloomy; but the next day, when I saw the plantation, the weather was pretty fair.

At this town of Tring, which is a very pretty and respectable place, I saw what reminded me of another of my endeavours to introduce useful things into this country. At the door of a shop, I saw a large *case* with the lid taken off, containing *bundles of straw for platting*. It was straw of spring wheat tied up in small bundles with the ear on; just as I myself have grown in England many times, and bleached for platting according to the instructions so elaborately given in the last edition of my *Cottage Economy*. I asked the shopkeeper where he got the straw; he said that it came from Tuscany. I told the shopkeeper that I wondered that they should send to Tuscany for the straw, seeing that it might be grown, harvested and equally well balanced at Tring.

My wife, wishing to have her bonnet cleaned some time ago, applied to a person who performs such work at Brighton, and got into conversation with her about the *English Leghorn* bonnets. The woman told her that they looked very well at first, but that they would not retain their colour, and added, 'They will not clean, m'am, like this bonnet that you have.' She was surprised on being told that this was an 'English Leghorn'. In short, there was no difference at all between the two, and if these people at Tring choose to grow the straw instead of importing it from Leghorn, and if they choose to make plat and to make bonnets just as beautiful and lasting as those which come from Leghorn, they have nothing to do but read my *Cottage Economy* paragraph 224 to paragraph 234 inclusive, where they will find, as plain as words can make it, the whole mass of directions for taking the seed of the wheat, and converting the produce into bonnets.

Of *'Cobbett's corn'** there is no considerable piece in the neighbourhood of Tring. If Mr Elliman were to have a patch of good corn by the side of his locust trees, and a piece of spring wheat by the side of the corn, people might then go and see specimens of the three great undertakings, or rather great additions to the wealth of the nation, introduced under the name of *Cobbett*.

I am the more desirous of introducing this manufacture at Tring on account of the marked civility which I met with at that place. I, to my great surprise, found that a *dinner had been organised*, to which I was to be invited. The company consisted of about forty-five gentlemen of the town and neighbourhood and certainly, though I have been at dinners in several parts of England, I have never found, even in Sussex, where I have frequently been so delighted, a more sensible, hearty, entertaining and hospitable company than this. From me, something in the way of a speech was expected as a matter of course, and though I was from a cold so hoarse as not to be capable of making myself heard in a large place I was so pleased with the company and with my reception that, from first to last, I dare say I addressed the company for an hour and a half. We dined at two and separated at nine. There was present the editor, or some other gentleman, from the newspaper called *The Bucks Gazette and General Advertiser*, who has published in his paper an account of what passed at the dinner.

After the reporter went away we had a great number of toasts. I must not omit to mention, in conclusion, that though I am no eater or drinker, and though I tasted nothing but the breast of a

* maize.

little chicken, and drank nothing but water, the dinner was the best that ever I saw called a *public dinner* and certainly unreasonably cheap. There were excellent joints of meat of the finest description, fowls and geese in abundance; and finally a very fine haunch of venison, with a bottle of wine for each person, and all for *seven shillings and sixpence per head*. Good waiting upon; civil landlord and landlady, and, in short, everything at this very pretty town pleased me exceedingly. Yet what is Tring but a fair specimen of English towns and English people?

NORTHERN TOUR
Little Brickhill
[Friday, 18th December, 1829]
I, with a daughter and two sons, set off from Kensington about three o'clock today, and reached this place about nine in the evening. The frost is not much as yet but still it is cold.

Birmingham
[20th Dec., 1829]
We came yesterday from Brickhill to this town. It had snowed very little in the night, but we found the fields here all covered with snow and the woods, having the snow sticking on the windward side of the trees, lying upon the limbs and clinging to the twigs, very beautiful. I have always thought coppices much more interesting in the winter, than in summer. In the summer they present you with a bank of solid green on the outside, and on the inside you cannot see a yard before you.

As we advanced on the way, the snow became deeper on the fields, and I really longed to be out in it and thought much more, for the time, about the tracking of hares than about the making of speeches. I could not help reflecting, and mentioning to my daughter, how strangely I had been by degrees pulled along, during my whole life, away from those pursuits and scenes which were most congenial to my mind. Being at Botley, I was disentangling myself from London by degrees. I had got very nearly to the smock-frock and I was inculcating in the minds of my children, as they grew up, a love of country life. I hated London, and saw it as seldom as possible. Just at this time venomous GIBBS laid hold on me and, having heard that it was the intention of the Government to crush me, my resentment urged me on to combat. My natural taste, my unsubduable bias for the country has never been, and can never be overcome as long as I have life. But to yield, to prostrate myself, to suffer myself to be subdued or humbled by *such men* was what my soul recoiled at.

Derby
[Monday, 21st December, 1829]

At Birmingham there had been an application for the theatre, or playhouse, for me to lecture in. But the lessee was at Liverpool and the theatre had been let this Christmas time to some Italian singers. Under these circumstances I decided to give up Birmingham for the present, to proceed to Derby and thence to Liverpool.

It has been said in London that Birmingham feels less of distress than other places. That the readers of the Register may have some idea of the state of Birmingham, I will state a fact or two which I have from unquestionable authority. The operative gun-lock maker, who used to earn, in *ordinary* times, from thirty to forty shillings a week, now earns *four shillings and sixpence a week*! The men in the iron-works are become little better than a set of beings fed from hand to mouth, in exchange for their labour. The ironmasters have taken to themselves the business of supplying the workmen with victuals, drink and other necessaries, supervising altogether the dealings with shop-keepers and victuallers, and suffering no money to pass between them and their labourers. Nay, to such a pitch is this carried, that they have their workmen SHAVED by contract, and pay the shavers *so much per dozen.*

We set off from Birmingham a little before three o'clock yesterday, and we stopped at Burton, the roads being heavy. The frost last night was pretty smart. In this part of England, the coals are so abundant and, of course, so cheap, that there is no want of plenty of fire and you are not put into a perishing room, as you are in the southern and western counties, where coals have to be brought from a great distance.

The situation of the greater part of the operative manufacturers in this county, in Nottinghamshire and in Leicestershire, is said to be truly deplorable. The wages of the weavers have declined to such a point as to leave the poor creatures scarcely the means of bare existence. One of the consequences of this state of things is the unsaleableness of the coarser parts of butcher's meat. Formerly, the richer part of the community purchased the best joints, while the working people took the remainder. But now, though there are customers enough for the *best*, there is nobody to buy the coarser parts of the meat. Workmen that used to purchase five or six pounds of meat at a time, now take a pound or half a pound and some of them none at all. Potatoes appear to be the best of their diet. Some live upon boiled cabbage and salt, and others are said to live on *scalded bran* which, as most readers know, is what we call mash, given to horses when they have colds.

One thing I have heard of in this county supposes the people to be treated not as slaves, not as negro slaves, but actually as beasts whose *sexual connexion* is superintended by their masters. The plain and horrible tale is this. In some places, those who have the command over the poor, keep the married women separated from their husbands for the odious, the shameful, the beastly purpose of preventing that increase of family which the parson at marriage has joined with the parties in praying God may take place! And this is ENGLAND! This is the envy of surrounding nations and the admiration of the world!

Liverpool
[28th December, 1829]
We set off from Derby at five o'clock yesterday morning and

reached this place about seven o'clock. The snow was pretty deep until we reached Knutsford, on this side of which there had been but little. But the frost has been, and is, pretty sharp, an evil hardly felt in the counties where coals are so cheap and excellent, and where so large a part of the people are employed within doors. Nature, which has been so prodigal in Hampshire, Sussex, Surrey and Kent and garnishing the country with woods, has here been very niggardly in that respect. But as far as fuel is concerned, she has made ample compensation by the endless resources which she has provided under ground.

I held my second lecture at Derby, on Saturday night, to an audience which filled the theatre to the utmost, pit, boxes and gallery. At the first lecture I adhered to the London charge of a shilling indiscriminately. But the kind, judicious and zealous friends which I found at Derby managed the matter otherwise at the second lecture, which was put off until Saturday, on account of the Christmas Even, and the Christmas Day, and charged the boxes at two shillings, the pit at a shilling and the gallery at sixpence. This judicious arrangement not only filled the house, but gave satisfaction to all parties. I and my sons and daughters were lodged at the house of friends, not known to us, however, for more than about a year, and known to us only in consequence of their good opinion with regard to the effect of my writings.

At Mr Joseph Johnson's, Smedley Lane, near Manchester [3rd Jan., 1830]

I came from Liverpool this morning, after having had three evenings of lecturing, or speech-making.

Today I am going to Oldham: tomorrow, to Bolton-le-Moors: on the 13th to Preston and the 14th to Rochdale: on the 15th to Todmorden . . . This is as near as I can lay down the route at present, but I think I shall be at Nottingham by the 27th, at farthest. The weather here now is clear ground and hard frost. Hitherto, the winter has been severe, and I think there is every likelihood of its continuance. However, my ten men and boys, with two maidservants, at the Farm, have got plenty to eat and drink and to burn, and to keep them warm at night. Notwithstanding the descriptions given of my farm and farm-yard by the infamous *Times* newspaper, there is not a farmyard in

England that presents greater abundance than does mine at this moment.

Todmorden
[17th January, 1830]

From Stockport, we returned back to Manchester, or rather to Smedley Lane, that night and, on Monday evening, went to Oldham. I was aware of the enthusiasm that would prevail among the good and sincere men of that very populous place and, therefore, I deferred my arrival in it to as late an hour as possible, wishing by all means to avoid the collecting of a great multitude together. In spite of all my precautions, and in spite of the darkness of the evening, the people were collected in great numbers. It was with great difficulty that we got into the inn to which we drove, and still with greater difficulty that we got into the place provided for the lecture; and I was compelled to take the carriage again to go from the inn to that place, it appearing absolutely impossible to go along on foot through the crowd.

The next day, Wednesday the 13th, we proceeded to Preston. The Quarter Sessions was holden there, and before the Grand Jury was dismissed, and while they were in the box, a bowl of soup was brought into the court and, after having been tasted by the Chairman, was handed round to the magistrates, and then to the Grand Jury, who appeared to have feasted upon this occasion *à la gamette*, as the French call it, that is to say, sitting round the mess in a circle, and handing the spoon from mouth to mouth. After the repast was over, the Chairman exhorted the Grand Jury to encourage the making of similar messes in all their districts, in order to relieve and comfort the poor. To this art thou come at last, bragging John Bull!

Here at Todmorden we are at the house, or rather houses, of friends. I never was induced to go into a factory, in England, before, but here is one for weaving by power-looms, belonging to the Messrs Fielding, consisting of *one room* on a ground floor, which is of the surprising dimensions of a hundred and eighty feet square and covering a statute acre of ground all but *twenty-eight rods!* In this room, which is lighted from above and in the most convenient and beautiful manner, there were five hundred pairs of looms at work, and five hundred persons attending those looms and, owing to the goodness of the masters, the whole looking healthy and well-dressed.

It was eight o'clock when we went to the theatre, and the audience had the patience to listen to me until nearly eleven. Then we had to return to the inn. Everyone wants to see me and shake me by the hand. I was particularly delighted with a very fine young man, very well dressed and about seventeen years of age, who squeezed himself through a crowd in the lower room to get up to me, to shake hands with me and, while he had hold of my hand, he said, 'I am coom'd a purpose to tak houd of the *fingers and the thumb that wrote the "Advice to Young Men"*'.

From this place to Halifax, you go nearly all the way upon a road which runs parallel with the canal, and there are mills and houses almost the whole of the way. The buildings, whether for manufactures or for dwelling, are all of solid stone, executed in the best possible manner. The window frames and door frames are generally of stone. The floors of passages to houses are of stone. The field fences are of stone walls: and the gate posts and stiles are made of stone. When I came to the North before, I used to call this country, on the side of Warwickshire, the *iron country*. Everything appears strong and hard and made to last for ever.

I am sitting at a window, and this is Sunday. Hundreds of the working people have passed by the window this day, and it is a very long time since I have seen working people so well-dressed as they are here. Probably it is partly owing to the uncrowded state of the people, to their being scattered in so long a line as this valley consists of. There may be, and there must be, less

immorality than in places like Blackburne and Preston, where there is such an immense mass in so small a circle. But something must also be owing to the conduct of the employers.

Leeds
[26th Jan., 1830, Night]
On Monday, the 18th, I went to Huddersfield where my friends had met with great difficulty in providing a suitable place. They at last got a room, which was well filled and yielded me much more money than I either expected or wished.

I have just returned from the theatre in this fine and opulent town, which may be called the London of Yorkshire, and in which I have been received with an enthusiasm which I should in vain endeavour to describe. Here, as in other places, there prevails *theatrical distress* to an exceeding degree, but I have filled, and over-filled, the whole house, pit, boxes and galleries.

The weather has been almost incessant hard frost, with a considerable quantity of snow. From Leeds to Ripley we went in a heavy snow-storm, and were compelled to take four horses on account of the heaviness of the road. The snow had fallen so fast, and the night was so dark, that the post-boys got out of the road on the edge of a moor, just on this side Harrogate and we were within a very few inches of being overset. But we got out of the carriage and assisted the post-boys and arrived at Ripley a little before eight o'clock. While I was standing out in the snow, I really began to blame myself for having so frequently jeered poor Burdett for having skulked from a Westminster meeting, on the ground of not daring to encounter a '*heavy fall of snow*'.

Sheffield
[31 January, 1830]
From Leeds I proceeded to this place, not being able to stop at either Wakefield or Barnsley, except merely to change horses. The people of those towns were apprised of the time that I should pass through them, and at each place great numbers assembled to see me, to shake me by the hand and to request me to stop. I was so hoarse as not to be able to make the post-boy hear me when I called him to stop. I promised to go back if my time and voice would allow me. They do not; and I have written

to the gentlemen of those places to inform them that when I go to Scotland in the spring, I will not fail to stop in these towns, in order to express my gratitude to them.

All the way along from Leeds to Sheffield it is coal and iron, and iron and coal. It was dark before we reached Sheffield, so that we saw the iron furnaces in all their horrible splendour of their everlasting blaze. Nothing can be conceived more grand, or more terrific, than the yellow waves of fire that incessantly issue from the top of these furnaces, some of which are close by the way-side. Nature has placed the beds of iron, and the beds of coal, alongside each other, and art has taught men to make one operate upon the other, as to turn the iron-stone into liquid matter which is drained off from the bottom of the furnace, and afterwards moulded into blocks and bars and all sorts of things. This Sheffield, and the land all about it, is one bed of iron and coal. They call it black Sheffield, and black enough it is, but from this one town and its environs go nine-tenths of the knives that are used in the whole world.

The ragged hills all around this town are bespangled with groups of houses inhabited by the working cutlers. They have not suffered, like the working weavers, for to make knives there must be the hand of man. The home demand has been very much diminished but still the depression has here not been what it has been, and what it is where the machinery can be brought into play.

Upon my arriving here on Wednesday night, the 27th instant, I by no means intended to lecture until I should be a little recovered from my cold. But to my great mortification, I found that the lecture had been advertised and that great numbers of persons had actually assembled. To send them out again, and give back the money, was a thing not to be attempted. I, therefore, went to the music hall, the place which had been taken for the purpose, gave them a specimen of the state of my voice, asked them whether I should proceed and they answering in the affirmative, on I went. I then rested until yesterday and shall conclude my labours here tomorrow, and then proceed to '*fair Nottingham*', as we used to sing when I was a boy celebrating the glorious exploits of 'Robin Hood and Little John'.

It is very curious that I have always had a great desire to see

Nottingham. This desire certainly originated in the great
interest that I used to take, and that all country boys took, in the
history of Robin Hood.

Barn Elm Farm
[10th February, 1830]
We arrived at Nottingham about six o'clock on Tuesday
evening and found a committee of gentlemen ready to receive us
and to give us an invitation to a public breakfast to be held the
next morning in the Thurland Hall, which is said to have been
the banqueting room of Charles the First. There were present
not much short of two hundred gentlemen and this, never
having seen one of the parties before in my life to my knowledge
except two gentlemen from Derby and one from Manchester, I
felt to be the greatest honour that I had ever received in the
whole course of my life. Here was no personal attachment at
work: it was purely the respect shown by this number of sensible
and well-educated men not to me personally, but to those
exertions for which I had endured twenty years of calumnies
from all the bribed and base reptiles of the country.

The breakfast itself was, in all respects, worthy of the donors,
worthy of the town which, in almost all respects that I can
mention, exceeds all the towns that I ever saw in my life. A fine,
most extensive and most beautiful market-place; lofty, strong
and neat buildings, elegant shops, clean-dressed people, active
and intelligent men and sprightly and beautiful women. The
environs of the town are as fine as the town itself. Open on all
sides; fine prospects; the town itself presents great inequality of
hill and dale. And all this without any of that beggarly, any of
that squalid misery which to me has been the great drawback in
the merits of so many other places.

EASTERN TOUR
Hargham
[22 March, 1830]
I set off from London on the 8th of March, got to Bury St
Edmunds that evening. At Bury St Edmunds I gave a lecture on
the 9th and another on the 10th March in the playhouse, to very

crowded audiences. I went to Norwich on the 12th and gave a lecture there on that evening and on the evening of the 13th. During the 14th and 15th I was at a friend's house at Yelverton, half way between Norwich and Bungay, at which place I lectured on the 16th. The next day I went to Eye, and there lectured in the evening in the neat little playhouse of the place. On the 19th I proceeded to Ipswich. In general, it would be useless for me to attempt to give anything like a *report* of these speeches of mine, consisting as they do of words uttered pretty nearly as fast as I can utter them during a space of never less than two, and sometimes three hours.

We were entertained at Ipswich by a very kind and excellent friend whom, as is generally the case, I had never seen or heard before. The morning of the day of the last lecture I walked about five miles, then went to his house for breakfast and stayed with him and dined. Here I heard the first singing of the birds this year; and I here observed an instance of that *petticoat government* which, apparently, pervades the whole of animated nature. A lark, very near to me in a ploughed field, rose from the ground and was saluting the sun with his delightful song. He was got about as high as the dome of St Paul's, having me for a motionless and admiring auditor, when the hen started up from nearly the same spot whence the cock had risen, flew up and passed close by him. I could not hear what she said, but I supposed that she must have given him a pretty sharp reprimand, for down she came on the ground and he, ceasing to sing, took a twirl in the air and came down after her. Others have, I dare say, seen this a thousand times over, but I never observed it before.

At twelve o'clock, my son and I set off for this place (Hargham), coming through Needham Market, Stowmarket, Bury St Edmunds and Thetford, at which latter place I intended to have lectured today and tomorrow, where the theatre was to have been the scene. But the major of the town thought it best not to give his permission until the assizes should be over, lest the judge should take offence, seeing that it is the custom, while his lordship is in the town, to give up the civil jurisdiction to him. Bless his worship! What in all the world should he think would take me to Thetford *except in being a time for holding the assizes*! At no *other* time should I have dreamed of finding an audience in so small a place, and in a country so thinly inhabited.

Finding Thetford to be forbidden ground, I came hither to Sir Thomas Beevor's, where I had left my two daughters, having, since the 12th inclusive, travelled 120 miles and delivered six lectures. Ipswich, to my surprise, we found a most beautiful town with a population of about twelve thousand persons. There is no doubt but that this was a much greater place than it is now. It is the great outlet for the immense quantities of corn grown in this most productive country, and by farmers the most clever that ever lived. I am told that wheat is worth six shillings a quarter more, at some times, at Ipswich than at Norwich, the navigation to London being so much more speedy and safe. Immense quanitites of flour are sent from this town. The windmills on the hills in the vicinage are so numerous that I counted, whilst standing in one place, no less than seventeen. They are all painted or washed white; the sails are black. It was a fine morning, the wind was brisk, and their twirling altogether added greatly to the beauty of the scene which, having the broad and beautiful arm of the sea on the one hand, and the field and meadows, studded with farm-houses, on the other, appeared to me the most beautiful sight of the kind that I had every beheld.

I know of no town to be compared with Ipswich, except it be Nottingham, and there is this difference in the two: that Nottingham stands high and, on one side, looks over a very fine country, whereas Ipswich is in a dell, meadows running up about it and a beautiful arm of the sea below it. The town itself is substantially built, everything good and solid, and no wretched buildings to be seen on its outskirts. From the town itself you can see nothing, but you can, in no direction, go from it a quarter of a mile without finding views that a painter might crave.

But observe that this has been a very *highly-favoured county*: it has had poured into it millions upon millions of money, drawn from Wiltshire and other inland counties. I should suppose that Wiltshire alone has, within the last forty years, had two or three millions of money drawn from it, *to be given to Essex and Suffolk*. At one time there were not less than sixty thousand men kept on foot in these counties.

Coming from Ipswich to Bury St Edmunds, you pass through Needham Market and Stowmarket, two very pretty market towns and, like all the other towns of Suffolk, free from the drawback of shabby and beggarly houses on the outskirts. I remarked that I did not see in the whole county one single instance of paper or rags supplying the place of glass in any window, and did not see one miserable hovel in which a labourer resided. The county, however, is *flat*. With the exception of the environs of Ipswich there is none of that beautiful variety of hill and dale and hanging woods that you see at every town in Hampshire, Sussex and Kent. Almost every bank and every field is studded with pollards, that is to say, trees that have been beheaded, at from six to twelve feet from the ground, than which nothing in nature can be more ugly. They send out shoots from the head, which are lopped off once in ten or a dozen years for fuel, or other purposes. To add to the deformity, ivy is suffered to grow on them which, at the same time, checks the growth of the shoots.

To conclude an account of Suffolk, and not to sing the praises of Bury St Edmunds, would offend every creature of Suffolk birth: even at Ipswich, when I was praising *that place*, the very people of the town asked me if I did not think Bury St Edmunds the nicest town in the world. Meet them wherever you will, they have all the same boast. And indeed, as a town *in itself*, it is the neatest place that ever was seen. It is airy, it has several fine open places in it, and it has the remains of the famous abbey walls and the abbey gates entire; and it is so clean and neat that nothing can equal it in that respect. It was a favourite spot in ancient times, greatly endowed with monasteries and hospitals. The

land all about it is good and the soil is of that nature as not to produce much dirt at any time of the year. But the country about it is *flat*, and not of that beautiful variety that we find at Ipswich.

Cambridge
[28 March, 1830]

I went from Hargham to Lynn on Tuesday, but owing to the disappointment at Thetford, everything was deranged. It was market-day at Lynn, but no preparations of any sort had been made. I therefore resolved to make a short tour and come back again.

I was particularly desirous to have a little political preaching at *Ely*, the place where the flogging of the English local militia under a guard of German bayonets cost me so dear. I got there about noon on Thursday, the 25th being market-day. I first walked round the beautiful cathedral, that honour to our Catholic forefathers and that standing disgrace to our Protestant selves. Ely is what one may call a miserable little town; very prettily situated but poor and mean. Everything seems to be on the decline, as indeed is the case everywhere, where the clergy are the masters. They say that this bishop has an income of £18,000 a year. He and the dean and chapter are the owners of all the land and the tithes for a great distance round about in this beautiful and most productive part of the country. And yet this famous building, the cathedral, is in a disgraceful state of irrepair and disfigurement.

The great and magnificent windows to the east have been shorted at the bottom, and the space plastered up with brick and mortar in a very slovenly manner for the purpose of saving the expense of keeping the glass in repair. Great numbers of the windows in the upper part of the building have been partly closed up in the same manner, and others quite closed up. One door-way, which apparently had stood in need of repair, has been rebuilt in modern style because it was cheaper, and the churchyard contained a flock of sheep acting as vergers for those who live on the immense income, not a penny of which ought to be spent on themselves while any part of this beautiful building is in a state of irrepair.

This cathedral was erected to 'to the honour of God and the Holy Church'. My daughters went to the service in the afternoon, in the choir of which they saw God honoured by the presence of *two old men*, forming the whole of the congregation. The cathedral and town stand upon a little hill, about three miles in circumference, raised up as it were for the purpose, amidst the rich fen land by which the hill is surrounded, and I dare say that the town formerly consisted of houses built over a great part of this hill, and of probably from fifty to a hundred thousand people. The people do not now exceed above four thousand.

Having no place provided for lecturing, and knowing no single soul in the place, I was thrown on my own resources. I picked up a sort of labouring man, asked him if he recollected when the local militia-men were flogged under the guard of the Germans, and receiving an answer in the affirmative, I asked him to go and show me the spot, which he did. He showed me a little common along which the men had been marched, and into a piece of pastureland, where he put his foot upon the identical spot where the flogging had been executed. On that spot I told him what I had suffered for expressing my indignation at that flogging. I told him that a large sum of English money was now every year sent abroad to furnish half pay and allowances to the officers of those German troops. When I opened, I found that the man was willing to open too. I discovered that there were two Ely men flogged upon that occasion, and that one of them was still alive and residing in the town. I sent for this man, who came to me in the evening when he had done his work, and who told me that he had lived seven years with the same master when he was flogged, and was bailiff or head man to his master. He has now a wife and several children, is a very nice-looking, and appears to be a hard-working, man and to bear an excellent character.

But how was I to harangue? For I was determined not to quit Ely without something of the sort. After I returned to the inn I walked back through the market among the farmers, then went to an inn that looked out upon the market place, went into an upstairs room, threw up the sash, and sat down at the window, and looked out upon the market. Little groups soon collected to survey me, while I sat in a very unconcerned attitude. The farmers had dined, or I should have found out the most numerous assemblage, and have dined with them. The next best thing was to go and sit down in the room where they usually dropped in to drink after dinner, and as they nearly all smoke, to take a pipe with them. This, therefore, I did, and after a time we began to talk.

The room was too small to contain a twentieth part of the people that would have come in if they could. It was hot to suffocation, but nevertheless I related to them the account of the flogging, and of my persecution on that account. And I related to them the account above stated, with regard to the English money now sent to the Germans, at which they appeared to be utterly astonished. I had not time sufficient for a lecture, but I explained to them briefly the real cause of the distress which prevailed. I portrayed to them the effect of the taxes, and showed them that we owed this enormous burden to the want of being fairly represented in the parliament. I strongly advised the farmers to be well with their work-people for that, unless their flocks were as safe in their fields as their bodies were in their beds, their lives must be lives of misery.

I walked on again from Ely on Friday morning. I found a public house at the end of nine miles and a half. The landlady here lamented the law about to be passed for throwing open the trade in beer. The house was her husband's own and he (probably some lord's late servant) had added to its value enormously by obtaining a license. It is a *free* house, but the man buys his beer of a brewer in Cambridge, not having premises whereon to brew it and, which is very curious, sells it at halfpenny a pot *cheaper* than the same beer is sold at houses that are not free. This landlady, a nice young woman with a very pretty little child, said that she hoped that the trade in beer would not be made free. I asked her *why*? She said that there would be everlasting drunkenness and rowing. I told her, that it did not seem reasonable to suppose that; for that drunkenness, and particularly rowing, arose from men congregating together in considerable numbers; that if the trade were free, the places of sale would be more numerous, the drinkers more dispersed, and that therefore the freedom of the trade, in my simple judgement, would have a tendency to produce a diminuation of the drunkenness and the rowing. She was not prepared for this, and hurried off to get my pint of beer.

BOSTON
[Friday, 9 April, 1830]
Quitting Cambridge on Monday, 29th March, I arrived at St Ives in Huntingdonshire about one o'clock in the day. In the evening I harangued to about 200 persons, principally farmers, in a wheelwright's shop, that being the only *safe* place in the town sufficiently strong. On the 31st I went to Stamford and in the evening spoke to about 200 farmers, and others, in a large room in a very fine and excellent inn, called Standwell's Hotel. On the 2nd April I met my audience in the playhouse at Peterborough: and though it had snowed all day, and was very wet and sloppy, I had a good audience. On the 3rd, I speechified at Wisbeach, in the playhouse, to about 220 people, I think it was. On the 6th I went to Lynn, and on that evening and on the evening of the 7th I spoke to about 300 people in the playhouse. And here there was more *interruption* than I have ever met with in any other place. Two or three or even *one* man may, if not tossed out at once, disturb and interrupt everything in a case where constant attention to *fact* and *argument* is requisite to ensure utility to the meeting. There were but three here, and though they were finally silenced it was not without great loss of time, great noise and hubbub. Two, I was told, were *deadweight* men, and one a sort of *higgling merchant*.

On the 8th I went to Holbeach, in this noble county of Lincoln, and gracious God! what a *contrast* with the scene at Lynn. I knew not a soul in the place. Mr Fields, a bookseller, had invited me by letter and had, in the nicest and most unostentatious manner possible, made all the preparations. Holbeach lies in some of the richest land in the world; a small market town, but a parish more than twenty miles across, larger, I believe, than the county of Rutland, produced an audience, in a very nice room, of 178. I was delighted with Holbeach; a neat little town; a most beautiful church with a spire; gardens very pretty; fruit trees in abundance with blossom-buds ready to burst; and land

dark in colour and as fine in substance as flour, and when cut
down deep with a spade, precisely as to substance like a piece of
hard butter.

The cathedral at Peterborough is exquisitely beautiful, and I
have great pleasure in saying that, contrary to the *more
magnificent* pile at Ely, it is kept in good order; the bishop
(Herbert Marsh) residing a good deal on the spot; and though
he *did* write a pamphlet to justify and urge on the war, and
though he *did* get a pension for it, he is, they told me, very good
to the poor people. My daughters had a great desire to see, and I
had a great desire that they should see, the burial place of that
ill-used, that savagely treated woman, and that honour to
womankind, Catherine, queen of the ferocious tyrant Henry
VIII. To the infamy of that ruffian and the shame of after ages,
there is no *monument* to record her virtues and her sufferings; and
the remains of this daughter of the wise Ferdinand and the
generous Isabella, who sold her jewels to enable Columbus to
discover the new world, lie under the floor of the cathedral,
commemorated by a short inscription on a plate of brass.

From Peterborough to Wisbeach, the road for the most part
lies through the *Fens*, and here we passed through the village of
Thorney, where there was a famous abbey which, together with
its valuable domain, was given by the savage tyrant Henry VIII
to Lord John Russell (made a lord by that tyrant), the founder
of the family of that name. This man got also the abbey and the
estate at Woburn; the priory and its estate at Tavistock: AND in
the next reign he got Convent Garden and other parts
adjoining. A history (a *true* history) of this family, which I hope I
shall have time to write, would be a most valuable thing. It
would be a nice little specimen of the way in which these families
became possessed of a great part of their estates.

Wisbeach, lying further up the arm of the sea than Lynn, is
like the latter a little town of commerce, chiefly engaged in
exporting to the south *the corn* that grows in this productive
country. It is a good, solid town, though not handsome, and has
a large market, particularly for corn.

To Crowland I went from Wisbeach, staying two nights at St
Edmunds. Here I was in the heart of the Fens. The whole
country as *level* as the table on which I am now writing. The

horizon like the sea in a dead calm; you see the morning sun come up just as at sea; and see it go down over the rim in just the same way as the sea in a calm. Everything grows well here; earth without a stone so big as a pin's head; grass as thick as it can grow on the ground; immense bowling greens separated by ditches; and not the sign of a dock or thistle or other weed to be seen. What a contrast between these and the heath-covered sand-hills of Surrey, amongst which I was born!

At Crowland was a great and rich *abbey*. They tell you that all the country at and near Crowland was a mere swamp, a mere bog *bearing nothing* until the *modern drainings* took place. The thing they called the 'Reformation' has lied common sense out of men's minds. So *likely* a thing to choose a barren swamp whereon, or wherein, to make the site of an abbey, and of a Benedictine abbey too! It has always been observed that the monks took care to choose for their place of abode pleasant spots, surrounded by productive land. The likeliest thing in the world for these monks to choose a swamp for their dwelling-place, surrounded by land that produced nothing good!

BOSTON
[Sunday, 11 April, 1830]
Last night I made a speech at the playhouse. I had given notice that I should perform *on Friday*, overlooking the circumstances that it was Good Friday. In apologising for this inadvertence, I took occasion to observe that, even if I had persevered, the clergy of the church could have nothing to object, seeing that

they were now silent while a bill was passing in parliament to put *Jews* on a level with *Christians*: to enable Jews, the blasphemers of the Redeemer, to sit on the bench, to sit in both Houses of Parliament, to sit in council with the king; to this bill *the clergy had offered no opposition*: and that therefore how could they hold sacred the anniversary appointed to commemorate the crucifixion of Christ by the hands of the blaspheming and bloody Jews?

The great pride and glory of the Bostonians is *their church*, which is both a land-mark and a sea-mark. To describe the richness, the symmetry, the exquisite beauty of this pile is wholly out of my power. Look at this church, then look at the heaps of white rubbish that the parsons have lately stuck up under the '*New-church Act*', and which, after having been built with money forced from the nation by odious taxes, they have stuffed full of *locked-up pens*, called *pews*, which they let for money as cattle and sheep-pens are let at fairs. Nay, after having looked at this work of the '*dark ages*', look at that great, heavy, ugly, unmeaning mass of stone called St Paul's, which an American friend of mine swore to me, when he first saw it, he was at a loss to guess whether it were a court-house or a gaol.

St Botolph, to whom this church is dedicated, has not the mortification to see his church treated in a manner as if the new possessor sighed for the hour of its destruction. Great care has been taken of it, and the inside is not disfigured and disgraced by a *gallery*, that great and characteristic mark of Protestant taste which, as nearly as may be, makes a church like a playhouse. Saint Botolph has the satisfaction of seeing that the base of his celebrated church is surrounded by an iron fence, to keep from it all offensive and corroding matter which is so disgusting to the sight round the magnificent piles at Norwich, Ely and other places.

HORNCASTLE
[12 April]
A fine, soft, showering morning saw us out of Boston. At Sibsey, a pretty village five miles out of Boston, we saw for the first time

since leaving Peterborough land rising above the level of the horizon. And not having seen such a thing for so long, it had struck my daughters who overtook me on the road (I had walked from Boston) that the sight had an effect like that produced by the first *sight of land* after a voyage across the Atlantic.

Horncastle
[13 April, Morning]
There is one deficiency, and that, with me, a great one throughout this country of corn and grass and oxen and sheep; namely, the want of *singing birds*. We are now just in that season when they sing most. Here, in all this country, I have seen and heard only about four skylarks and not one other singing bird of any description, and of the small birds that do not sing, only one *yellowhammer* and it was perched on the rail of a pound. Oh! the thousands of linnets all singing together on one tree in the sand-hills of Surrey. Oh! the carolling in the coppices and the dingles of Hampshire and Sussex and Kent. At this moment (5 o'clock in the morning) the groves at Barn-Elm are echoing with the thousands upon thousands of birds. The *thrush* begins a little before it is light; next the *blackbird*; next the *larks* begin to rise; all the rest begin the moment the sun gives the signal.

Spittal, near Lincoln
[19 April, 1830]
Here we are at the end of a pretty decent trip since we left Boston. At Hull I *lectured* (I laughed at the word) to about 700 persons on the same evening that I arrived from Louth, which was on Thursday the 15th. We had what they called the summer theatre, which was crowded in every part except on the stage.

The three mornings that I was at Hull, I walked out in three different directions and found the country everywhere fine. I used to wonder that Yorkshire, to which I, from some false impression in my youth, had always attached the idea of *sterility*, should send us of the south those beautiful cattle with short horns and straight and deep bodies. You have only to see the country to cease to wonder at this.

The appelation 'Yorkshire *bite*', the acute sayings ascribed to

Yorkshiremen, and their quick manner I remember in the army. When speaking of what country a man was, one used to say, in defence of another, 'York, but honest.' Everyone knows the story of the gentleman who, upon finding that a boot-cleaner in the south was a Yorkshireman and expressing his surprise that he was not become master of the inn, received for answer, 'Ah, sir, but master is York too!' And that of the Yorkshire boy who, seeing a gentleman eating some eggs, asked the cook to give him a little salt: and upon being asked what he could want with salt, he said 'perhaps that gentleman may give me an egg presently'. In truth, I long ago made up my mind that this hardness and sharpness ascribed to Yorkshiremen arose from the sort of envy excited by that quickness, that activity, that buoyancy of spirits which bears them up through adverse circumstance, and their consequent success in all the situations of life. They, like the poeple of Lancashire, are just the reverse of being *cunning* and selfish: be they farmers, or be they what they may, you get at the bottom of their hearts in minutes. Everything they think soon gets to the tongue and out it comes, head and tails, as fast as they can pour it.

The town of Hull is a little city of London. Streets, shops, everything like it; clean as the best parts of London, and the people as bustling and attentive. The town of Hull is *surrounded* with commodious docks for shipping. The town on the outside of the docks is pretty commodious and the walks from it into the country beautiful. I went about a good deal and nowhere saw marks of beggary or filth, even on the outskirts; none of those nasty, shabby, thief-looking sheds that you see in the approaches to London. I hate commercial towns in general: there is generally something so loathsome in the look, and so stern and unfeeling in the manners of sea-faring people that I have always, from my very youth, disliked sea-ports; but really, the sight of this nice town, the manner of its people, the clean streets and especially the pretty gardens in every direction, has made Hull, though a sea-port, a place that I shall always look back to with delight.

Beverley, which was formerly a very considerable city with three or four gates, one of which is yet standing, had a great college, built in the year 700, by the archbishop of York. It had three famous hospitals and two friaries. There is one church, a very fine one, still standing and the minster still left; of which a bookseller in the town was good enough to give me a copperplate representation. It is still a very pretty town; the market large, and it is particularly famous for horses, those for speed being shown off here on the market days at this time of year. The farmers and gentlemen assemble in a very wide street on the outside of the western gate of the city; and at a certain time of the day, the grooms come from their different stables to show off their beautiful horses. When I was asked at the inn to go and see '*the horses*' I had no curiosity, thinking it was such a parcel of horses as we see at a market in the south. But I found it a sight worth going to see for, besides the beauty of the horses, there was the adroitness, the agility and the boldness of the grooms, each running alongside his horse, with the latter trotting at the rate of ten or twelve miles an hour.

It is time for me to speak of the state of *the people*, and of the manner in which their affairs are affected by the workings of the system. With regard to the labourers they are, everywhere, miserable. The farmers, for want of means of profitable employment, suffer the men to fall upon the parish and they are employed in digging and breaking stone for the roads so that the roads are nice and smooth for the sheep and cattle to walk on in their way to the all devouring jaws of the jews and other tax-eaters in London and its vicinity. None of the best meat, except by sheer accident, is consumed here. Today (the 20th April) we have seen hundreds upon hundreds of sheep as fat as hogs go by this inn door, their toes, like those of the footmarks at the entrance of the lion's den, all pointing towards the Wen. And the landlord gave us for dinner a little, skinny, hard leg of old ewe mutton!

One of the great signs of the poverty of people in the middle rank of life is the falling off of the audiences at the playhouse. There is a playhouse in almost every country town where the players used to act occasionally, and in large towns almost always. In some places they have of late abandoned acting altogether. In others they have acted, very frequently, to no more than *ten or twelve persons*. At Norwich, the playhouse had been shut up for a very long time. I heard of one manager who has become porter to a warehouse and his company dispersed. In most places, the inside of the buildings seem to be tumbling to pieces, and the curtains and scenes they let down seem to be abandoned to the damp and the cobwebs. *My* appearance on the boards seemed to give new life to the drama.

Lord Stanhope cautioned his brother peers, a little while ago, against the angry feeling which was *rising up in the poor against the rich*. Nor is this angry feeling confined to the counties of the south. When I was at St Ives in Huntingdonshire I sat with the farmers and smoked a pipe by way of preparation for evening service, which I performed on a carpenter's bench in a wheelwright shop. While we were sitting, a handbill was handed round the table, advertising *farming stock* for sale; and amongst the implements of husbandry '*an excellent fire-engine,** several steel traps and spring guns*'. And that is the life, is it, of an English farmer? I walked on about six miles of the road from Holbeach to Boston. I have before observed upon the inexhaustible riches of this land. At the end of about five miles and three-quarters I came to a public house, and thought I would get some breakfast, but the poor woman, with a tribe of children about her, had not a morsel of either bread or meat! At a house called an inn a little further on, the landlord had no meat except a little bit of chine of bacon. Just the state of things that existed in France on the eve of the Revolution. On the very spot I looked round me and counted more than two thousand fat sheep in the pastures!

Another respect in which our situation so exactly resembles that of France on the eve of the Revolution is the *fleeing from the country* in every direction. When I was in Norfolk there were four hundred persons, generally young men, labourers, carpenters, wheelwrights, smiths and bricklayers, most of them with some money. These people were going to Quebec, in timber ships. At Hull the scene would delight the eyes of the wise Burdett. Ten large ships have gone this spring, laden with these fugitives from the fangs of taxation, some bound direct to the ports of the United States, others, like those at Yarmouth, for Quebec. This emigration is a famous blow to the borough-mongers. The way to New York is now as well known and as little expensive as the way from old York to London.

---

* i.e. steam-engine, for threshing.

EASTERN TOUR ENDED – MIDLAND TOUR BEGUN
Lincoln
[23 April, 1830]
From the inn at Spittal we came to this famous, ancient Roman
station. It was the third or fourth day of the *Spring fair* which is
one of the greatest in the kingdom and lasts the whole week.
Horses begin the fair, then come sheep and today the horned
cattle.

The country from Spittal to Lincoln continued to be much
about the same as from Barton to Spittal. As you get towards
Lincoln, the ground gradually rises, and you go on the road
made by the Romans. When you come to the city, you find the
ancient castle and the magnificent cathedral on the *brow* of a sort
of ridge which ends here, for you look all of a sudden down into a
deep valley, where the greater part of the remaining city lies. It
once had *fifty-two churches*; it has now only eight, and only about
9,000 inhabitants. The cathedral is, I believe, the finest in the
world. To the task of describing a thousandth part of its striking
beauties I am inadequate; it surpasses greatly all those I have
anticipated, and oh! how loudly it gives the lie to those brazen
Scotch historians who would have us believe that England was
formerly *a poor* country!

We got to Leicester on the 24th at about half after five o'clock.
Leicester is a very fine town; spacious streets, fine inns, fine shops
and containing, they say, thirty or forty thousand people. It is
well stocked with gaols, of which a new one, in addition to the
rest, has just been built. And as if proud of it, the grand portal
has little turrets in the castle style. Nothing speaks the want of
reflection in the people so much as the self-gratulation they
appear to feel in these edifices in their several towns.

WORCESTER
[18 May, 1830]
In tracing myself from Leicester to this place I begin at
Lutterworth, one of the prettiest country towns that I ever saw;
that is to say, prettiest *situated*. At this place they have, in the
church (they say), the indentical *pulpit* from which Wickliffe
preached! This was not his birthplace, but he was, it seems,
priest of this parish.

I set off from Lutterworth early on the 29th April, stopped to breakfast at Birmingham, got to Wolverhampton by two o'clock (a distance of about 50 miles), and lectured at 6 in the evening. On the 6th May I went to Dudley and lectured there, on the 10th of May at Birmingham, on the 12th and 13th at Shrewsbury; and on the 14th came here.

In the iron country, of which Wolverhampton seems to be a sort of central point, and where thousands perhaps two or three hundred thousand people are assembled together, the *truck* or *tommy* system prevails, and this is a very remarkable feature in the state of this country. I have made inquiries with regard to the origin, or etymology, of this word *tommy*, and could find no one to furnish me with information. It is certainly, like so many other good things, to be ascribed to *the army*: for when I was a recruit at Chatham barracks in the year 1783 we had brown bread served out to us twice a week. And, for what reason God knows, we used to call it tommy. Any one that could get white bread called it bread; but the brown stuff that we got in lieu of part of our pay was called *tommy*. When the soldiers came to have bread served out to them in the several towns in England, the name of 'tommy' went down by tradition, and doubtless it was taken up and adapted to the truck system in Staffordshire and elsewhere.

The manner of carrying on the tommy system is this. Suppose there be a master who employs a hundred men. That hundred men, let us suppose, earn a pound a week each. These men lay out weekly the whole of the hundred pounds in victuals, drink, clothing, bedding, fuel and house rent. Now the master, finding the profits of his trade fall off very much, and being at the same time in want of money to pay the hundred pounds weekly, and perceiving that these hundred pounds are carred away at once, and given to shop-keepers of various descriptions, and knowing that on average these shop-keepers must all have a profit of *thirty per cent* or more, he determines to keep this *thirty per cent to himself*. He therefore sets up a tommy shop, a long place containing every commodity that the workman can want, liquor and house-room excepted. Here the workman takes out his pound's worth, and his house rent he pays in truck, if he do not rent of his master; and if he will have liquor, beer or gin he must get it by trucking with the goods that he has got at the tommy shop. Now there is nothing essentially unjust in this. The only question is, whether the master charges a higher price than the shop-keeper would charge, and while I have not heard that the masters do this, I think it improbable that they should. They must desire to avoid the charge of such extortion, and they have little temptation to do it because they buy at best hand and in large quantities.

A view of the situation of things at Shrewsbury will lead us in a minute to the real cause of the tommy system. Shrewsbury is one of the most interesting spots that man ever beheld. It is the capital of the county of Salop, and Salop appears to have been the original name of the town itself. It is curiously enclosed by the river Severne, which is here large and fine, and which in the form of a *horse-shoe* completely surrounds it, leaving in the whole of the two miles around it only one little place whereon to pass in and out on land. There are two bridges, one on the east and the other on the west, the former called the English and the other the Welsh bridge. The environs of this town, on the Welsh side especially, are the most beautiful that can be conceived. The town lies in the middle of fine agricultural country, of which it is the great and almost only mart.

It was a fair-day when I arrived at Shrewsbury. Everything was on the decline. Cheese, which four years ago sold at sixty shillings the six-score pound, would not bring forty. I took particular pains to ascertain the fact with regard to the cheese, which is a great article here. I was assured that shop-keepers in general did not now sell half the quantity of goods in a month that they did in that space of time four or five years ago. The *ironmongers* were not selling a fourth part of what they used to sell five years ago. Now it is impossible to believe that a somewhat similar falling off in the sale of iron must not have taken place all over the kingdom. And need we wonder then that the iron in Staffordshire has fallen, within these five years, from thirteen pounds to five pounds a ton or perhaps a great deal more: and need we wonder that the *ironmasters*, who have the same rent and taxes to pay that they had to pay before, have resorted to the tommy system, in order to assist in saving themselves from ruin!

TOUR IN THE WEST
[3 July, 1830]

Just as I was closing my third lecture (on Saturday night) at
Bristol, the news of the above event (the death of George IV)
arrived. I had advertised, but under the circumstances thought
it would not be proper to proceed thither. But never shall I see
another place to interest me, as Bristol and its environs, taking
the whole together. A great commercial city in the midst of
cornfields, it surpasses all that I ever saw: the ships coming into
the centre of it, miles from anything like sea, up a narrow river
and passing between two clefts of rock probably a hundred feet
high. So that from the top of these clefts you *look down* upon the
main-topgallant masts of lofty ships that are gliding away.

SOUTHERN TOUR
Havant
[23rd of July, 1832]

At Winchester I put up at the Barley Mow, a house that I would
recommend to anyone who has not more money than he knows
what to do with, and who can eat a mutton chop without having
a waiter dancing in and out of the room with a knapkin in his
hand, and making more clatter with his plates and his other stuff
than you hear in a crockery-ware shop where there are half-a-
dozen women engaged in the choosing of tea-tackle. In this
house I found quietness, good bed, and reasonable charges. I
was engaged in writing all the day. It was at the time of what
they call 'THE COLLEGE ELECTIONS', and they told me
that there were swarms of parsons *waiting upon poor boys and girls
while they were eating*. Alas! the working people are not to be
cajoled in this way. In Norfolk, when money and blankets were
given to them in the winter of 1831, they called them '*scare-
money*' and '*scare-crows*'.

From Winchester, I came on towards Botley, and a more
beautiful ten miles there is not in all England. From Botley I
came on to Titchfield that evening and slept at the house of MR
WILLIAM STARES, who had met us at the chopstick* festival

---

* chopstick: Cobbett's affectionate nickname for farm labourers.

at Sutton Scotney. From the house of Mr Stares, who is both miller and farmer and a most excellent man, we came on very early in the morning of 12th July to Portsmouth, or rather to PORTSEA, which is just outside the town of PORTSMOUTH and which is now included in the borough of PORTSMOUTH. Mr Sweet, who keeps the WHEATSHEAF INN, which is near the gate of the dockyard at PORTSEA; this gentleman and other friends met us about two miles from his house, took me into a landau decorated with flags and thus conducted us to the inn. On Sunday the 15th we went over to the Isle of Wight, taking horse and carriage over with us. On Monday, I lectured at the little town of BRADLING, and on Tuesday at Newport.

From Newport we returned that evening to the beautiful and pleasant farm of Mr Smith and spent the whole of Wednesday in walking or lounging about. The accounts which people give of the ISLE OF WIGHT are by no means fabulous. It is a very beautiful spot, an endless variety of views: hill, dale and water being almost constantly under your eye at the same time. On Thursday, the 19th, we set off to return to Portsmouth, quitting one of the pleasantest houses I ever was in in all my life.

TO THE PEOPLE OF MANCHESTER
Brighton, 28th July, 1832
My Friends
After holding the CHOPSTICK FESTIVAL of SUTTON SCOTNEY, going from the north-west to the south-easternmost part of Hampshire, taking into my tour the beautiful Isle of Wight, I arrived on the 26th of July at this town of Brighton, certainly surpassing in beauty all other towns in

the world. The neatest of carriages stand about the streets for you to step into at your pleasure. To accommodate the children there are abundance of beautiful chaises and coaches in miniature, elegantly harnessed, drawn by goats and attended by lads dressed in a manner bespeaking the high pay that they receive for their trouble. In short, it is all a scene of evident wealth, of pleasure, and of luxury.

It is impossible *for me* to behold all this without calling to my recollection the weavers, stripped naked to their waists, and the sweat running down their bodies, in the dismal cellars of PRESTON. Everything that I behold here is *created by the taxes*. This is a place of no trade, of no commerce at all. It has no harbour. It is all a pure creation of the taxing and funding system.

No great nation has ever experienced a fall or a dreadful revolution, without that fall or revolution having been preceded by show and luxury which have astonished the world. This is precisely the case of England now. In the passing of the Reform Bill an effort has been made to save the country from Revolution; but saved from Revolution it cannot be unless that Reform Bill produce such a change as shall restore to the labouring part of the community that share in the fruits of the earth which is their unquestionable right.

IT IS MY INTENTION TO BE AT MANCHESTER IN THE LAST WEEK OF AUGUST, on my way probably to the very northern counties of England, if not to Paisley and Glasgow. In the meanwhile, I repeat an expression of my great anxiety to be elected for MANCHESTER. Until I have the pleasure of seeing you again face to face I conjure you all to bear in mind that the fate of the country now depends upon the public virtue, upon the good sense and the resolution of the great towns of the north.

I am your faithful friend, and
most obedient servant,
Wm. COBBETT

PROGRESS IN THE NORTH
Newcastle-upon-Tyne
[23 September, 1832]
From Bolton, in Lancashire, I came through Bury and Roch-

dale to Todmorden, on the evening of Tuesday the 18th of September. I have formerly described the valley of Todmorden as the most curious and romantic that was ever seen, and where the water and the coal seemed to be engaged in a struggle for getting foremost in point of utility to man.

Having heard and read so much about the 'Northern Harvest', about the 'Durham ploughs' and the Northumberland system of husbandry, what was my surprise at finding that there is not as much corn grown in the North Riding of Yorkshire, which begins at Ripon, and in the whole county of Durham, as is grown in the Isle of Wight alone. The land appears to be divided into very extensive farms. The corn, when cut, you see put up into little stacks of a circular form, each containing about *three* of our southern waggon-loads of sheaves, which stacks are put up round about the stone house and buildings of the farmer. How they thrash them out I do not know, for I could see nothing resembling a barn, or a barn's door. By the corn being put into such small stacks, I should suppose the thrashing places to be very small, and capable of holding only one stack at a time.

But this by no means implies that these are beggarly countries, even exclusive of their waters, coals and mines. This is not a country of farmers, but a country of graziers; a country of pasture and not a country of the plough, and those who formerly managed the land were not husbandmen, but herdsmen. St Augustine, in writing to the pope an account of the character and conduct of his converts in England, told him that he found the English an exceeding good and generous people but that they had one fault: their fondness for flesh-meat was so great, and their resolution to have it so determined, that they would return to their horrible heathenism rather than submit to the discipline of the church in this respect. The pope, who had more sense than the greater part of his bishops have ever had, wrote for answer, 'Keep them within the pale of the church at any rate, even if they slaughter their oxen in the churchyards.' The taste of our forefathers was by no means for the potatoe; for the 'nice *mealy* potatoe'. The pope himself would not have been able to induce them to carry 'cold potatoes in their bags' to the ploughfield, as it was in evidence before the special commissions.

I looked with particular care on the side of the road all the way through Yorkshire and Durham. The distance, altogether, from Oldham in Lancashire to Newcastle-upon-Tyne, is about a hundred and fifty miles; and, leaving out the *great* towns, I did not see so many churches as are to be seen in any twenty miles of any of the valleys of Wiltshire. All these things prove that these are by nature counties of pasturage. It is curious that there are none of those lands here which we call 'meadows'. The rivers run in *deep beds*, and have generally very steep sides; no little rivulets and occasional overflowings that make the meadows in the south.

North Shields
[25 September, 1832]
I came here this afternoon and am to *lecture* at the theatre this evening. This place is about eight miles from Newcastle, down the river Tyne towards the sea, and as much like Wapping it is as any two peas were ever like each other. South Shields is just opposite on the other side of this 'LITTLE THAMES' called the TYNE, and such places for stir and bustle never were seen except at London itself, and, really, these places seem to surpass even London in this respect.

As you go over the bridge from GATESHEAD to Newcastle, there are the ships innumerable, lying below the bridge as far as you can see down the river. NEWCASTLE is a really solid fine town, just such streets as the city of London; just such shops; and just such industrious and busy-looking people.

Sunderland
[26 Sept., 1832]
From North Shields you look across the water to SOUTH SHIELDS, and there is a steamboat taking passengers across every half-hour. By this steam-boat I crossed today, and got to this place about two. SUNDERLAND is seven miles from South Shields, near the mouth of a river called the Wear. To go into the town you go over an iron bridge of very beautiful architecture. The river is narrow, running between rocks which are nearly perpendicular and of great height. The bridge crosses this river from rock to rock and is so far above water that ships of considerable size go under the bridge by only lowering their top-

gallant masts. The main street of Sunderland is, they say, *a mile and three quarters long*, and it has innumerable shops, finer, on an average, than those of the STRAND, FLEET-STREET, or CHEAPSIDE; so that, though there is nothing but coals produced here, they cause the other parts of the world to bring hither all manner of conveniences and fineries. There are considerable glass manufactories here and in the neighbourhood of Newcastle, but these are also occasioned by the coals.

Durham
[27 Sept., 1832]
The great business of life here relates to the produce of the subsoil still more than to that which comes from the surface. The *collieries* are the chief part of the property of the county. Here is the most surprising thing in the world: thousands of men and thousands of horses continually living under ground: children born there and who sometimes, it is said, seldom see the surface at all, though they live to a considerable age. The thing is not like the mining in Cornwall, which causes so much tumbling about the surface and disfiguring of the face of the country. You see here and there a group of large buildings, and see the smoke issuing from some place where there is a steam engine amidst those buildings. Out of a hole somewhere amidst that group of buildings come everlasting shiploads of coals. There is a railway from the pit to carry the coals to the ships: the wagons carrying the coals are made of sheet iron; they are all of a size. A whole train of them marches one after another, sometimes drawn by a horse, but more frequently impelled by the pulling of a chain, which passes along a little gutter below the surface of the ground, which rope or chain is pulled by the force of an engine and thus you see a score of wagons loaded going one way, and another score of empty ones passing them going the other way, without your being able to discover any cause for their motion. Then there are *railways down under ground for bringing the coals to the mouth of the pit*, and horses living there draw the wagons upon these railways. Some of the horses go down and live there for ten or a dozen years, and a gentleman told me that Lord DURHAM, or his father, had eight hundred horses under ground for years together.

In the vicinage of each colliery there are extensive rows of small houses, in which the families of the *pit-men* and other workman reside. These are built of stone, and covered with tile. All very solid and very good, and invariably well furnished; hardly one without a good chest of drawers and other evidences of good living. Kept very clean too. I particularly observed, ay, and I observed it with singular pleasure, that there were scarcely any potatoes to be seen. Everything here shows that this root is used here merely as *garden-stuff* and that the people live, as they ought to do, on bread and meat.

This city of DURHAM is, like all old towns and cities, of shape very irregular and the streets are by no means what we call handsome. But the inequality of the ground is so great, and the situation of the castle and tower of the cathedral church; the little hill on which these are situated is so lofty, and so nicely guarded and ornamented by the river Wear, which comes pretty nearly round it in the form of a horseshoe and then goes off under two bridges; all these make the site of the city the most interesting and beautiful that it is possible to conceive. The bishop is a sort of sovreign prince here. He has his court of Registry, and all manner of offices such as belong to regal dominion and revenue. The Dean and Chapter are a sort of petty sovereigns too: they have '*royalties*' of coal-mines and lead mines: they have the tithe of the lands above: they have the rents of the lands above and of the mines beneath. I wonder what law, MOSAIC, APOSTOLIC, CANONICAL, COMMON or STATUS, gave them the right to sell, *and cause to be carried away*, the soil of the lands given to them in trust?

Hexham
[1 Oct., 1832]
I left Morpeth this morning pretty early in a post-chaise to come to this town, which lies on the bank of the Tyne at thirty-four miles distant from Morpeth and at twenty distant from Newcastle. Morpeth is a great market town, for cattle especially. It is a solid old town, but it has the disgrace of seeing an enormous new gaol arising from it.

From Morpeth to within about four miles of Hexham, the land is but very indifferent; the farms of an enormous extent.

The country seems to be almost wholly destitute of people. Immense tracts of corn-land, but neither cottages nor churches. There is here and there a spot of good land, just in the deep valleys that I crossed but, generally speaking, the country is poor.

At night I gave a lecture at an inn, at Hexham, in the midst of the domains of that impudent and stupid man, Mr BEAUMONT, who, not many days before, in what he called a speech, thought proper, as was reported in the newspapers, to utter the following words with regard to me; never having, in his life, received the slightest provocation for so doing. '*The liberty of the press* had nothing to fear from the Government. It was the duty of the administration to be *on their guard* to prevent *extremes*. The company, he believed, as much disapproved of *that political traveller* who was now going through the country – *he meant Cobbett* – as they detested the servile effusions of the Tories.' BEAUMONT, in addition to his native stupidity and imbecility, might have been drunk when he said this, but the servile wretch who published this was not.

It is my fashion to meet, if I can, every assailant upon his own dunghill. BEAUMONT knew I was to be in HEXHAM; this is his dunghill. But he took very good care not to be seen in the neighbourhood at the time, though, which is curious enough, the dirty fellow made his appearance there when he found I was gone off to Newcastle. Such a wretch, such a truly comtemptible fellow, cannot be an object of what is properly called *vengeance* with any man who is not worth a straw. But, I say with Swift, 'If a *flea* or a *bug* bite me, I will kill it if I can,' and, acting upon this principle, I, being at Hexham, put my foot upon this contemptible creeping thing who is offering himself as a candidate.

Sunderland
[4 Oct., 1832]
This morning I left North Shields in a post-chaise in order to come hither through Newcastle and Gateshead, this affording me the only opportunity that I was likely to have of seeing the plantation of Mr ARMORER DONKIN, which had been made according to the method prescribed in my book called the 'WOODLANDS', and to see which I had previously com-

municated a request to Mr Donkin. That gentleman received
me in a manner which will want no describing to those who have
had the good luck to visit Newcastle. The plantation is most
advantageously circumstanced to furnish proof of the excellence
of my instructions as to planting. As a sort of reward for having
thus contributed to this very rational source of his pleasure, Mr
Donkin was good enough to give me an elegant copy of the fables
of the celebrated BEWICK, who was once a native of Newcastle
and an honour to the town, and whose books I had had from the
time that my children began to look at books. At Mr Donkins I
saw a portrait of Bewick, which is said to be a great likeness. Mr
Wm. ARMSTRONG was kind enough to make me a present of
a copy of the last performance of this so justly celebrated man. It
is entitled 'WAITS FOR DEATH', exhibiting a poor old horse
just about to die and preceded by an explanatory writing which
does as much honour to the heart of Bewick as the whole of his
designs put together do to his genius.

From Mr Donkin's I came off to SUNDERLAND, through
GATESHEAD. Away to my left, down on the side of the
TYNE, lay the various works for drawing up of coals, for the
making of copperas, for the making of magnesia, of Epsom salts,
of soda, of soap, of glass, and of God knows what besides. Here
are hills of *lime-stone* out of which, it seems, they get the means of
doing these things. Why the salts are called *Epsom salts* I always
wondered, seeing that Epsom is a pretty village in my native
county of Surrey, famous for nothing that I ever heard of but the
horse-races upon its down, where liars and scoundrels meet to
waste time, or to gamble with money they have got out of taxes.

Edinburgh
[14 Oct., 1832]

My proceedings at this city must be reserved for description
after I have brought my readers forward from ALNWICK, in
Northumberland, at which place I wrote my last Register, to
this famous capital of Scotland.

From Alnwick to Belford we first leave behind us with every
feeling of contempt which haughtiness and emptiness can excite
in the human mind, the endless *turrets* and *lions* of the
descendants of SMITHSON, commonly called PERCY. There

was a flag flying on the battlements to indicate to the vassals around that the descendant of HOTSPUR was present in the castle. As we advanced, the farms grew larger and the land better. Here we get amongst the mischief. The farms are enormous. Here the thrashing machines are turned by STEAM-ENGINES: here the labourers live in a sort of *barracks*, that is to say, long sheds with stone walls and covered with what are called pantiles. They have neither gardens, nor privies nor back-doors and seem altogether to be kept in the same ways as if they were under military discipline. There are no villages: no scattered cottages: one little window and one door-way to each dwelling in the shed or barrack. One farmer, drawing to one spot the produce of the whole country all around; a sort of manufactory of corn and meat, the proceeds of which go, with very little deduction, into the pocket of the big landlord, there being no such thing as a small proprietor to be seen.

I descend to the TWEED: and now for the 'antalluct'! As I went over the bridge my mind filled with reflecting on those who had crossed it before; saying to myself, 'This has been the pass of all those pestiferous *"feelosofers"* whom I have been combatting so long and who have done so much mischief to their own country as well as mine'. With my mind thus filled I could not help crossing myself as I passed this celebrated bridge.

BERWICK, which is a good solid town and has a river into which small vessels come to take away the corn from the *corn-factories* and which was formerly a strongly fortified place, is regarded, by law, as being in neither England nor Scotland but a separate dominion; and thinking this was a safe place to stay here the night of Monday, the 8th, in order to prepare myself a little before I actually got into Scotland; but seeing placards up enjoining the observance of the *fast* on account of the cholera morbus, and being rather hungry at the time, I, travelling by post-chaise, resolved to push on another stage, in order to avoid giving offence by indulging my appetite in such a state of things.

At about four miles from Berwick, we come down to the village of Ayton, a parcel of very homely stone houses.

At the end of fourteen miles from Berwick, I came to Hounds-wood Inn, a place for changing horses, and I liked the look of the place so well that I resolved to stop here all night, which I did: in order to steady my head a little, and to accustom it to that large and fresh supply of '*antalluct*' which it had been imbibing ever since I crossed the Tyne, and more particularly since my crossing the Tweed. All these new ideas about thrashing machines *worked by steam*; cornweavers kept in barracks without backdoors or privies; all these new ideas of such vast importance in rural philosophy; especially when I found myself in Dr BLACK's *native country* and recollected with what urgency he had pressed upon us of the South, the '*prudence*' of his countrymen in *checking population* by resorting to illegitimate indulgencies, instead of *loading* themselves with wives; all these ideas wanted a little digesting in my mind.

Between HOUNDSWOOD and DUNBAR we came to ROXBURGH Park, which has near it a sort of village consisting of very bad-looking houses, with the people looking very hearty and by no means badly dressed, especially the little boys and girls, whose good looks I have admired ever since I came to Scotland. They do not put boys to work hard when they are young, as they do in England, and, therefore, they are straighter and nimbler on foot. But there is a total carelessness about the *dwelling-place*. You see no such things as a little garden before the door and none of those numerous ornaments and those conveniences about labourers' dwellings, which are the pride of England and by which it is distinguished from all the other countries in the world.

COBBETT'S ADVICE TO
THE CHOPSTICKS OF
all the counties in the South of England
Edinburgh, 14 Oct., 1832

My Friends – This is the finest city that I every saw in my life, but neither the beauty of this city, nor its distance from your and my home has made me forget you. I have some *advice* to offer you, the object of which is to induce you resolutely to maintain the rights which, agreeably to the laws of our country, we all inherit from our forefathers.

There is a reform of the Parliament, and it is touching your conduct as connected with this reform, that I am about to offer you my advice. But before I can do that, I must speak to you about what I have seen in Scotland, of which this fine city is the capital. You know that many gentlemen in England have *Scotch bailiffs*, and that these Scotch bailiffs were principal witnesses against the men that were brought to trial for breaking threshing machines and other acts of that sort in 1830. You know that these bailiffs are always telling you how good and obedient the labourers are in Scotland and how WELL OFF they are.

Now, then, I will tell you how well off the Scotch labourers are, and then you will judge whether you have been wise or foolish in what you have been lawfully doing for two years past, with a view of making your living a little better than it was.

This city is fifty-six miles from the river TWEED which separates England from Scotland. With the exception of about seven miles, the land is the finest I ever saw in my life, though I have seen very fine vale in every county of England. You will know what the land is when I tell you it is by no means uncommon for it to produce seven English quarters of wheat upon one English acre and forty tons of turnips upon one English acre.

Oh! how you will wish to be here. 'Lord,' you will say to yourselves, 'what pretty villages there must be. What nice churches and churchyards; oh! and what preciously nice alehouses. Come, Jack, let us set off for Scotland! What nice gardens shall we have to our cottages there! What beautiful flowers our wives will have climbing up about the windows! And what prancing, barking pigs we shall have, and what a flock of geese grazing on the green!'

Stop! Stop! I have not come to listen to you, but to make you listen to me. Let me tell you, then, there is neither village, nor church, nor garden, nor cottage nor flowers, nor pig, nor goose, nor common, nor green; but the thing is thus: 1) The farms of a whole country are, generally speaking the property of one lord: 2) They are so large that the corn-stacks frequently amount to more than a hundred upon one farm: 3) The farmer's house is a house big enough and fine enough for a gentleman to live in: the farm-yard is a square, with buildings on the side of it for horses, cattle, and implements:

the stack yard is on one side of this and the place is as big as a town: 4) On the side of the farm-yard next to the stack-yard there is a place to thrash the corn in: and there is, close by this, always a thrashing machine, sometimes worked by horses, sometimes by water, sometimes by wind, and sometimes by steam, there being no such thing as a barn or a flail in the whole country.

The single labourers are kept in this manner: about four of them are put into a shed quite away from the farm-house and out of the farm-yard. Here these men live and sleep, having a certain allowance of oat, barley, and pea meal upon which they live, mixing it with water or with milk when they are allowed the use of a cow. They hire for the year, under very severe punishment in case of misbehaviour or quitting service, and cannot have fresh service without a *character* from the *last master* and also a character from the *minister of the parish*.

Pretty well that, for a knife-and-fork chopstick of Sussex who has been used to sit around the fire with the master and the mistress, and to pull about and tickle the laughing maids. Pretty well *that*! But the life of a married labourer will delight you. Upon a steam-engine farm there are perhaps eight or ten of these. There is, at a considerable distance from the farm, a sort of *barrack* divided into a certain number of *boothies*. Each distinct boothie is about seventeen feet one way and fifteen feet the other. There is no ceiling, and no floor but the earth. In this place, a man and his wife and family have to live. When they go into it there is nothing but the four bare walls, and the tiles over their heads, and a small fireplace. To make the most of the room they, at their own cost, erect *berths* like those in a barrack room which they get up into when they go to bed.

But if their dwelling place is bad, their food is worse, being fed upon exactly that which we feed hogs and horses upon. The married man receives in money about four pounds for the whole year, and he has besides sixty bushels of oats, thirty bushels of barley, twelve bushels of peas and three bushels of potatoes, with ground allowed him to plant the potatoes. They never have one bit of wheaten bread, nor of beef, nor mutton, though the land is covered with wheat and cattle.

The labourer is wholly at the mercy of the master, who, if he will not keep him beyond the year, can totally ruin him by refusing him a character. This family has NO HOME: and no home can any man be said to have who can thus be dislodged every year at the will of his master.

There, chopsticks of Sussex, you can now see what English scoundrels, calling themselves 'gentlemen', get Scotch bailiffs for. These bailiffs are generally the sons of some of these farmers, recommended to the grinding ruffians of England by the grinding ruffians of Scotland. Six days, from daylight to dark, these good and laborious and kind people labour. But, say you, what do they do with all the wheat and beef and the mutton, and what becomes of the money they are sold for? Why, the cattle and sheep walk into England on their legs; the wheat is put into ships, to be sent to London or elsewhere; and as to the money these are sold for, the farmer is allowed to have a little of it. But almost the whole of it is sent away to the landlord, to be gambled or otherwise squandered away at LONDON, at PARIS, or at ROME.

I remain, your faithful friend,
  Wm Cobbett

I hereby direct my printers to print ten thousand copies of this address; to put at the bottom of them PRICE ONE PENNY: and I hereby direct the person keeping my shop at Bolt Court, to sell these addresses at *five shillings a hundred*, or at three shillings for fifty.*

There, Dr Black, now talk about your '*antalluct*' as long as you please. What a Sussex chopstick would say if he were asked to live with his family in one of these *boothies* I do not exactly know. But this I know, that I should not like to be the man to make the proposition to him, *especially if he had a bill-hook in his hand*!

I now come back to this delightful and beautiful city. I thought that Bristol, taking in its heights and CLIFTON and its rocks and the river, was the finest in the world. But EDIN-BURGH with its castle, its hills, its pretty little seaport

---

* This direction to the printer precedes the Address in the original Register, and the Address is itself here much shortened.

conveniently detached from it, its vale of rich land lying all around, its lofty hills in the background, its views across the FIRTH: I think little of its streets and its rows of fine houses, though all built of stone and though everything in London and Bath is beggary to these. I think nothing of *Holyrood House*, but I think a greal deal of the fine and well-ordered streets of shops; of the regularity which you perceive everywhere in the management of business. The *people*, however, still exceed the place: here all is civility: you do not meet with rudeness, or even with the want of disposition to oblige. A friend took me round the environs of the city: he had a turnpike ticket received at the first gate which cleared five or six gates. It was sufficient for him to *tell* the future gate-keepers that he had it. When I saw that, I said to myself, 'Nota bene: gate-keepers take people's word in Scotland, a thing I have not seen before since I left *Long Island*.'

Glasgow
[19 October, 1832]
On Monday morning, the 15th October, I went in a carriage furnished by my kind friends at EDINBURGH, who accompanied me in it to a place called Queen's-Ferry where you cross the FIRTH of FORTH, to go over to a little place called North Ferry, whence I went in a post-chaise to the ancient town of DUNFERMLINE. In leaving Edinburgh we came close by the castle, which I had not seen at so short a distance before, and up into which I would not go, seeing that there were *soldiers* there; for merely speaking to one of whom (he choosing to swear that I had endeavoured to seduce him to desert) *I might have been hanged by the neck until I was dead*, according to a law originally drawn up by Scott Eldon. This castle, like the Christian church, is built upon a rock, which rock is very lofty and almost perpendicular, so that it is a most interesting and magnificent spectacle, especially if you are on any eminence at a little distance from the city; infinitely grander and more interesting than St Paul's from BATTERSEA RISE.

When we got to Glasgow, we alighted at a hotel, and as I had not breakfasted I therefore set to that work at the inn, without loss of time, upon everything that is good, but particularly upon some *tender beef-steaks*, a thing which I have not met with before in more than one out of ten beef-steaks in my life. And, I may as well stop to observe here that which I have omitted before, that all the beef I have tasted in Scotland has been excellent. It appears to come from the little oxen which the Highlands send down in such droves and a score of which, please God to give me life, I will have next year in Surrey.

So much for the meat of Scotland, and now I am talking about victuals, let me observe, first, that the wheaten bread, of which there is an abundance in all the towns, is just about as good as it is in London. That, besides this, there are oat-cakes made very thin, which are very nice things of the break kind. Then the oatmeal, when ground and dressed in a nice manner, is made into porridge, just in the same manner as the Americans make corn-meal into *mush*, and it is eaten with milk just in the same manner.

This is the living in Scotland. Everywhere you see a sufficiency of good victuals, and as to the drink, just as in England, you always see ten times too much of it. Everybody drinks too much.

Greenock
[21 October, 1832]

After lecturing at Glasgow on Wednesday, Thursday and Friday nights, I set off by steamboat for this town yesterday morning at eight o'clock. I had not time in writing at Glasgow to notice several things which I should not have omitted. There is the finest, most convenient, best conducted *cattle-market* that I ever saw in my life. I do not like to see manufactories of any sort, but that of Mr MONTEITH for the dyeing and printing of calicoes and shawls and handkerchiefs and upon a scale of prodigious magnitude, I did go to see and I saw it with wonder that I cannot describe. First there was a large room full of men, engaged in drawing, upon paper, the flowers and other things which were to be imprinted on their cotton: then there was another set to put these drawings upon blocks of wood; then there was another to fasten on little pieces of copper upon the wood; then there were others to engrave upon the copper in order to print, pretty nearly as printing work is carried out; then came the men to mark the copper with the blocks according to the drawings, and lastly came the printers, who carry out their work by rollers. The buildings belonging to this dyeing and printing concern are as large as no very inconsiderable country town.

I was not aware that Glasgow was an ancient city, but I now find it was the see of one of the archbishops of Scotland. Of the cathedral, only the nave and the chancel remain, the transepts appearing to have been demolished.

Paisley
[26 October, 1832]
In my last I had not time to say anything about my passages down the Clyde from Glasgow to Greenock. The whole of the way down the Clyde is interesting beyond belief. It is a fine wide river at Glasgow, gets wider and wider of course, but for several miles down it is walled in the most complete manner. At about half way down the town of DUMBARTON lies on our right: the Castle of Dumbarton on a round and almost perpendicular rock standing out in the water; an object worth travelling from the Isle of Wight to this spot barely to see.

At about seven miles from Glasgow we pass the mouth of the famous canal which goes from Glasgow and which connects the Firth of Clyde with the Firth of Forth and thus connects the water of the ATLANTIC with the German Ocean.

The harbour and bay at Greenock are very fine. The town, which consists of thirty thousand people, is built on a little flat, the highland beginning to rise up immediately behind it to the south; the streets are regular, conveniently wide; the houses built of stone and everything wearing the appearance of ease, competence and great solidity. The great curiosity here, and the thing upon which the people pride themselves, and most justly, is what they call the 'SHAWSWATER'. Greenock lies to the north of very high, rocky hills. No fresh water stream or river comes near it. On the high land about six miles to the south of it, there was a little stream or bourne. By means of dams the water proceeding from this bourne was formed into a lake, but between the lake and Greenock was a chain of lofty hills.

After various schemes about tunnels to go under the hills, and steam pumping and God knows what besides, Mr THOM, a native I believe of the Isle of Bute, made a proposition for carrying the water to Greenock by acqueduct, which he finally accomplished. There is all this water brought to the side of the high hills behind Greenock, and there it comes tumbling down the various acqueducts, not only supplying the town amply at all times but furnishing the means of turning flour-mills, cotton-mills or anything of the sort, at the cheapest possible rate. They say that the people were wholly incredulous of effecting this thing and that, on the day on which the acqueduct was opened for the water to proceed, not less than ten thousand people were assembled to watch the result of this brilliant experiment. Mr THOM, who did me the honour to accompany me in riding round the lake, is a man of too much sense and too much merit to set any value upon an empty title. But if George the Fourth had made him a baronet instead of COUTTS TROTTER, WALTER SCOTT, or PARSON BATE DUDLEY, he would have in some degree diminished the contempt and disgust with which men now view that hackneyed hereditary honour.

Dalzell House, near Hamilton
[28 Oct., 1832]
I went to see the beautiful manufacture of silk, carried on by Mr Fulton and Son. I never like to see these machines, lest I should be tempted to understand them. I constantly resist all the natural desire which people, out of kindness, have to explain them to me. This silk affair, however, afforded one very pleasing circumstance. It was all put in motion by a wheel, turned by three men; and there was a great number of young women and girls employed at the work, and all very neatly and nicely dressed. The things they make are beautiful beyond description. In these fabrics our countrymen now surpass, not only all the rest of Europe, but those of India, too, and I understand that PAISLEY surpasses all the rest of the kingdom in this respect.

New Lanark
[1 November, 1832]
Here I am upon the most interesting spot of earth that I ever set

foot on in my life. But before I proceed to give an account of what I have seen, I must go back again, as in reality I did, from Dalzell House to Glasgow.

I lectured at HAMILTON on Saturday 27, went that night and slept at DALZELL HOUSE. The lecturing place was in what is called the Burgher church, that is to say, the dissenting church. Here is an established church in Scotland, an established *Presbyterian* church, the priests of which are paid by what are called Tiends (which is only another word for tithes or tenths). But there is the seceding church; that is to say there is, in every considerable place, a large part of the people that have *seceded* or *drawn off* from this established church. So that there are here *two churches*, one of which is pretty nearly as extensive as the other, and as the seceders have generally the most able and most diligent ministers, they are daily gaining ground over the established church.

It will easily be conceived that the established church, exclusively under the patronage of the nobility, and trembling for the stability of the TIENDS, are not *very warm friends of any change at all*, particularly of that very great change, the absolute necessity of which is the great burden of all my lecturings. Parsons have noses as keen as that of the crow; they smell danger at a greater distance than any other part of God's creation. It is said that the *Bald-Eagles* in North America, they being in Canada, will smell a dead horse upon the borders of the Gulf of Mexico. But wonderful as this may appear, my belief is that the noses of parsons are still finer than those of these Bald-Eagles. No wonder, then, that I have everywhere found the established churches shut against me, while the seceding churches have, wherever necessary, flung open their doors for my reception. This was the case at HAMILTON, where the fine-nosed gentry carried their hostility a little farther than merely shutting the doors of their church. They spread about the assertion that I was an *infidel*, and did everything in their power to prevent people attending the lecture, in which however they by no means succeeded.

From Hamilton I went back to Glasgow to a dinner. This dinner is a matter of great importance, not as it concerns me but as it shows the temper in which the people of Scotland now are. I shall insert a report of it, as given in the Glasgow *Chronicle* of the 31 of October.

On Tuesday evening, after having been at the lecture before mentioned, I went to see the Royal Exchange by *Candlelight*. I wished to be able to notice it, in a rather particular manner, because their 'exchanges' are the subjects of boast with LEEDS, MANCHESTER, LIVERPOOL, BRISTOL and other great commercial places. I have never viewed any of them in a particular manner, having no very good opinion of the politics of the persons generally assembled in them. Here, the case is different.

This edifice is placed between two of the principal streets of the city, *Queen-street* and *Buchanan Street*, looking eastward, having a noble *Corinthian* portico formed of two rows of pillars. Above rises a cupola, or lantern, supported by about a dozen columns with a vane surmounting the whole. Here is a place intended for a clock which, being to be lighted by gas, is to show the time at night as well as day.

After passing under the lofty portico, you pass through a grand entrance hall into an oval-shaped saloon, having a cupola above for the purpose of light. You then enter The Great Room, or, as they call it, the NEWSROOM. The floor above is supported by several lofty pillars, each pillar consisting of *one single stone*. Thus there is a grand promenade in the middle of the room, while the two sides, each of which has three large and elegant fire-places, are fitted up with highly polished mahogany tables for the subscribers, merchants and strangers to read magazines, newspapers and other periodical publications. They say there are a hundred newspapers taken in and, amongst the rest, I cast my eye, without seeming to know it, upon a little octavo weekly publication in the fate of which I am somewhat interested but which, in an account of a building so magnificent, the reader will consider too unimportant to be named. This splendid room is lighted by several brilliant gas-chandeliers and very beautiful as to its decorations.

Very much to the credit of the directors and proprietors of this establishment, and, indeed, bespeaking the character of the city itself, this NEWSROOM, which is opened about seven in the morning, and is not closed till ten at night is quite free for the

admission of all strangers gratuitously without even an introduction by a subscriber, as is the case of all news-rooms which I
have seen in England. The subscribers are about fourteen or
fifteen hundred in number, who pay, I am told, not forty
shillings a year apiece.

A gentleman who appeared to be a West India merchant told
me that the grand room up-stairs was devoted entirely to the
exhibiting of samples of all sugar imported into the *Clyde*. Below
the ground floor of the Exchange are, a coffee-house, private
room, a larder most beautifully and abundantly furnished. After
coming from the lecture, I went down into these apartments
with some friends, where we were furnished with tea and other
things according to our fancy, amongst which were oysters,
which are very abundant both here and at Edinburgh, small
and white and as good as ever I tasted in London.

Thus I quit this very elegant building and, for the present,
Glasgow itself. I am here at the famous NEW LANARK, which
is near the celebrated FALLS OF THE CLYDE.

New Milns
[Sunday, 4 November, 1832]
No man living has every beheld, in my opinion, a river the banks
of which presented a greater number and a greater variety of
views, or more beautiful views, than those which are presented
to the eye on the banks of the Clyde.

The Clyde has three grand *falls*: the first is going up the river, a little nearer Glasgow than the borough of Lanark: the second about three miles further up, and the third about a mile above that. The middle falls are just above the manufacturing village of NEW LANARK, the vast and various machinery of which is put in motion by the waters, taken in a most curious manner out of the river, and applied to these purposes. This NEW LANARK, of which we have heard so much as connected with the name of Mr OWEN, stands upon a little flat, which nature has made on one bank of the river. The village is about a mile and a half from the town of LANARK. In coming from the town of Lanark, down to the new village, you come to a spot as you descend the hill where you have a full view of the great falls of the Clyde.

We went up to the very edge of the falls, stood upon the tips of the rocks and looked down upon the smoking water. In the crevices near the tops of the rocks, the jackdaws have discovered inaccessible places for depositing their nests, and here I saw such multitudes of that bird, such as I have never seen before. There were thousands upon thousands of them skimming about over a sort of bay, formed by the twirling water as it came over the falls.

After having been at the falls, we came back through the manufacturing village. Being at New Lanark, I was rather curious to know whether there was any reality in what we had heard about the effects of the Owen *'feelosofy'*. I had always understood that he had been the author of his own great fortune, and the founder of the village. But I found that the establishment had been founded by a Mr DALE, who had had two or three daughters with great fortunes; that Mr Owen had got one of these daughters and one of these fortunes; that Mrs Owen had been dead for some years; that the concern had long been in other hands; that the only part of it which was ever of his own invention, was a large building in which the *'feelosofical'* working people were intended to eat and drink in common; that they never did this; that there had been a place at some distance from Lanark, fixed upon for the execution of the 'OWEN PLAN': that a large space had been surrounded with a high stone wall for the purpose; that the scheme had been abandoned; and that the wall had been taken down, and sold as *old stones*!

The building, in NEW LANARK, which Owen had erected for the *'feelosofers'* to carry on their community of eating and drinking, is used as a *school-room*. And here I saw boys in one place, and girls in another place, under masters appointed for the purpose, carrying on what is called 'education'. There was one boy pointing with a stick to something stuck upon the wall, and then all the rest of the boys began bawling out what it was. In one large room they were all *singing out something* at the word of command, just like the little tribe of things at Bolt-court who there stun the whole neighbourhood with singing *God Save the King*, the *'Apostle's Creed'* and the *'Pence Table'*, and the fellow, who leads the lazy life in the teaching of whom, ought to be sent raking the kennel or filling a dung-cart. In another apartment of this house there were eighteen boys and eighteen girls, the boys dressed in Highland dresses, naked from three inches above the knee down to the foot, without shoes on, a tartan plaid close around the body, each having a girl by the arm duly proportioned in size, the girls without caps, and without shoes and stockings, marching arm in arm, in regular files, with a lock-step, slow march to the sound of a fiddle which a fellow, big enough to carry a quarter of wheat or to dig ten rods of ground in a day, was playing in a corner of the room with an immense music book lying open before him.

It is difficult to determine whether, when people are huddled together in this unnatural state, this sort of soldier-ship discipline may or may not be necessary to effect the purposes of schooling. It is altogether a thing that I abhor. It is the reverse of *domestic life*; it reverses the order of nature; it makes minds a fiction and, which is amongst the greatest of its evils, it fashions the rising generation to habits of *implicit submission*. However, the consolation is that it is impossible that it should ever become anything like general in the nation. The order of the world demands that nine-tenths of the people should be employed on *the land*: being so employed, they must be scattered about widely and there must be *homes* and domestic life for the greater part of the rising generation.

From this account of the 'OWEN-PLAN' I come to something a great deal more pleasant, the numerous and plentiful and beautiful orchards on the banks of the Clyde, on its two great tributary rivers, the CAULDER and the AVEN, and on the banks of the numerous *glens* which terminate when they arrive at one or other of these rivers. These fine orchards are *general* all the way from very near Glasgow to the falls of the river. Mr Prentice, the editor of the *Glasgow Chronicle*, has the good sense to have a pretty considerable farm at about six or seven miles from Glasgow. About three English acres of his land form a garden and orchard, the trees of which are about six years old, very fine, free from canker and bearing fine fruit. The cherry-trees are very fine also: the plum-trees are fine, and an orchard is not a mere matter of ornament or pleasure here, but of prodigious profit.

There are, besides coal-mines, innumerable iron works on the banks of the Clyde as you approach Glasgow. We went over the bridge, called BOTHWELL-BRIDGE, where the famous battle was fought in 1679, between the Covenanters and the army of Charles I, or rather between the Covenanters and the Royal *Scotch troops united*. And this has always been the case with Scotland and Ireland; always kept down by domestic defection. But it was Cromwell who was the great *destroyer*. He must have been in reality, what Burke calls an 'architect of ruin', for everywhere in Scotland as well as England, when they show you a disfigured and partly demolished edifice, they ascribe the mischief to Cromwell.

On Saturday, the 3 of November, I set off from Glasgow towards England in a post-chaise accompanied by my friends, Mr BELL and Mr TURNER, who took their leave of me at an inn on the road, about fourteen miles from Glasgow, where I changed horses. Kingswell, the little place where we changed horses, is in Ayrshire, famous for its beautiful breed of milking cows. From Kingswell we soon began to descend into a country of fields and woods. We were yet a mile and a half from New Milns, that public spirited manufacturing village, a deputation from which had come on foot, twenty-four miles to Glasgow to present that address to me which was published in the *Register* dated from Glasgow.* The chaise was yet a mile and a half from the village when the *boys* (always the advance guard) began to

*See entry for November 1, page 191.

meet us in groups. As we advanced, the groups grew more and more numerous. Arrived at the first house in the village, the committee accompanied by three flags met us, with a request that I would be so kind as to get out of the chaise, and walk in the procession to the inn, a request with which I instantly complied, and on we went preceded by a drum and fife. It was a general holiday in the village, every soul of which seemed to be present, from the oldest person down to the baby in arms. Arrived at the inn, I found the magistrates of the BURGH, who are called bailiffs, assembled with a great number of burgesses, to present me with the freedom of the Burgh, which they did in due form, delivering to me the necessary document and I going through the usual solemnities; the chief Bailiff stating, as to the grounds of this mark of their respect and attachment, that the people of the Burgh owed their political knowledge to me; that the nation owed the reform, in their opinion to me more than to any other man, and more than to all other men put together; and that they had more reliance upon my future exertions than upon those of all other men, to make the reform productive of good to the people.

Bolt Court, Fleet Street
[7 Jan., 1833]

And now I, for the present, take my leave of Scotland with expressing a hope that, going from and returning to, that very identical room, in *Bolt Court*, from which DR JOHNSON went, to which he returned to spread over England the belief that there was not a tree in Scotland, and that all was sterility and worthlessness, I have done something at any rate to remove the errors which he so largely contributed to plant in the minds of Englishmen, relative to Scotland. I never do things by halves. While I am writing this upstairs, I have to exhibit below a beautiful sample of apples from the banks of the Clyde, and a cheese of excellent flavour, and of half a hundredweight, which I brought from the country of Ayr.

I could not bring Scotland itself to London; but I have brought indubitable proofs that all we have been told about its sterility has been either sheer falsehood, or monstrous exaggeration.

LETTERS TO CHARLES MARSHALL
Editorial note. Cobbett's description of his Irish tour is in the form of ten letters, all addressed to Charles Marshall, Labourer, Normandy Tithing, Parish of Ash, County of Surrey, and signed: I remain, Your Master and Friend, William Cobbett.

Dublin
[22 Sept., 1834]
Marshall, I have seen this morning more than one thousand of working persons, boys and girls, all the clothes upon the bodies of all of whom were not worth so much as the smock-frock that you go to work in. I have seen the *food* and the *cooking* of the food, in a LARGE HOUSE: cast iron coppers are employed to boil *oatmeal* in water or skim-milk; and that is the food given to these poor creatures. The *white cabbage*, the *barley meal*, the pot-fat, the *whey* and the *butter-milk* which George boils daily for our little pigs and their mothers, is a dish to obtain a mouthful of which thousands of these people would go on their knees. Marshall, you know how I have scolded Tom Denman and little Barratt, and your own son Dick, on the Saturday before I came away, for not sweeping the sleeping-place of the *yard-hogs* out clean, and what a strict charge I gave George to fling out the old bed, and to give them a bed of fresh straw every Saturday. O, how happy would thousands upon thousands in this city be, if they could be lodged in a place like the roughest hog bed!

The LARGE HOUSE of which I have spoken to you above, is called the MENDICITY. The word *mendicant* means beggar, and the word MENDICITY means *beggary*. From this house there are sent forth, every day, begging carts drawn by women to collect what is called '*broken victuals*'. The carts, when they come in, have their contents taken and examined by persons appointed for the purpose, who separate all that can become food from the mere rubbish and filth. A gentleman has in evidence given by him before the commissioners here, stated that out of *seventy odd hundredweight* taken out of the carts, the examiners found only *nine hundredweight* that could by any *possibility* become human food.

Dublin
[27 September, 1834]
After I wrote to you, the other day, about MENDICITY, I went again at the *dinner-time*. In one long room, there were about 500 women, each with some potatoes in a bowl, mashed, as you mash them to mix with *meal*, for your hogs. There were about a hundred little girls in a *school* and about as many boys in another: neither had shoes or stockings, and the boys had *no shirts*. In another place I saw a great crowd of women sitting and doing nothing, each with a *baby* in her arms. They were sitting in rows waiting, I believe, for their messes. Some of them were young and naturally handsome, but made ugly by starvation, rags and dirt. In another place, I saw the most painful sight of all: *women*, with heavy hammers, *cracking stones* into very small pieces, *to make walks in gentlemen's gardens*.

I hear that discontents are arising again in England, on account of the *lowering of the wages*. Mr Dean will not lower the wages of anybody. He knows that I never gave a *full* working man *less* than 15*s*. a week, though found a good house and garden and plenty of fuel. Two things, I hope, you will attend in my absence: first, cheerful obedience to Mr Dean: the other thing is my hope that none of you will go to any *drinking place* on my account.

Waterford
[6 Oct., 1834]
I have now been over 180 miles in Ireland, in the several counties of Dublin, Wicklow, Kildare, Carlow, Kilkenny and Waterford. In coming from Kilkenny to Waterford I and my friend (Mrs O'Higgins), in a post-chaise, came through a little town called Mullinavat where there was a fair for *cattle* and *fat hogs* and *apples*. There might be 4,000 people: there were about 7 acres of ground covered with cattle, mostly fat, and all over the street of the town there were about THREE THOUSAND BEAUTIFUL FAT HOGS lying all over the road and the streets: and our chaise was *actually stopped and blocked up by fat hogs*. Ah, but there arose out of this fine sight reflections that made my blood boil; that the far greater part of those who bred and fatted those hogs were never to taste one morsel of them. The hogs are

to be killed, dried or tubbed and sent out of the country to be sold for money to be *paid* to the *landowners* who spend it in London, Paris, Bath, Rome or some other place of pleasure.

The case is this: the owners of all the great estates *live in England or France or Italy.* The *rents are sent to them*, and as there are no poor-rates, they get all the produce of the land from the miserable farmer, except just enough to keep him alive: the working people here, who might eat meat three times a day, are compelled to live on *lumpers*, which are such bad potatoes that the hogs will not thrive on them and will not touch them if they can get other potatoes.

Marshall, mind me well. You know that at Peperharrow (only about four miles from your cottage) there lives LORD MIDDLETON. You know that he was a long while Lord Lieutenant of our county. Now, Marshall, HE is one of the GREAT LANDOWNERS OF IRELAND. He is the owner of a town called Middleton, half as big as Guildford. He is the owner of the lands for many miles round and it is supposed that he draws, yearly, *from twenty-five to thirty thousand pounds from this estate.* Lord Middleton may say that he is not the *landlord* of these wretched people. Ah, but his *tenant*, his *middleman*, is their landlord, and Lord Middleton gets the *more rent from him* by enabling him to let these holes in this manner.

Dublin
[4 November, 1834]

I dare say that my letters have made you stare; but staring is not all that they ought to make you do; they ought to make you think about how you would like to have a naked wife and children; how you would like to have no shoes, or stockings, or shirt; and the mud spewing up between your toes when you come down the road to your work in the morning. They ought to make you think about what you shall *do, all of you*, to prevent this state of starvation, nakedness and filth coming upon you. Do not think that it is IMPOSSIBLE that it should ever come upon you. Do not think this; for there is no *reason* for you thinking it. The countries are very close to one another. The county of Cork is but a very little way from Somersetshire. I am not so far from you now as I should be if I were at Morpeth in the county of Northumberland. This miserable people have been brought to this state little by little and for want of beginning in time to *do the things which they ought to have done in their own defence* to make use of the faculties which God has given them; that is to say, in legally and constitutionally and according to the good custom of our wise and brave forefathers petitioning to the King and the Parliament, and otherwise legally doing that which the laws of this our country bid us do, sanctioned as they are by the laws of God.

Index

[place names only]